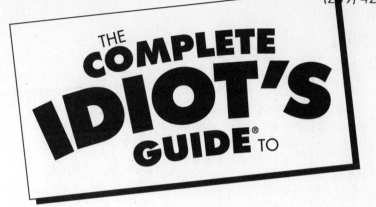

THE
COMPLETE IDIOT'S GUIDE® TO

High-Fiber Cooking

by Liz Scott

D1072847

ALPHA

A member of Penguin Group (USA) Inc.

ALPHA BOOKS

Published by the Penguin Group

Penguin Group (USA) Inc., 375 Hudson Street, New York, New York 10014, USA

Penguin Group (Canada), 90 Eglinton Avenue East, Suite 700, Toronto, Ontario M4P 2Y3, Canada (a division of Pearson Penguin Canada Inc.)

Penguin Books Ltd., 80 Strand, London WC2R 0RL, England

Penguin Ireland, 25 St. Stephen's Green, Dublin 2, Ireland (a division of Penguin Books Ltd.)

Penguin Group (Australia), 250 Camberwell Road, Camberwell, Victoria 3124, Australia (a division of Pearson Australia Group Pty. Ltd.)

Penguin Books India Pvt. Ltd., 11 Community Centre, Panchsheel Park, New Delhi—110 017, India

Penguin Group (NZ), 67 Apollo Drive, Rosedale, North Shore, Auckland 1311, New Zealand (a division of Pearson New Zealand Ltd.)

Penguin Books (South Africa) (Pty.) Ltd., 24 Sturdee Avenue, Rosebank, Johannesburg 2196, South Africa

Penguin Books Ltd., Registered Offices: 80 Strand, London WC2R 0RL, England

Copyright © 2008 by Liz Scott

International Standard Book Number: 978-1-59257-820-7
Library of Congress Catalog Card Number: 2008929018

10 09 08   8 7 6 5 4 3 2 1

Interpretation of the printing code: The rightmost number of the first series of numbers is the year of the book's printing; the rightmost number of the second series of numbers is the number of the book's printing. For example, a printing code of 08-1 shows that the first printing occurred in 2008.

Printed in the United States of America

Note: This publication contains the opinions and ideas of its author. It is intended to provide helpful and informative material on the subject matter covered. It is sold with the understanding that the author and publisher are not engaged in rendering professional services in the book. If the reader requires personal assistance or advice, a competent professional should be consulted.

Most Alpha books are available at special quantity discounts for bulk purchases for sales promotions, premiums, fundraising, or educational use. Special books, or book excerpts, can also be created to fit specific needs.

For details, write: Special Markets, Alpha Books, 375 Hudson Street, New York, NY 10014.

Publisher: *Marie Butler-Knight*
Editorial Director: *Mike Sanders*
Senior Managing Editor: *Billy Fields*
Acquisitions Editor: *Tom Stevens*
Senior Development Editor: *Christy Wagner*
Production Editor: *Megan Douglass*
Copy Editor: *Jan Zoya*

Cartoonist: *Steve Barr*
Cover Designer: *Kurt Owens*
Book Designer: *Trina Wurst*
Indexer: *Johnna Vanhoose Dinse*
Layout: *Ayanna Lacey*
Proofreader: *Laura Caddell*

Contents at a Glance

Contents

Introduction

There are any number of reasons you may have decided to explore high-fiber cooking. Maybe your doctor suggested you increase the amount of daily dietary fiber you consume to help with a digestive issue. Maybe you heard that fiber can help lower cholesterol and, consequently, be beneficial for people with heart disease. Maybe some of these health problems exist in your family history and you're hoping to ward off any potential diseases that might be waiting to emerge by consuming a diet higher in fiber as a preventive move. Or your weight may be the issue at hand—losing it or maintaining it. Or perhaps all those things the experts are saying about the importance of fiber are finally starting to make sense to you.

No matter what brought you here, the question for everyone is, no doubt, *How do I do this fiber thing? Apart from eating bran and chomping on raw veggies, how do I get fiber into a normal, daily eating routine that's easily accomplished and perhaps, most importantly, not just edible, but delicious?*

In your hands is the answer to those questions. In the following pages you'll not only learn about the basics of fiber and nutrition, you'll discover more than 180 amazing recipes that will add excitement and taste to your fiber quest. Highly user-friendly and even a bit entertaining at times, you'll find everything you need right here.

So without further ado, let's begin our journey toward high-fiber health and great eating!

How This Book Is Organized

There are seven parts to this book:

Part 1, "The Lowdown on High Fiber," answers any questions you may have about what fiber is, where to find it, and how much you should shoot for. Included are many helpful tips for setting up your pantry with some essential high-fiber ingredients.

Part 2, "Breakfast and Brunch," launches you straight into the first meal of the day with terrific ideas for hot and cold cereals, as well as muffins, pancakes, and egg dishes.

Part 3, "Fiberful Snacks and Beverages," shows you how you can snack and drink your way to your fiber goals with some incredible munchies and mixes.

Part 4, "The Lunch Menu," is chock full of sensational soups, salads, and sandwiches, all made with an eye toward fiber and incredible taste.

Part 5, "What's for Dinner?" provides delicious recipes for everything from chicken to fish to beef, as well as some outstanding vegetarian entrées and pasta dishes that will astound you with flavor and variety while still keeping the focus on fiber.

Part 6, "Supplemental Sides," introduces you to fiber-rich vegetable, bean, and grain recipes that bring great taste and rich fiber to any meal.

Part 7, "Desserts and Sweet Treats," shows that even your sweet tooth can be happily catered to when cooking high fiber.

Extras

You'll come across many boxed notes throughout the book that offer you a little extra information. Watch for these:

Fiber Optics _____

Here you'll find helpful definitions of some unusual terms and ingredients.

Grist for the Mill _____

These boxes contain a wealth of facts, figures, and amusing trivia.

Smooth Move _____

Check out these tips and hints to make your high-fiber cooking a bit easier and more fun.

Acknowledgments

No book ever sees the light of day without the hard work and loving care of many, many people.

I'd like to thank the staff at Alpha, in particular, Tom Stevens and Christy Wagner, for their terrific support and patience. Marilyn Allen and Coleen O'Shea are my heroes at the Allen O'Shea Literary Agency. Kudos to Larry Chilnick for sending me in their direction. Thanks also to Raj Kumari for her indispensable help with nutrition analysis.

I am blessed with a wonderful group of friends and family who have always been my biggest fans. Thanks to Jennifer, Anna, Jimmy, Rich, Nancy, and Connie for always being there. Thanks also to Mom—who would have really enjoyed hearing snippets from this book and sampling the recipes. Finally, to Baby—my feline best friend of 18 years—how you put up with me I'll never know.

Special Thanks to the Technical Reviewer

The Complete Idiot's Guide to High-Fiber Cooking was reviewed by an expert who double-checked the accuracy of what you'll learn here, to help us ensure that this book gives you everything you need to know about cooking delicious high-fiber meals at home. Special thanks are extended to Lisa Vislocky.

Trademarks

All terms mentioned in this book that are known to be or are suspected of being trademarks or service marks have been appropriately capitalized. Alpha Books and Penguin Group (USA) Inc. cannot attest to the accuracy of this information. Use of a term in this book should not be regarded as affecting the validity of any trademark or service mark.

Part 1

The Lowdown on High Fiber

Let's get up close and personal with this amazingly healthy thing called fiber. What exactly is it, why do you need it, and where can you find it? All these questions and more are addressed in Chapter 1 as we pave the way toward one of the most important and, surprisingly, neglected facets of healthy cooking. From recommendations for daily intake to lists of top-performing ingredients, you'll find all you need to know to embark on a high-fiber cooking and eating plan that's simple and delicious.

Getting your kitchen geared up for cooking the high-fiber way is the focus of Chapter 2. We compare and contrast some common ingredients in your pantry to determine which ones suit you best in your fiber quest. We take a quick look at the pros and cons of fresh versus frozen versus canned ingredients and get a lesson on the optimal way to store and care for these ingredients. We also see how fiber-conscious cooking fits into any type of eating plan and can be an ally in any overall healthy food approach.

Finding Fiber in a Refined World

In This Chapter

- ◆ The fuss about fiber
- ◆ Your daily dietary goals
- ◆ Fiber-rich foods

Fiber is an essential part of your diet, but how much do you need and where can you find it? In a world where our food has become fast, mass-produced, and highly processed, dietary fiber is more important than ever.

All the furious fuss you may have noticed on food manufacturer labels ("good source of fiber") as well as ads on TV encouraging you to eat more fiber is actually good advice. Without it, your health can be way below par, prompting problems with digestion, obesity, glucose tolerance, and the like. With fiber, you can be well on your way to enjoying excellent physical condition and vigor, while warding off potential calamities such as heart attacks, diabetes, and even cancer. Sounds pretty important, right?

Fiber 101

So what exactly is this miracle nutrient called fiber, and where do you find it? Simply put, dietary fiber is the indigestible part of plant foods that moves through the digestive system. It can be *soluble* (dissolves in water) or *insoluble* (stays intact).

Fiber Optics _____

Soluble fiber dissolves in water, lowering fats and blood sugar by slowing digestion. **Insoluble fiber** does not dissolve in water, but clears out toxins and makes you regular.

When soluble fiber travels through your stomach and intestines, it binds with fatty acids to slow digestion, lowering cholesterol and regulating blood sugar. When insoluble fiber moves through you, it bulks up and clears the colon of toxins as well as encouraging regular visits to the bathroom, avoiding constipation. It's what you may remember your grandmother calling "roughage" when she was force feeding you those lima beans. Both types are readily available in the plant kingdom, and both types are equally important to your health.

Ready, Aim, Shoot for 35

The American Dietetic Association (ADA) recommends that the average healthy adult consume between 20 and 35 grams dietary fiber a day. Most of us eat barely 50 percent of this amount, often even less, which experts say may, in part, account for the huge increase in obesity in the United States. (Interestingly, the British Nutrition Foundation recommends a minimum of only 12 to 24 grams, which may account for that look everyone has on their face over there!)

Grist for the Mill _____

The ADA's recommendation for children is age in years plus 5 grams a day. So a 6-year-old should consume 6 grams + 5 grams = 11 grams daily.

Health gurus here and abroad, however, suggest a much higher intake, even up to 45 grams a day. What should be your goal? Aiming for the higher end of the ADA's recommendation—35 grams—and even a few grams more—is a sensible number to shoot for. It's also very easily accomplished when you know what to eat and how to cook the high-fiber way.

A Typical Day in the Rough

What would an average menu that meets your goal of at least 35 fiber grams per day look like? Here's one example:

Breakfast:

> Old-Fashioned Apple-Cinnamon Oats   12 grams
> (recipe in Chapter 3)

Lunch:

> Garden Vegetable–Barley Soup   10 grams
> (recipe in Chapter 10)

> Quick Cornbread (recipe in Chapter 21)   2 grams

Dinner:

> Whole-Grain Linguine with Turkey Sausage   8 grams
> (recipe in Chapter 17)

> Spinach Salad with Blackberries and Almonds   5 grams
> (recipe in Chapter 11)

> Deep Chocolate Brownie (recipe in Chapter 23)   2 grams

> *Total:*   39 grams

Not too shabby for a day in the rough. I know what you're thinking. *Where's all the mushy bran stuff and prune juice? Isn't that what high-fiber is all about?* Oops—I forgot to mention one very important point—eating and cooking with fiber, contrary to popular belief, is totally awesome and delicious!

Now that I've got your taste buds' attention, let's take a closer look at our menu. As you can see, breakfast is one of the best times to kick off your fiber intake with selections that include oats and whole grains, fruit, and other fiber-rich ingredients. With a good breakfast under your belt to start the day, the rest is pretty much downhill. It's also important if you're looking to lose or maintain weight, because a high-fiber breakfast keeps you satiated and makes it less likely you'll visit the candy vending machine before lunch.

Of course, there's nothing wrong with a healthful, fiber-rich snack in between meals. In fact, you'll find many recipes within the pages of this book for nibbles and treats you can take along with you to work or keep on hand at home when your stomach rumbles.

Easy Does It

One word of fiber-related caution: if you're not used to eating much fiber, you might want to ease into the higher-gram goals. A sudden large intake may cause a few stomach rumblings of its own as your digestive system becomes accustomed to handling it.

Just drink lots of water, which helps move fiber through the intestines. It won't be long before you'll be enjoying a fiber-rich diet on a daily basis without excess bloating and—let's be blunt—enough gas to float a helium balloon.

Smooth Move

Remedy excess gas or flatulence naturally by eating fennel, dill, or ginger, or by drinking peppermint or chamomile tea.

Be Fruitful and Pulpify

We all know fruit is an important part of a balanced diet. Full of essential vitamins and minerals, including antioxidants that fight free radicals and help prevent disease, fruit can be a real powerhouse of nutrition. It's also a great place to look for fiber.

Some members of the fruit family are much better sources of fiber than others. For example, an apple eaten out of hand, including the peel, can contain up to 5 grams dietary fiber, depending on its size and variety. A cup of cantaloupe, on the other hand, contains only slightly more than 1 gram.

Keep Your Skin On

At first glance, it might appear that any fruit with an edible skin offers a greater amount of fiber than one whose skin you discard. In part, this is true. However, the pulp of a fruit can often be just as fiber-rich as its outer epidermis. Surprisingly, a peeled apple provides up to 4 grams dietary fiber, still more than the rindless melon. Ounce for ounce, the apple is the better choice for fiber-conscious folks.

Still, it's always a good idea to eat the skin of fruits such as apples, pears, and peaches because not only are you gaining a bit of fiber, but you're also ingesting some very valuable plant-based nutrients that are only available in the exterior of the fruit.

For instance, the apple skin's red pigment is caused by a substance called antho-cyanin, an important *phytochemical* linked to cancer prevention. And grape skins are enormously rich in resveratrol, the anti-oxidant most often talked about in relation to wine consumption and its effect on car-diovascular health. For our fiber purposes, however, the skin of the fruit is something you should include in your cooking when-ever possible, as every little bit of fiber helps bump up your gram goals.

Incidentally, unlike other nutrients such as vitamin C that can be destroyed by cook-ing, high temperatures do not reduce the amount of fiber in food.

> **Fiber Optics**
>
> **Phytochemicals,** also called *phytonutrients,* are specific plant-based chemicals that protect the plants in which they're found from environmen-tal threats, giving them a better chance of survival. Experts believe that when we ingest these nutrients, we also obtain these protective characteristics.

Can I Drink to That?

Unfortunately, for fruit juice fans, fiber is pretty much lost in the juicing process, par-ticularly in commercial juices. Despite misleading claims of "lots of pulp," there's no more fiber present than in original versions. Fiber must be added and is usually done in the form of maltodextrin, a soluble fiber substance made from cornstarch and the same stuff found in fiber supplements. If you think you're getting the extra fiber from the actual fruit, you're not. The only way to ensure that you're ingesting valuable fruit fiber from say, oranges, is to eat the orange itself.

What about expensive juicers that extract all the nutrients from fruit and veg-etables? Aren't they good for high-fiber eating and cooking? The real aim of juicing machines is to avoid consuming additives like preservatives and corn syrup often pres-ent in commercially bottled juices, not to retain fiber. In fact, die-hard juicers don't want the fiber in their drinks because it slows the absorption of all those vitamins and minerals they're trying to flood into their systems for quick energy.

Using a blender, however, like in smoothie-making, breaks down the fiber of fruits and vegetables into a thick and hearty drinkable concoction. This is most certainly the way to go if you're looking to drink your fiber as well as eat it. You'll find a great vari-ety of smoothies and shakes in Chapter 9

> **Smooth Move**
>
> Opting to eat a whole fruit rather than its juice always provides more fiber as well as important vitamins, minerals, and phytonutrients.

that you can make in a blender, all of which contain high-fiber fruits as well as other fiber goodies such as nuts and cocoa powder.

Your Top-Ten Fibrous Fruits

So which fruits give you the most bang for your fiber buck? Happily, you have many to choose from. The question is which ones will you be most likely to include in your diet and cooking on a regular basis? What's the practicality factor? After all, it's all well and good to know that only $1/4$ cup fresh coconut contains a whopping 10 grams fiber, but how likely are you to rush out to the market and come home with a lovely bunch? More important, how apt will you be to fetch the ice pick and sledgehammer in the name of fiber consumption? Just as I thought.

Here are your "top bananas":

1 large orange	7 grams
1 medium pear, skin on	5 grams
1 large apple, skin on	5 grams
$1/2$ cup blackberries	4 grams
1 large banana	4 grams
$1/2$ cup raspberries	4 grams
8 medium strawberries	4 grams
$1/4$ cup raisins	2 grams
1 medium peach	2 grams
$1/2$ cup blueberries	2 grams

Other fiber-friendly fruits include pineapple, mango, and grapefruit, as well as nearly all dried fruits such as apricots, plums (prunes), cranberries, and cherries.

By the way, coconut is indeed a great source of fiber. I call for it often in the recipes as shredded (from a bag) or creamed (from a can). You can put away your ice pick.

Eat Your Vegetables!

If you're hearing the voice of your mother right about now, good. She was right ... at least about eating your veggies.

For many of the same reasons that fruit is an all-important part of your diet, vegetables are indispensable to good health. No matter how you slice it, that carrot sitting in your fridge has the potential to improve your eyesight, ward off a cold, prevent cancer, and keep heart disease at bay. It also has a good amount of fiber. Whether you shred it, boil it, mash it, or chomp on it like Bugs, 1 cup contains about 4 grams.

Like other members of the root vegetable family to which it belongs, such as sweet potatoes, Idahoes, beets, and parsnips, carotene-rich fibrous carrots lend themselves to any number of delicious cooking preparations, either on their own or in the company of other great-tasting ingredients, as you'll see.

Cruciferous Magniferous

Another family of veggies that's fiber friendly is the cruciferous bunch. These guys, all related in some way to the cabbage, are the dream team of nutritionists. Broccoli, cauliflower, brussels sprouts, and kale, to name a few, possess specific antioxidants shown to reduce the risk of lung cancer and other respiratory diseases. Fiber-wise, their makeup is both soluble and insoluble, so they offer the best of both worlds when it comes to fighting the good fight against disease and clearing out the trenches of toxic enemies.

They work the offense as well as the defense. In the process, however, they tend to release a rather strong sulfur odor during cooking and, sometimes, after eating. We can excuse them, of course—or excuse ourselves, as the case may be—because the benefits they provide outweigh the slight indiscretion.

Beans, Beans, the More You Eat ...

Speaking of indiscretion, our most outspoken allies in the fiber arena are surely beans. They have unfairly been on the receiving end of much bathroom humor as well as getting a bad rap from kids and carnivores. But the truth is, proper preparation and cooking can greatly limit their vivacity, allowing them to emerge as the hero fiber foods they so richly deserve to be. Also, like the cruciferous family, they're an excellent source of both types of fiber, soluble and insoluble, not to mention their ability to step in as a low-fat protein from time to time.

From black beans to cannellini to chickpeas, these members of the larger group

> **Grist for the Mill**
>
> Beans, beans, the magical fruit! Beans perform their magic by producing carbon dioxide and hydrogen when their sugars combine with bacteria in the large intestine.

called legumes are an essential part of high-fiber cooking. Where would we be, after all, without chili on Sunday, or barbecued baked beans on the Fourth of July? Life as we know it would be far less nutritious and delicious, not to mention quiet and subdued.

A Leg Up on Legumes

A bit of confusion always arises when we begin to speak of *legumes, beans,* and that other odd classification, *pulses.* Here's some help so you can easily converse with other fiber-seeking individuals.

First, all beans are legumes. Lentils are also legumes as are common vegetables like peas and string beans. And legumes, for all intents and purposes, are really just pulses by another name. Pretty simple.

Now, what if I tell you that peanuts are also legumes, but nuts are not. Or that grain legumes are grown for their seeds but seeds are not legumes. You'd probably say I'm just showing off, and you'd be right.

All we really need to know as high-fiber cooks is that beans and other legumes are a great source of fiber and a delicious addition to your repertoire. From split peas to navy beans, you can't go wrong by including them in your diet. And as far as we are concerned, they all fall under the umbrella of vegetables.

Here are the best of the bunch, the top 10 veggies, fiber-wise:

¹/₂ cup lentils	8 grams
¹/₂ cup kidney beans	7 grams
¹/₂ cup lima beans	7 grams
¹/₂ acorn squash	5 grams
1 cup fresh broccoli	4 grams
¹/₂ cup green peas	4 grams
1 sweet potato	4 grams
¹/₂ cup canned corn	3 grams
1 Idaho potato, skin on	3 grams
¹/₂ cup cooked spinach	2 grams

Numerous other beans and veggies are a good source of fiber, and variety is certainly the spice of life, especially a high-fiber one. You'll be meeting lots of them in the following chapters, many familiar, and some delightfully new. For now, we need to go sow a few oats.

Go With the Grains

Over the centuries, wheat has come full circle. There was a time when hunters and gatherers collected these little grains and ground them up by hand to cook and bake with. They were hearty and nutty—the grains, that is—and still full of good things like the bran and germ.

Eventually, machines took over the grinding process, and the result was much less coarse, making wheat far more suitable for mass production. And of course, before we knew it, the proverbial "best idea" ever, sliced bread, arrived on the scene, virtually unrecognizable compared to those wonderful little grains from whence it came.

And as far as our health was concerned, the finer and finer wheat grains became, the less nutrition came along with them. Now, and for the last few years or so, everybody's seen the error of their ways and is trying to put all that good stuff back in—or a more sensible approach—not take it out in the first place.

A Whole Lotta Fiber

Fiber is only one of the amazing offerings whole grains present, but for our purposes, it's surely the most important. After maize, or corn, wheat is the largest-produced cereal crop, with rice following close behind. There are a huge number of varieties, from durum, used primarily in pasta-making, to soft or hard winter wheat, used mostly in flour production.

In just about all cases, however, the best part of the grain is removed during processing, and "enriching" as well as bleaching usually happens as well. Whole wheat, as opposed to refined wheat, still retains the bran and germ and, consequently, a whole lot of fiber. This is also why it's darker in color than white flour or bread.

Sow Those Oats ... and Barley, and Groats

Wheat is, of course, only one type of grain. Barley, oats, rice, buckwheat, rye, and a number of others, for example, are also classified as grains and are subject to the same processing or nonprocessing, as the case may be.

Oats are a good example, as you're no doubt familiar with old-fashioned oats as opposed to quick-cooking oats. The latter are more processed and, therefore, refined, while the former are less messed with and, as a result, contain more fiber. And you can certainly tell the difference when you're eating it. One is chewy and flavorful, while the other is bland and highly processed. Unless you're a baby or someone with an extremely delicate constitution, opt for the chewy, old-fashioned type. The even less-refined steel-cut oats taste better still.

All About Bran

Whole grains contain primarily insoluble fiber, the type that bulks up in your digestive tract, sweeping it clean as it passes through and out. Bran is the epitome of this action and is why some people mistakenly think fiber must be a laxative.

Have you ever watched a bowl of bran cereal after you pour the milk in, as it poufs up and grows to twice its size? (I suppose you don't sit and watch paint dry either.) Watch it sometime at breakfast. That's pretty much what's going on inside you when you eat insoluble fiber. Most laxatives don't do that. They stimulate movement, usually through chemicals or some kind of lubricant. Dietary fiber, on the other hand, encourages the muscles of your GI (gastrointestinal) system to do the work, and that's a good thing. All your musculatory system requires exercise, including your digestive tract. It's essential for healthy aging and disease prevention.

Grist for the Mill

"Separating the wheat from the chaff" means to separate things of value from things of no value. The chaff is the dry, outer casing of the grain, which is discarded and not, as is sometimes thought, the bran.

Your Top-Ten Grain Products

So who ranks best in fiber power in the category of grains? Before we open the envelope, bear in mind, these grains are tops not only because they're fiber-rich but also because they're the ones you and your family are most likely able to enjoy on a regular basis. I could tell you that amaranth grains have more than 17 grams fiber per $1/2$ cup, or that teff and spelt offer 16 grams in the same amount, but would you drop everything and hurriedly go seek them out? No. In fact, you might hurriedly drop this book and decide that high-fiber is just way too high-minded for you. Practicality again.

The envelope, please …

¹/₂ cup steel-cut oats	8 grams
2 slices whole-wheat bread	6 grams
1 cup whole-wheat spaghetti	6 grams
1 cup bran flakes cereal	5 grams
10 whole-wheat crackers	5 grams
3 cups popcorn	4 grams
1 cup brown rice	4 grams
¹/₄ cup whole-wheat flour	4 grams
¹/₂ cup barley	3 grams
3 TB. toasted wheat germ	3 grams

Surprised to see popcorn on the list? Bet you didn't know it's not a bad snack choice, provided you go easy on the butter and salt.

We'll be meeting some other terrific grains and grain products later on such as bulgur wheat, wheat berries, and quinoa, learning to cook them with agility and confidence. For now, put your reading glasses on as we take a close look at product labels and their fiber-related claims.

Reading Labels

Packaging is always designed to grab your attention. Because your first impression of a product is the front of its packaging, whether box or bag, manufacturers try to draw you in with the use of color, attractive photographs and drawings, and bold statements that are short and memorable.

The savvy shopper knows, however, that the most important part of the packaging is the nutrition label that appears on the back or side. It's there that you really discover what the true benefits are and whether or not the contents meet your needs. For fiber seekers, learning to read these labels with discernment is of paramount importance.

Fiber grams always appear as part of the carbohydrate grams. Sometimes labels differentiate between soluble and insoluble fiber, and sometimes the listing simply gives the amount of dietary fiber per serving, which is, frankly, all you really need to worry about.

A more recent inclusion on the nutritional label is something called the Daily Reference Value (DRV), which can be a bit misleading. Determined by the Food and Drug Administration (FDA), it tells you the percentage of the daily recommended amount that each nutrient contains. The problem is that, in the case of fiber, the DRV is based on a daily recommendation of 25 grams, which we've already seen is on the low side. Calculating your goals based on these percentages won't get you where you want to be, fiber-wise, so it's best just to ignore them. Concentrate on the grams, and you'll be good to go.

Deciphering Claims

For product manufacturers to make health claims on their packaging, they must meet certain government regulatory criteria. Otherwise, you'll see one of those tiny asterisks that lead you to even tinier print that says, "These statements have not been evaluated by the FDA" or some other type of disclaimer.

Fortunately, pretty specific definitions have been created for fiber content, which can help you when shopping:

- *High fiber* means there are 5 or more grams per serving.

- *Good source of fiber* means there are between 2.5 and 4.9 grams per serving.

- *More fiber than* … means there's at least 2.5 grams more per serving than the food it's being compared to.

Grist for the Mill _____

Claims like "high in oat bran" or "made with wheat bran" only mean that there's a decent amount of that ingredient in their product. It doesn't mean it's necessarily high in fiber.

It can be a little tricky, all this deciphering, but for the most part, sticking to the number of grams per serving and looking for the words *high fiber* or *good source of fiber* will assist you in your goals and make life a lot simpler.

The Carb Connection

Fiber is only present in carbohydrates. It's not found in animal protein or fat. But isn't it a bad thing to eat too many carbs? Yes and no. It depends on the type of carb you're consuming.

Refined carbohydrates, as opposed to complex carbohydrates, can wreak havoc with blood sugar, particularly for diabetics. Because refined carbs are less processed and, consequently, your body has less processing to do of its own, they tend to raise blood sugar levels quickly, putting stress on the pancreas to pump out insulin.

Complex carbs take a longer time to metabolize (or process), so the effect on blood sugar is more gradual. This is a good thing, not only for glucose control but also for hunger control. You get full a bit faster and stay full a bit longer when you eat less-refined foods.

It's not surprising that fiber plays a large role in this phenomenon. Chances are, the more complex a carb is, the more fiber it contains.

Recently, the glycemic index has gained attention as an indicator of good and bad carbs. It provides a number, from 1 to 100, for common carbohydrates, ranking them according to how quickly they increase blood sugar. In very simple terms, foods with low numbers are better for us than those with higher numbers, and more often than not, carbs that are low on the glycemic index are high in fiber. So eating a high-fiber diet automatically puts you in good stead with carbs and can assist tremendously in maintaining healthy glucose levels and avoiding insulin resistance.

Calories—Stand Up and Be Counted ... or Not!

What if I told you that calories from fiber don't really count? How is that possible? Well, as fiber moves through the digestive tract, remember, it's not digested so it doesn't contribute any calories to the food it's in. Fiber also prevents the absorption of some calories—about 7, to be exact, per gram of fiber. Over time, this could be a significant amount and is one of the reasons that high-fiber eating can result in weight loss.

Before you zip over to the nearest wholesale retail store and start stocking up on cases of bran cereal, however, be aware that super-extreme amounts of fiber (if you're even capable of ingesting them) are not recommended and may even prevent the absorption of some vital nutrients.

Just be happy that an added benefit to your high-fiber plan is the ability to control weight primarily through the pacification of hunger, which keeps you from grabbing empty calories, and to a lesser degree, calorie elimination through nonabsorption.

 Grist for the Mill

Calories are measurements of energy provided by nutrients. To look at some numbers: 1 gram protein or carbohydrate contributes 4 calories, while 1 gram fat contributes 7 calories. Fiber, on the other hand, contributes 0 calories per gram.

What About Supplements?

The powers that be tell us that if we aren't eating enough fiber in our diet, we needn't worry because there's always that handy variety of supplements available to us in the supermarket or the pharmacy to fill in the blanks. At least that's what the supplement manufacturers proclaim.

Powders, pills, chewable tablets, wafers, and even shakes and energy bars are all poised and ready to help us reach our fiber goals. Isn't it easier to just take them up on their offer and dispense with all this figuring and label reading and, in their view, unnecessary high-fiber cooking business?

No, no, and no again. Eating foods rich in fiber is by far the healthiest and surest way to consume this all-important nutrient. Eating your fiber naked, as the experts say, not only proves inefficient but also deprives you of all the amazing nutrients found in plants that you need so badly to keep your body running smoothly and staying disease-free. All those fabulous phytochemicals and antioxidants would be sorely missed.

So would a lot of really delectable meals, like the ones in this book. Who wants to trade in their favorite food for a pill? Not even the astronauts have to do that. Eating your fiber the whole-food way is the only real way to go.

It's Psyllium, Silly!

Psyllium is a form of supplemental dietary soluble fiber you may have heard about, and it may be the exception to the rule of supplement avoidance. It's often seen in trendy food stores and health food shops. Derived from the husks of psyllium seeds, it's generally sold in powder form to be added to water or other beverages and can be found in some laxatives and breakfast cereals as well. It's been touted as a super fiber supplement, containing more fiber than oat bran (about 71 grams per 100 grams psyllium). It's also been studied as a cholesterol-lowering agent with modest success.

If you add psyllium powder to your diet, be aware that regular use in large quantities should really be monitored by a doctor or dietitian. Sometimes recommended for extreme cases of constipation and for those suffering from inflammatory or irritable bowel syndrome (IBS), psyllium is a supplement that's worth

Smooth Move

Before taking any type of vitamin, mineral, herb, or fiber supplement, be sure to check with your physician for potential drug interactions and side effects.

looking into. For the most part, however, if you're a healthy adult looking to increase dietary fiber, don't go silly with supplementation, and instead opt for getting your fiber from food.

The Facts on Flax

Flaxseeds have received a lot of attention lately, and rightly so. They have so many benefits that it's hard to know where to begin to toot their horn.

First, flax is one of the very few plant sources of healthful omega-3 fatty acids, so it's often recommended for those who follow a vegetarian diet or shun fish like salmon and sardines. Most importantly for us, however, it's an excellent source of both soluble and insoluble fiber.

To reap the benefits of flaxseeds, they need to be ground. You can do it yourself, or you can buy flaxseeds that are already ground, often referred to as flax meal. You'll see it pop up a few times in the recipes because it's a terrific addition to baking.

Because flaxseeds have a high oil content and are super perishable, keep your flax meal and seeds in the refrigerator. It's also the best place for other types of seeds, nuts, and whole-grain flours for the same reason, but we'll get to all that in the next chapter when we set up our high-fiber kitchen and pantry.

The Least You Need to Know

- Dietary fiber is the indigestible part of plant foods, and is either soluble or insoluble in water.
- Fiber is a necessary part of your diet and can help you ward off disease and maintain a healthy weight.
- The average adult should consume about 35 grams fiber, or a bit more, per day to reap its benefits.
- Many fruits, vegetables, and grains are great sources of dietary fiber.
- High-fiber cooking is simple, satisfying, and delicious.

Chapter 2

Cooking High Fiber

In This Chapter

◆ Stocking your pantry

◆ Choosing and storing fresh ingredients

◆ A handful of helpful tips

Cooking the high-fiber way doesn't require any special equipment or impossible-to-find ingredients. For the average cook, and even for those who aren't that confident in the kitchen, preparing and cooking food with an eye toward fiber is by no means a formidable task. All that's required is a love of quality ingredients and an eagerness to eat great food. True, there are a few things to consider, which I address in this chapter, but for the most part, high-fiber cooking is simple, stress-free, and overwhelmingly satisfying.

Take a quick inventory of your pantry to check that the ingredients you'll be using on a regular basis are handy and fresh. Doing a little label reading also helps you determine if the products you already have meet the high-fiber goals you've set for yourself and your family. Swapping out the least healthy desirable items for fiber-rich ones on the cereal shelf, as well as in the pasta, rice, and grain cupboards, is a good place to start.

Learning a bit about fresh ingredients such as specific fruits and vegetables that will be popping up in the recipe chapters, and knowing how to store and care for them, is also a good idea. We look at the benefits of fresh versus frozen or canned and discuss which ingredients need refrigeration.

When all's said and done, you'll be ready to plunge head-first into the high-fiber kitchen, knowing you've got everything you need at your fingertips and the knowledge to put it all to work for you.

Taking Stock of Your Pantry

Fling open the door to your pantry, and take a cold, hard look inside. If you see an abundance of boxes that say *quick-cooking* and no sign of bags or boxes containing dried beans and grains or the words *whole wheat*, you've got some work to do.

Rice that cooks in minutes or oatmeal that's zappable in seconds needs to be replaced with their better-for-you counterparts. Cans of ingredients like kidney beans, corn, or apricot halves will get you a feather in your cap. Things like Hamburger Helper and Dinty Moore are better off donated to the next food drive. You'll want to make room for all those wonderful fiber-rich boxes of pasta and cans of legumes to come.

If you're feeling at all daunted by this exercise, let's take it category by category.

Cereals—Swap Out for Extra Fiber

Beginning with breakfast fare, cold cereals that don't offer a decent amount of fiber per serving (at least 4 grams) need to be phased out. Replace those fruity loopy things with whole-grain squares. Puffy, crispy, overly processed rice cereals need to be usurped by whole-wheat flakes and morsels, and even better, by those that offer a scoopful of dried fruit and nuts. At least one box should have the word *bran* on the front, whether it be buds, bits, or flakes.

Grist for the Mill _____

Products labeled *quick-cooking* or *ready in minutes* are often highly processed and sorely lacking in fiber. Be sure to read nutrition labels to determine how many grams of fiber per serving you can expect.

Hot cereals like oatmeal should say *steel cut* or *old-fashioned* rather than *instant*. Multigrain mixes for microwave or stovetop are great additions, while creamed wheat and rice cereals are okay provided they're the "original" versions with fiber.

You might also want to keep your dried fruit supply nearby to encourage a quick sprinkling just before serving. Things like golden raisins, dried cranberries, and banana chips are perfect.

Beans—Dried or Canned?

If you're wondering whether cooking beans from dry provides you with more fiber than the same bean from a can, the answer boils down to convenience.

If you're more likely to open a can than soak and simmer, the can is the choice for you. There's not a whole lot of difference, fiber-wise, although taste-wise, cooking from dry is always preferred. But in a pinch it's a good idea to have cans on hand. Keep both types for recipes that require dry versions and for those times when you're feeling no time constraints. Split peas, lentils, and some types of small beans don't actually require hours and hours of cooking, so opting for the bags of dried are the best bet in some cases. A few types of beans, like black-eyed peas, come frozen as well and are great to keep on hand.

> **Smooth Move**
>
> To cut down on cooking time for dried beans and legumes, soak them in cold water overnight or boil them for 1 hour.

Always give yourself the choice so you won't have any excuses not to make use of these wonderfully fiber-rich ingredients in your cooking.

Pasta and Rice—Choosing Wisely

Although traditional pasta made from durum wheat has been pushed aside by health enthusiasts in favor of whole-wheat and whole-grain varieties, there's still a place for them in the high-fiber kitchen, as you'll discover in the pasta recipes later in the book. Sometimes an ingredient that has less to offer, fiber-wise, can be kicked up with other ingredients that have a lot to offer, resulting in a terrific high-fiber dish. Still, keep a supply of the whole-grain type as well, for those times when a pasta needs to deliver a more powerful fiber punch.

Same goes for your rice selections. Brown rice of all varieties, whether they be short grain, long grain, basmatic, or arborio, is certainly the choice of rice champions, but don't toss out their less-fibrous cousins. They can be doctored up to meet your fiber goals in plenty of ways.

Tin Can Alley—Good in a Pinch

As mentioned before, canned ingredients can be your best friends when your time and energy are low. A variety of beans and many types of fruit are just as good to use from the can in most recipes. Obviously, when certain fresh fruit is in season, nothing can compare to the quality of taste and the level of nutrition you can gain. But for times when seasonality is not on your side, canned fruits are terrific helpers in your fiber endeavors. Frozen fruits can be excellent as well, particularly in the berry department.

Vegetables are often another story. Although there's nothing wrong with canned corn, beets, and peas, to name a few, I've never been a big fan of mushy asparagus or spinach from a can. Frozen, or even better, fresh, is clearly the choice in these instances. Canned vegetables also tend to be higher in sodium if that's a concern of yours, although many products are now available with reduced salt.

The true exception to the rule is canned tomatoes. Whole, chopped, diced, or puréed, canned tomatoes are great to have on hand for myriad purposes. Tomato paste, naturally high in fiber, is also an important staple.

How Fresh You Are!

From now on, you should make a point of hanging out in the produce aisle of your supermarket. There you'll find your most fiber-friendly ingredients just waiting for you to take them home and give them a taste of your creativity. From winter squash to spring peas, the seasonal choices you'll encounter will shower your senses with color, aroma, and flavor. Look for sales on super-fresh vegetables and fruit, and plan to high-light them in one or more recipes where their qualities will shine.

It's okay to poke at them, and squeeze a bit—I have it on good authority they actually enjoy it! Adoringly make your choice, and transport them home to your kitchen of love. Just don't do what they fear the most: shove them in the fridge behind the soy milk and forget about them.

Storing Fruits and Vegetables

Take a hint from your produce manager, and store your fresh ingredients the same way they were on display at the market.

Greens belong in the fridge; potatoes and root vegetables don't. Fruit that's not quite ripe will benefit from a couple days at room temperature before chilling. And never, ever, refrigerate tomatoes. Their luscious flavor and perfect texture will quickly change to bland and mealy.

Although the method of storage won't affect the fiber content of vegetables and fruit, it will make a huge difference in how long they keep and how flavorful and crisp they stay.

Caring for Your Grains, Nuts, and Seeds

These terrific fiber-rich ingredients need to be coddled and cared for if you hope to prolong their life and usability.

Flours made from whole wheat and whole grains need to be kept cold to avoid the bran and germ present in them from going rancid. When you get them home, store them in the fridge or even the freezer—they'll last many months away from warmth.

Dried grains and beans are fine on the pantry shelf, but nuts and seeds, which contain high levels of oil, are also subject to turning quickly. Keep them well sealed in airtight bags or containers and store them in the fridge.

Shelled nuts can even be stored in the freezer for up to a year. Any oils that come from nuts and seeds, like walnut or sesame, also need refrigeration. If your oil starts to smell like art class (the linseed oil base of paints), its time to replace it with a new bottle. Oils used past their freshness will not only perform and taste bad but may also cause digestive distress, so keep an eye (and nose) on them from time to time.

Smooth Move

Keep a box or container in one corner of your freezer and fridge to hold bags of perishable nuts, seeds, and flours, so you can find them quickly when needed.

The Matter of Organics

Nearly every large supermarket now has an organic produce aisle. There you can find everything from mushrooms to apples, labeled *pesticide-free* and boasting about a 20 percent higher price. When it comes to high-fiber cooking, does it really matter? Fiber content is unaffected by this distinction. But buying organic, if you're inclined to and can afford to, is a good move.

Certain types of produce absorb more pesticide residue than others, so if possible, you may want to begin there. White mushrooms, strawberries, and spinach are just a few items that have been shown to be far safer in organic form.

Fresh produce, however, is not the only food category that can be found in organic form. Many whole grains, including flours, are also available pesticide-free.

A Quick Look at Protein and Fat

High-fiber cooking is not low-carb cooking, but that aspect certainly can be incorporated into a diet that carefully monitors healthful carbohydrates.

Regardless of your carb preferences, it's always smart to make good use of lean proteins such as chicken, pork, and fish in your cooking. And don't forget that some of the stars of a fiber-rich diet such as beans, including soybeans, as well as many grains, are low-fat sources of protein as well. All around, it's a healthy approach.

Similarly, cooking high-fiber doesn't imply low-fat. It's not because fiber-rich ingredients are high in fat, but because many recipes that focus on fiber tend not to worry terribly about fat grams. Having said that, healthy fats like olive oil are used quite often, and many recipes in the book lend themselves to substitutions. For example, swapping low-fat milk for whole milk, or nonhydrogenated margarine for butter, is certainly okay to do.

No matter what your leaning, you'll find plentiful recipes and ingredient suggestions to suit your taste and requirements.

The Least You Need to Know

- ◆ Keeping a good supply of fiber-rich cereals and grains in your pantry as well as canned vegetables and fruit encourages you to cook high fiber.

- ◆ Fresh ingredients are usually best, but good-quality frozen versions and those in cans can be used without losing fiber or flavor.

- ◆ Incorporating other dietary concerns such as organic ingredients, carb watching, or low fat, can be easily worked into a high-fiber plan.

Part 2

Breakfast and Brunch

A sensible start to any day is surely a nourishing breakfast, and this is where fiber can really shine. From hot cereals to muffins to pancakes, learn to create some mighty tasty selections to satisfy the pickiest of eaters, and pick up a few tricks on how to add a bit of fiber here and there to really jump-start your daily intake. You'll meet a great group of delectable grains, fruits, and nuts, as well as some healthy whole-grain flours to assist you in your fiber-rich breakfast-baking.

Hearty brunch ideas are on the menu, too, from omelets to frittatas, giving you your first look at how fiber-rich carbohydrates can combine with protein for a healthful, well-rounded meal.

Wholesome Hot and Cold Cereals

In This Chapter

◆ Jump-starting your daily fiber intake

◆ Hot and hearty breakfast grains

◆ Convenient, fiber-rich cold cereals

With cereals as your staunchest allies, there's no better time than breakfast to get a head start on meeting your daily fiber goals. Whether as part of a larger morning repast, or simply on its own, a good helping of wholesome grains can account for almost $1/3$ of your total daily fiber when you're aiming for 35 grams. *Wholesome* is the key distinction here, and if you've stocked your pantry with steel-cut oats, kasha, and flax meal, to name a few staples, you're halfway there.

Still, you may be wondering how to cook these fiber powerhouses without resulting in a bowl of what might taste akin to the cardboard box they came in. Not to worry! Contrary to popular belief, fiber and good taste are not mutually exclusive, and in this chapter, you'll quickly see why.

Stirring Up a Good Habit

Cooking methods for hot cereals don't always entail slaving over a hot stove, repetitively stirring until carpal tunnel syndrome sets in. Many grains such as barley, wheat, and even steel-cut oats do just fine with an initial stir, a low flame, and a somewhat watchful eye. Your trusty microwave can even step in on occasion to speed up the process. This leaves no excuses about not having enough time for a good, nutritious breakfast.

As with anything else, once you start preparing wholesome hot cereals on a regular basis, it becomes second nature. And after you've tasted the overwhelmingly delicious difference, you'll wonder why it took you so long to come on board with the rest of us.

DIY Cold Cereal

Cold breakfast cereals that contain fiber usually tout this fact on their boxes, along with various other health claims and self-boasting. Reading the nutrition labels, however, and remembering the criteria the government uses to define fiber claims in food, quickly helps you determine whether these products fit in with your high-fiber goals.

Remember, for a manufacturer to claim "high fiber," the food must have at least 5 grams fiber per serving, while a designation of "good source of fiber" requires between 2.5 and 4.9 grams per serving. Although not bad, these numbers are far from impressive. They may even be coming mostly from those pebbly bits of stale dried fruit that get stuck in your teeth as well as clusters of unknown origin.

By making your own versions of granola, muesli, and even cold cereal blends, you'll have the power to kick up the fiber content per serving while also munching on nutritious bits you like. What better way to start your "fiberful" day?

Steel-Cut Oatmeal with Brown Sugar and Walnuts

After one taste of this hearty, chewy, and delicious oatmeal, featuring sweet, soft brown sugar and the delightful crunch of walnuts, you'll never go back to instant!

1½ cups water	1 TB. dark brown sugar
½ tsp. salt	2 TB. chopped walnuts
½ cup steel-cut oats	Splash milk (optional)
½ tsp. unsalted butter	

1. In a medium saucepan over high heat, bring water to a boil. Stir in salt and oats. Reduce heat to low, cover, and cook for about 20 minutes or until most of water is absorbed.

2. Remove from heat, stir in butter, and let stand until thickened to desired consistency.

3. To serve, divide oatmeal between 2 cereal bowls, sprinkle with brown sugar and walnuts, and add milk (if using).

Variation: Other nut topping combinations like honey and hazelnuts, maple syrup and pecans, or raw sugar and almonds are also delicious. A sprinkling of dried berries or raisins adds an extra boost of fiber.

> *Yield: 2 servings*
>
> **Prep time:** 1 minute
>
> **Cook time:** 25 to 30 minutes
>
> **Serving size:** ¾ cup
>
> **Each serving has:**
>
> **11 g fiber**
> 475 calories
> 15 g fat
> 73 g carbohydrate
> 14 g protein

 Smooth Move

To make your hurried weekday mornings easier, double or triple this recipe and store the extra in the fridge. When you're ready for a quick and delicious breakfast, all you need is a 1-minute zap in the microwave.

Old-Fashioned Apple-Cinnamon Oats

Fresh-tasting diced, unpeeled apple makes this oatmeal even more delicious and fiber-rich, while the snappy taste of cinnamon will please every taste bud.

Yield: 2 servings
Prep time: 3 minutes
Cook time: 7 minutes
Serving size: about 1 cup
Each serving has:
12 g fiber
438 calories
8 g fat
84 g carbohydrate
13 g protein

2 cups water

½ tsp. salt

1 cup old-fashioned rolled oats

1 medium Golden Delicious apple, cored and diced

1 TB. sugar

¼ tsp. ground cinnamon

1. In a medium saucepan over high heat, bring water to a boil. Stir in salt and oats. Reduce heat to medium-low, and simmer, stirring occasionally, for 3 minutes.

2. Stir in apple, sugar, and cinnamon, and continue cooking on low for 2 minutes or until thickened. Serve immediately.

Variation: Try substituting pears, especially the fiber-packed *Asian pear*, for a change of pace.

Fiber Optics

Asian pears, those apple look-alikes with brown skins similar to Bosc pears, are one of the five most fiber-rich plant foods in the world. Look for them in the specialty fruit section of your supermarket.

Microwave Multigrain Cereal Blend

This multigrain bowl of goodness has just the right amount of sweetness and crunch, not to mention loads of hidden fiber.

¼ **cup quick-cooking oats**

¾ **cup multigrain hot cereal with rye, barley, oats, and wheat**

1 TB. **ground flax meal**

1 TB. **firmly packed light brown sugar**

Pinch salt

1½ **cups water**

2 TB. **Grape Nuts Cereal**

2 TB. **strawberry preserves**

Splash milk (optional)

Yield: 2 servings
Prep time: 5 minutes
Cook time: 2 minutes
Serving size: 1 cup
Each serving has:
10 g fiber
330 calories
3 g fat
55 g carbohydrate
5 g protein

1. In a large microwave-safe bowl, combine oats, multigrain cereal, ground flax meal, brown sugar, and salt. Add water and stir until well combined.

2. Microwave on high for 2 minutes, and stir again.

3. To serve, divide mixture between 2 cereal bowls. Sprinkle each bowl with 1 tablespoon Grape Nuts, top with 1 tablespoon preserves, and add milk (if using).

 Grist for the Mill

Adding just 1 tablespoon ground flax meal to any hot cereal provides 2 extra grams fiber.

Kasha with Banana Chips and Honey

Kasha, or roasted buckwheat, has a wonderful nutty flavor that pairs perfectly with banana. The vanilla soy milk and honey add just the right finish.

Yield: 2 servings
Prep time: 2 minutes
Cook time: 10 minutes
Serving size: about 1 cup
Each serving has:
9 g fiber
400 calories
13 g fat
65 g carbohydrate
5 g protein

3 cups water

½ tsp. salt

1 TB. sugar

⅔ cup coarse-grain *kasha*

½ cup dried banana chips

2 TB. honey

½ cup vanilla soy milk

1. In a medium saucepan over high heat, bring water to a boil. Stir in salt, sugar, and kasha.

2. Reduce heat to medium-low and cook, stirring occasionally, for 8 to 10 minutes or to desired consistency.

3. To serve, divide kasha between 2 cereal bowls, top each with ¼ cup banana chips, drizzle with 1 tablespoon honey, and pour ¼ cup soy milk around edges.

Fiber Optics

Kasha, the result of roasting nutritious buckwheat groats, is a popular ingredient in Jewish and Middle Eastern cooking, and is an excellent source of fiber for those with wheat and gluten intolerance. It's available in fine, medium, coarse, and whole grain.

Tropical Sunrise Granola

The intoxicating flavors of Hawaii beckon in this easy, homemade granola that includes sweet pineapple, coconut, and the rich taste of macadamia nuts.

3 cups old-fashioned rolled oats

½ cup toasted wheat germ

¼ cup sesame seeds

½ cup sweetened flaked coconut

½ cup canola oil

½ cup honey

¼ cup firmly packed light brown sugar

Pinch salt

½ cup diced dried pineapple

½ cup chopped macadamia nuts

Yield: 8 servings
Prep time: 12 minutes
Cook time: 25 minutes
Serving size: ¾ cup
Each serving has:
9 g fiber
510 calories
26 g fat
70 g carbohydrate
13 g protein

1. Preheat the oven to 325°F.

2. In a medium mixing bowl, combine oats, wheat germ, sesame seeds, and coconut.

3. In a small saucepan over medium heat, cook canola oil, honey, brown sugar, and salt, stirring often, until sugar has dissolved. Pour over oat mixture, and stir well to coat.

4. Transfer mixture to a large baking sheet with a rim and spread out evenly. Bake for 20 to 25 minutes or until golden and crisp, occasionally shaking the pan to evenly brown. Remove from the oven.

5. Stir in dried pineapple and macadamia nuts. Allow to cool completely, and store in an airtight container for up to 3 weeks.

Variation: Substitute different dried fruits and nuts such as Australian ginger and cashews or dried peaches and Georgia pecans to take you to other sunny locales.

Smooth Move

Think outside the cereal bowl by using homemade granola as a topping for ice cream, yogurt, and puddings.

Toasted Oat and Almond Muesli

If the mere mention of *muesli* conjures up visions of chomping on cardboard, this wonderfully crunchy version that includes succulent yogurt-covered raisins will quickly change your mind.

Yield: 4 servings
Prep time: 3 minutes
Cook time: 20 minutes
Serving size: 1 cup
Each serving has:
11 g fiber
495 calories
12 g fat
77 g carbohydrate
17 g protein

2 cups old-fashioned rolled oats

½ cup sliced almonds

1 cup multigrain or corn flakes

½ cup yogurt-coated raisins

1. Preheat the oven to 350°F.

2. On a baking sheet with a rim, combine oats and almonds. Toast in the oven, shaking the pan occasionally, for 20 minutes or until lightly browned. Transfer to a medium mixing bowl and allow to cool.

3. Add multigrain flakes and yogurt-coated raisins, mix well, and store in an airtight container for up to 3 weeks.

Grist for the Mill

Muesli was created by the Swiss doctor Maximilian Bircher-Benner in 1900 as a therapy for his patients. Authentic fresh muesli requires an overnight oat soaking and the addition of lemon juice and mushy fruit.

Kicked-Up Bran Flakes

Here's your chance for designer cereal fame. Start with a good base like hearty bran flakes, and mix it up from there. Use this honey-sweet and golden fruity version to get started and then try it with your favorite cereals.

3 cups bran flakes

1 cup All-Bran cereal

1 cup Wheat Chex cereal

1 cup Honey Nut Cheerios cereal

½ cup golden raisins

Yield: 6 servings
Prep time: 3 minutes
Serving size: 1 cup
Each serving has:
8 g fiber
210 calories
1 g fat
40 g carbohydrate
5 g protein

1. In a large mixing bowl, combine bran flakes, All-Bran, Wheat Chex, Honey Nut Cheerios, and raisins.

2. Store in an airtight container for up to 1 month.

 Smooth Move

For added fiber and nutrition, always consider topping your dry cereal with fresh fruit like blueberries, sliced strawberries, or banana when serving.

Chapter 4

Muffins, Scones, and Griddle Favorites

In This Chapter

- ◆ Whole-grain breakfast baking
- ◆ Fruits and nuts go to bat for you
- ◆ Old favorites with a fiber twist

Whether it's a muffin hot from the oven or a stack of perfect pancakes, making your own rather than relying on store-bought versions guarantees the fiber outcome you're after. When your average supermarket muffin barely contains 1 gram fiber, you might as well proclaim "Let them eat cake!" at the family breakfast table. Although your kids probably won't protest, you know those empty calories won't sustain them much past their walk out the door.

The Whole Answer

Whole-grain ingredients that are fiber rich can make the difference in a breakfast that carries everyone through to lunch. Not only will they feel full and satisfied, their energy levels won't take a dive midmorning, so they'll stay alert and focused. Stone-ground flours, bran, and flax meal are just a few of the ingredients that provide a good amount of fiber and contribute to a healthy muffin or waffle.

Another way to boost the fiber content of breakfast selections is to let fruit, nuts, seeds, and on occasion even vegetables, assist you in your cause. Raisins, walnuts, sunflower seeds, and puréed pumpkin are just a few of the additions that can make your breakfast baking not only healthier, but tastier as well.

He Ain't Heavy, He's My Muffin

If your experience with whole-grain baking has led you to conclude that your muffin would make a better baseball than a breakfast item, you're in for a surprise. Proper whole-grain baking does not result in the inedible.

On the contrary, added flavor and texture always accompany the use of wholesome stone-ground flours.

Golden Raisin Bran Muffins

Applesauce adds moistness and flavor to these healthful and delicious morning muffins.

2 cups All-Bran cereal

1 cup milk

¾ cup applesauce

¼ cup vegetable oil

1 large egg

1 cup all-purpose flour

½ cup whole-wheat flour

½ cup firmly packed brown sugar

2 tsp. baking powder

½ tsp. salt

¼ tsp. baking soda

¾ cup golden raisins

Yield: 12 muffins
Prep time: 20 minutes
Cook time: 25 minutes
Serving size: 1 muffin
Each serving has:
4 g fiber
140 calories
2 g fat
27 g carbohydrate
4 g protein

1. Preheat the oven to 400°F. Grease a 12-cup muffin pan or line with cupcake liners.

2. In a medium mixing bowl, stir together All-Bran, milk, applesauce, vegetable oil, and egg. Let stand for 10 minutes.

3. In a separate medium mixing bowl, whisk together all-purpose flour, whole-wheat flour, brown sugar, baking powder, salt, and baking soda. Stir in raisins. Add dry ingredients to bran mixture, and stir just until combined.

4. Divide batter evenly among muffin cups, and bake for about 25 minutes or until tops are golden brown and a toothpick inserted in the middle comes out clean.

5. Cool on a rack for 5 minutes, gently remove from the pan, and store muffins in an airtight container for 3 to 5 days.

Smooth Move

If a full batch of muffins is too much for you to consume in a few days, try freezing half of them for the future. Cool completely, wrap tightly in plastic, and store in a zipper-lock freezer bag.

Pumpkin-Flax Muffins

Convenient canned pumpkin provides both fiber and moistness in these tasty breakfast treats brimming with cinnamon-rich flavor.

Yield: 12 muffins
Prep time: 15 minutes
Cook time: 30 minutes
Serving size: 1 muffin
Each serving has:
2 g fiber
150 calories
5 g fat
24 g carbohydrate
0 g protein

1 cup canned puréed pumpkin	2 TB. ground flax meal
½ cup water	1 TB. whole flaxseeds
¼ cup vegetable oil	1 tsp. baking powder
1 tsp. vanilla extract	½ tsp. baking soda
1 cup all-purpose flour	½ tsp. cinnamon
⅔ cup whole-wheat flour	½ tsp. salt
1 cup sugar	⅛ tsp. ground nutmeg

1. Preheat the oven to 350°F. Grease a 12-cup muffin pan or line with cupcake liners.

2. In a small mixing bowl, combine pumpkin, water, vegetable oil, and vanilla extract.

3. In a medium mixing bowl, whisk together all-purpose flour, whole-wheat flour, sugar, flax meal, flaxseeds, baking powder, baking soda, cinnamon, salt, and nutmeg. Add pumpkin mixture to dry ingredients, and stir well to combine.

4. Divide batter evenly among muffin cups, and bake for about 30 minutes or until a toothpick inserted in the middle comes out clean.

5. Cool on a rack for 5 minutes, gently remove from the pan, and store muffins in an airtight container for 3 to 5 days.

Smooth Move

In a pinch, 1 tablespoon ground flaxseeds and 3 tablespoons water can replace 1 large egg in baking recipes.

Peanut Butter–Banana Muffins

Creamy peanut butter and sweet, ripe bananas come together in these delicious golden muffins flavored with a hint of honey.

1¼ cups all-purpose flour	**½ cup chunky peanut butter**
½ cup whole-wheat flour	**½ cup honey**
¼ cup toasted wheat germ	**2 large eggs**
1 tsp. baking soda	**⅓ cup vegetable oil**
½ tsp. salt	**¼ cup firmly packed brown sugar**
1 cup mashed ripe bananas (about 3 medium)	**1 tsp. vanilla extract**

Yield: 12 muffins
Prep time: 15 minutes
Cook time: 20 minutes
Serving size: 1 muffin
Each serving has:
3 g fiber
290 calories
12 g fat
38 g carbohydrate
7 g protein

1. Preheat the oven to 400°F. Grease a 12-cup muffin pan or line with cupcake liners.

2. In a medium bowl, whisk together all-purpose flour, whole-wheat flour, wheat germ, baking soda, and salt.

3. In a separate medium bowl, and using an electric mixer on medium-high speed, beat together bananas, peanut butter, honey, eggs, vegetable oil, brown sugar, and vanilla extract. Beat in flour mixture until well combined.

4. Divide batter evenly among muffin cups, and bake for about 20 minutes or until a toothpick inserted in the middle comes out clean.

5. Cool on a rack for 5 minutes, gently remove from the pan, and store in an airtight container for 3 to 5 days.

Smooth Move

When bananas are ready for baking but you're not, store them in the freezer. Slip the bananas, peel and all, into a plastic freezer bag and store them for up to 3 weeks. Allow to defrost before peeling and mashing.

Raspberry Crumb Muffins

Succulent raspberries and healthful oats provide a fiberful twist in this delectable muffin based on a classic breakfast cake.

Yield: 12 muffins
Prep time: 15 minutes
Cook time: 25 minutes
Serving size: 1 muffin
Each serving has:
2 g fiber
220 calories
10 g fat
30 g carbohydrate
3 g protein

1½ cups plus 3 TB. all-purpose flour

½ cup granulated sugar

2 tsp. baking powder

⅛ tsp. salt

½ cup (1 stick) unsalted butter, melted

1 large egg

½ cup milk

1 tsp. vanilla extract

1¼ cups fresh raspberries

⅓ cup quick-cooking oats

¼ cup firmly packed brown sugar

½ tsp. ground cinnamon

3 TB. unsalted butter, softened

Confectioners' sugar (optional)

1. Preheat the oven to 350°F. Grease a 12-cup muffin pan or line with cupcake liners.

2. In a medium bowl, whisk together 1½ cups flour, sugar, baking powder, and salt.

3. In another medium bowl, whisk together melted butter, egg, milk, and vanilla extract. Add flour mixture, and stir just until combined. Gently fold in raspberries.

4. For crumb topping: in a small bowl, using a fork or a pastry blender, combine oats, brown sugar, remaining 3 tablespoons flour, cinnamon, and softened butter.

5. Divide batter evenly among muffin cups, and sprinkle each with crumb topping. Bake for about 25 minutes or until a toothpick inserted in the middle comes out clean.

6. Cool on a rack for 5 minutes, gently remove from the pan, and sprinkle tops with confectioners' sugar (if using). Store in an airtight container for 2 or 3 days.

Grist for the Mill

The fiber content in raspberries accounts for 20 percent of their total weight, making them one of the top fiber providers in the fruit world.

Whole-Grain Cranberry-Orange Scones

Orange is a natural flavor partner for whole-grain baking, and the oat flour ups the fiber ante.

1½ cups whole-wheat flour

1 cup *oat flour*

½ cup all-purpose flour

⅔ cup sugar

2 tsp. baking powder

½ tsp. baking soda

½ tsp. salt

½ cup (1 stick) unsalted butter, cut into ½-in. dice

1 cup dried cranberries

½ cup buttermilk

¼ cup frozen orange juice concentrate, thawed

1 large egg

Yield: 12 scones	
Prep time: 30 minutes	
Cook time: 20 to 24 minutes	
Serving size: 1 scone	
Each serving has:	
4 g fiber	
250 calories	
14 g fat	
25 g carbohydrate	
4 g protein	

1. Preheat the oven to 375°F. Line a large baking sheet with parchment paper.

2. In a large mixing bowl, whisk together whole-wheat flour, oat flour, all-purpose flour, sugar, baking powder, baking soda, and salt.

3. Using the back of a fork or a pastry blender, cut butter into flour mixture until it resembles a coarse meal. Stir in cranberries.

4. In a small bowl, whisk together buttermilk, orange juice concentrate, and egg. Gradually add to flour mixture, stirring with a fork until evenly moistened.

5. Turn dough out onto a lightly floured surface, and form 2 balls. Pat each out into ¾-inch-thick circles, cut each circle into 6 wedges, and carefully transfer to the baking sheet.

6. Bake for 20 to 24 minutes or until lightly browned and a toothpick inserted in the middle comes out clean. Serve warm or store in an airtight container for up to 5 days.

Fiber Optics

Oat flour is simply finely ground oats. You can make your own by grinding quick-cooking oats in a blender or food processor.

White Chocolate–Cherry Scones

Classic scones get a sweet fiber makeover with dried cherries and a drizzle of melted white chocolate.

Yield: 12 scones
Prep time: 25 minutes
Cook time: 15 minutes
Serving size: 1 scone
Each serving has:
3 g fiber
325 calories
15 g fat
40 g carbohydrate
7 g protein

1 cup white whole-wheat flour

1 cup all-purpose flour

¼ cup sugar

1 TB. baking powder

¼ tsp. salt

⅓ cup unsalted butter, cut into ½-in. dice

1 cup dried cherries, roughly chopped

1 cup whipping cream

1 (4-oz.) bar white chocolate, broken and melted

1. Preheat the oven to 400°F. Line a large baking sheet with parchment paper.

2. In a medium mixing bowl, whisk together white whole-wheat flour, all-purpose flour, sugar, baking powder, and salt.

3. Using the back of a fork or a pastry blender, cut butter into flour mixture until it resembles a coarse meal. Stir in cherries. Gradually add whipping cream, and stir with a fork until evenly moistened.

4. Turn dough out onto a lightly floured surface, and knead 3 or 4 times until well combined, adding flour if necessary.

5. Roll out to a ½-inch thickness and, using a biscuit cutter or the open end of a glass dipped in flour, cut out dough and transfer to the baking sheet. Gather scraps, re-roll, and cut until all dough is used.

6. Bake for 12 to 15 minutes or until tops are golden and a toothpick inserted in the middle comes out clean. Cool completely, transfer scones to a rack set over parchment paper, and drizzle each with white chocolate. Store single layered in an airtight container for up to 5 days.

Grist for the Mill

White chocolate isn't really chocolate because it only contains cocoa butter and not chocolate liquor (essence of cocoa bean).

Cinnamon Bun Hazelnut Scones

Two treats in one, it'll be hard to resist reaching for another of these intoxicating cinnamon treats laced with flavorful hazelnuts. No problem—hazelnuts have one of the highest fiber ratings in the nut world.

2 cups all-purpose flour

1 cup whole-wheat flour

¼ cup plus 2 TB. granulated sugar

1 TB. baking powder

¼ tsp. salt

½ cup (1 stick) unsalted butter, cut into ½-in. dice

¾ cup milk

1 large egg

1 tsp. vanilla extract

¾ cup chopped hazelnuts

2 tsp. ground cinnamon

1 cup confectioners' sugar

¼ cup orange juice or water

Yield: 12 scones
Prep time: 30 minutes
Cook time: 10 to 13 minutes
Serving size: 1 scone
Each serving has:
3 g fiber
325 calories
15 g fat
40 g carbohydrate
7 g protein

1. Preheat the oven to 425°F. Line a large baking sheet with parchment paper.

2. In a medium bowl, whisk together all-purpose flour, whole-wheat flour, ¼ cup sugar, baking powder, and salt.

3. Using the back of a fork or a pastry blender, cut butter into flour mixture until it resembles a coarse meal.

4. In a small bowl, whisk together milk, egg, and vanilla extract, and add to flour mixture, stirring with a fork until evenly moistened.

5. In another small bowl, combine remaining 2 tablespoons sugar, hazelnuts, and cinnamon. Sprinkle evenly over dough, and stir in only slightly. Do not blend in.

6. Drop dough onto baking sheet by ¼ cupfuls 2 inches apart. Bake for 10 to 13 minutes or until golden and a toothpick inserted in the middle comes out clean. Remove from the oven, and transfer scones to a wire rack set over parchment paper and cool for 5 minutes.

7. In a small bowl, whisk together confectioners' sugar and orange juice, and drizzle generously over each warm scone. Serve immediately or store single layered in an airtight container for up to 5 days.

 Grist for the Mill

Although hazelnuts and filberts are referred to interchangeably, the filbert nut is actually a subspecies of the common hazelnut. The other 17 subspecies are also edible but are rarely seen commercially.

Whole-Wheat Blueberry Pancakes

Plump, delicious blueberries complement the heartiness of these healthful and easy-to-prepare pancakes. Serve with blueberry syrup for an extra-special treat.

Yield: 10 to 12 pancakes
Prep time: 20 minutes
Cook time: 20 minutes
Serving size: 2 pancakes
Each serving has:
5 g fiber
325 calories
11 g fat
45 g carbohydrate
10 g protein

1¼ cups whole-wheat flour
¾ cup all-purpose flour
3 TB. sugar
4 tsp. baking powder
½ tsp. salt

2 cups milk
2 large eggs
¼ cup (½ stick) unsalted butter, melted
1½ cups fresh blueberries

1. In a medium bowl, whisk together whole-wheat flour, all-purpose flour, sugar, baking powder, and salt.

2. In a small mixing bowl, whisk together milk, eggs, and melted butter. Add to flour mixture, and stir with a fork until well combined. Stir in blueberries, and let rest for 10 minutes.

3. Heat a large, nonstick griddle or pan over medium heat. Coat lightly with oil. Drop batter by ⅓ cupfuls onto the griddle, and cook pancakes for 2 minutes per side or until lightly golden.

4. Serve immediately or keep warm on a heated platter.

Variation: Substitute raspberries, sliced strawberries, or halved blackberries for the blueberries and serve with matching fruit syrups, or simply dust with confectioners' sugar.

 Grist for the Mill

Ever wonder why pancake batters always seem to need a rest before pouring? Blame the baking powder. It needs time to come to its full raising power, particularly important when cooking with heavier whole-grain flours.

Buckwheat Pancakes with Apricot Preserves

Nutritional powerhouse buckwheat flour teams up with fiber-rich apricots for a sensational breakfast they'll flip over.

½ cup buckwheat flour

½ cup all-purpose flour

1 TB. sugar

2 tsp. baking powder

¼ tsp. ground cinnamon

¼ tsp. salt

1 cup milk

2 large eggs

¼ cup (½ stick) unsalted butter, melted

Sour cream

Apricot preserves

Yield: 8 to 10 pancakes
Prep time: 20 minutes
Cook time: 15 minutes
Serving size: 3 pancakes
Each serving has:
3 g fiber
375 calories
18 g fat
40 g carbohydrate
12 g protein

1. In a medium bowl, whisk together buckwheat flour, all-purpose flour, sugar, baking powder, cinnamon, and salt.

2. In a small bowl, whisk together milk, eggs, and melted butter. Add to flour mixture, and stir with a fork until well combined. Let rest for 10 minutes.

3. Heat a large, nonstick griddle or pan over medium heat. Coat lightly with oil. Spoon batter onto griddle to make 3-inch wide pancakes, and cook for 1 or 2 minutes per side or until golden.

4. To serve, place 3 pancakes single layered on a plate, and top each with a dollop of sour cream and a spoonful of apricot preserves.

Smooth Move

Leftover pancakes can be kept up to 5 days in the fridge for spontaneous breakfasts. Heat in the microwave for 1 minute and enjoy!

Hearty Cornmeal Flapjacks

Hearty stone-ground cornmeal provides rich flavor and fiber in these delicious, buttery flapjacks.

Yield: 10 to 12 flapjacks
Prep time: 20 minutes
Cook time: 20 minutes
Serving size: 3 flapjacks
Each serving has:
3 g fiber
325 calories
10 g fat
45 g carbohydrate
10 g protein

¾ cup stone-ground cornmeal

¾ cup all-purpose flour

3 TB. sugar

1 tsp. baking powder

½ tsp. baking soda

¼ tsp. salt

1 cup buttermilk

2 large eggs

3 TB. unsalted butter, melted

Maple syrup or fruit jam

1. In a medium bowl, whisk together cornmeal, all-purpose flour, sugar, baking powder, baking soda, and salt.

2. In a small bowl, whisk together buttermilk, eggs, and melted butter. Add to flour mixture, and stir with a fork until well combined. Let rest 10 minutes.

3. Heat a large griddle or pan over medium heat. Coat lightly with oil. Thin batter, if necessary, with a little buttermilk, and pour by ¼ cupfuls onto the griddle. Cook for about 2 minutes per side or until lightly golden.

4. Serve immediately with maple syrup or jam, or keep warm on a heated platter.

Variation: Kick up your fiber content even more by adding ½ cup canned, drained, corn kernels to the batter and serving as a side dish at dinnertime.

 Grist for the Mill

Stone-ground cornmeal, as opposed to common steel-ground, retains some of the hull and germ of the corn kernel, providing more fiber and flavor. Consequently, it's more perishable and should be stored in the refrigerator.

Nutty Whole-Grain Waffles

After you try these healthful and flavorful waffles, packed with the bold taste of whole grains and nuts, you'll never reach for store-bought frozen waffles again!

¾ cup whole-wheat flour

½ cup all-purpose flour

¼ cup toasted wheat germ

¼ cup flax meal

¼ cup ground walnuts

2 TB. sugar

4 tsp. baking powder

¼ tsp. salt

1¾ cups milk

2 large eggs

½ cup vegetable oil

1 tsp. vanilla extract

Yield: 9 or 10 waffles
Prep time: 20 minutes
Cook time: 20 minutes
Serving size: 2 waffles
Each serving has:
6 g fiber
465 calories
18 g fat
38 g carbohydrate
6 g protein

1. In a medium bowl, whisk together whole-wheat flour, all-purpose flour, wheat germ, flax meal, ground walnuts, sugar, baking powder, and salt.

2. In a small bowl, whisk together milk, eggs, vegetable oil, and vanilla extract. Add to flour mixture, and stir with a fork until well combined. Let rest for 10 minutes.

3. Heat waffle iron according to manufacturer's instructions and coat lightly with cooking spray. Pour batter into waffle iron in batches, and cook for about 3 minutes or until crisp and golden.

4. Serve immediately or keep warm on a baking sheet in a 200°F oven.

 Smooth Move

Aunt Jemima's not the only game in town. Freeze your leftover waffles in plastic wrap and toast them up in the morning for a quick, tasty breakfast.

Buttermilk Waffles with Butter Pecan Syrup

Classic waffles get healthy with white whole-wheat flour and a delectable fiber-rich topping made from soft, sweet pecans drenched in a buttery, maple syrup.

Yield: 6 to 8 waffles
Prep time: 25 minutes
Cook time: 15 minutes
Serving size: 2 waffles
Each serving has:
7 g fiber
495 calories
20 g fat
50 g carbohydrate
9 g protein

⅔ **cup pure maple syrup**

¼ **cup (½ stick) unsalted butter**

½ **cup pecans, roughly chopped**

1 **cup** *white whole-wheat flour*

½ **cup all-purpose flour**

2 **tsp. baking powder**

1 **tsp. baking soda**

¼ **tsp. salt**

1¼ **cups buttermilk**

3 **large eggs**

¼ **cup vegetable oil**

2 **medium-size ripe bananas, peeled and sliced**

1. In a small saucepan over medium heat, combine maple syrup, butter, and pecans. Cook, stirring occasionally, for 3 or 4 minutes or until butter has melted and syrup begins to boil. Remove from heat and keep warm.

2. In a medium bowl, whisk together white whole-wheat flour, all-purpose flour, baking powder, baking soda, and salt.

3. In a small bowl, whisk together buttermilk, eggs, and vegetable oil. Add to flour mixture, and stir with a fork until well combined. Let rest 10 minutes.

4. Heat waffle iron according to manufacturer's instructions and coat lightly with cooking spray. Pour batter into waffle iron in batches, and cook for about 5 minutes or until crisp and golden.

5. To serve, place a few banana slices on each waffle and ladle butter pecan syrup over top.

Fiber Optics

White whole-wheat flour is milled from hard white spring wheat and is lighter in color and taste than traditional whole-wheat flour. It can be substituted for 100 percent of the all-purpose flour called for in most baking recipes.

Classic Cinnamon French Toast

No one will guess this "neo"-classic favorite actually contains terrific fiber as well as taste. Aromatic cinnamon and vanilla provide the flavor, while a healthy white bread alternative soaks up the richness.

4 large eggs

¼ cup milk

2 tsp. sugar

1 tsp. ground cinnamon

½ tsp. vanilla extract

6 slices whole-grain white bread

Yield: 6 slices	
Prep time: 10 minutes	
Cook time: 12 minutes	
Serving size: 2 slices	
Each serving has:	
4 g fiber	
275 calories	
9 g fat	
32 g carbohydrate	
14 g protein	

1. In a large, shallow bowl, whisk together eggs, milk, sugar, cinnamon, and vanilla extract.

2. Heat a large griddle or pan over medium heat and coat lightly with oil.

3. Dip each bread slice into egg mixture to saturate, and transfer to griddle. Cook for about 3 minutes per side or until golden and puffed, adding oil to griddle as necessary.

4. Serve immediately or keep warm on a heated platter.

 Smooth Move

Instead of the usual maple syrup, try topping your French toast with fresh fruit and confectioners' sugar for a healthful fiber boost.

Baked Multigrain French Toast

The perfect solution for make-ahead hosting, this hearty French toast flavored with a hint of orange and vanilla couldn't be easier or more delicious, especially when served up with whipped butter and sweet maple syrup.

Yield: 8 slices
Prep time: 70 minutes or overnight
Cook time: 15 minutes
Serving size: 2 slices
Each serving has:
5 g fiber
240 calories
7 g fat
30 g carbohydrate
13 g protein

4 large eggs

½ cup orange juice

½ cup vanilla soy milk

8 (1-in.-thick) slices multigrain bread loaf or baguette

1. In a medium bowl, whisk together eggs, orange juice, and soy milk.

2. Place bread, cut side down, in a 9×13-inch baking dish. Pour egg mixture over bread, turn slices to absorb liquid, cover with foil, and refrigerate for 1 hour or overnight.

3. Preheat the oven to 400°F. Lightly coat a large baking sheet with cooking spray or butter.

4. Place bread slices on the baking sheet 1 inch apart, and bake for about 15 minutes or until golden brown, turning over slices halfway through to cook evenly.

5. Serve immediately or keep warm on a heated platter.

 Smooth Move _____

Instead of hitting your husband over the head with that stale baguette, use it to make *pain perdu,* or "lost bread" as the French call "French toast." Once it's soaked in the egg mixture, it'll come back to life … unlike your husband.

Chapter **5**

Eggs, Omelets, and Frittatas

In This Chapter

- ◆ Egg-ceptional beginnings
- ◆ Ingredients to *egg* you on
- ◆ Hidden ways to include fiber

The answer to the proverbial "which came first?" question has to be the egg. After all, eggs contain many vitamins and minerals our bodies require. And now that they've survived the cholesterol hysteria of the last few decades, eggs are surely a great beginning for a healthy breakfast.

Unfortunately, like all other sources of animal protein, they don't possess a smidgeon of fiber, so to get them to work for you, you'll need to introduce them to some fiber-rich friends in the form of grains, vegetables, and fruit.

Fiber in a Supporting Role

Eggs work very nicely with other ingredients and are quite congenial when it comes to sharing their role in a recipe. Scrambled egg wraps and omelets would be nothing without the support of tortillas and fillings.

It's the fiber content of these supporters that you want to be aware of when attempting to play matchmaker. You'll get a much better fiber boost with a whole-wheat tortilla than a plain floured one, while omelets and frittatas that include spinach or beans definitely outweigh traditional ham and cheese. Still, there's a place for everyone, as these recipes deliciously show.

Hide and Seek

Another great attribute of egg dishes is that they can be the perfect foil for hidden fiber additions such as a sprinkle of wheat germ for those who aren't yet bran-friendly. No one will notice, but everyone will benefit from a few grams of fiber here or there, so feel free to sprinkle at will. Even a little ground flaxseed in a frittata won't be detected. The frittata won't mind, either. After all, it's made up of some very "good eggs."

Scrambled Egg Multigrain Wrap

As easy to scramble together as it is to eat, this wholesome breakfast wrap, filled with creamy eggs and oozing with melted cheddar beats fast-food versions every time.

2 (10-in.) multigrain wraps or tortillas

1 TB. unsalted butter

4 large eggs

2 TB. water

1 TB. toasted wheat germ

Salt and pepper

½ cup shredded cheddar cheese

Yield: 2 wraps
Prep time: 15 minutes
Cook time: 2 minutes
Serving size: 1 wrap
Each serving has:
2 g fiber
425 calories
28 g fat
12 g carbohydrate
23 g protein

1. Preheat the oven to 250°F.

2. Cover wraps in foil and keep warm in the oven.

3. Melt butter in a large, nonstick skillet over medium-high heat.

4. In a medium bowl, whisk together eggs, water, wheat germ, salt, and pepper. Pour egg mixture into the skillet, reduce heat to medium-low, and stir to scramble for about 2 minutes or until firm yet moist.

5. Divide cooked eggs between warmed wraps, sprinkle with cheese, and fold. Serve immediately.

Variation: "Beef" it up by adding crumbled cooked sausage or diced ham.

 Smooth Move

To avoid rubbery eggs, always stop the cooking while the eggs are still a bit runny. They'll continue to firm up before serving.

Home on the Range Huevos Rancheros

Hey, amigo! Add both zip and fiber to your morning with this version of a Mexican classic that features the tang of peppered Jack and salsa and the creamy richness of avocado.

Yield: 2 servings
Prep time: 15 minutes
Cook time: 8 minutes
Serving size: 1 topped tortilla
Each serving has:
4 g fiber
510 calories
41 g fat
10 g carbohydrate
23 g protein

2 (8-in.) corn tortillas

3 TB. vegetable oil

4 large eggs

½ cup shredded hot pepper or plain Monterey Jack cheese

½ cup prepared mild or hot salsa

½ ripe avocado, peeled and diced

2 tsp. finely chopped fresh cilantro

1. In a large, nonstick skillet, fry tortillas in 2 tablespoons vegetable oil over medium-high heat, about 1 minute per side. Wrap in foil and keep warm.

2. Add remaining 1 tablespoon vegetable oil to the skillet, reduce heat to medium, and crack eggs into the skillet. Cook for 1 or 2 minutes or until whites are almost firm.

3. Sprinkle cheese over eggs, cover, and reduce heat to low. Cook 1 more minute until cheese has melted and whites are firm. Remove from heat.

4. To assemble, place each tortilla on a serving plate, top with 2 eggs, ½ of salsa, and ½ of avocado. Sprinkle with chopped cilantro.

Variation: Try black bean and corn salsa or other prepared vegetable salsas in place of tomato to boost your fiber.

 Smooth Move

At brunch or lunchtime, serve up huevos rancheros the traditional way with sides of refried beans and country-style potatoes for even more fiber.

Eggs Benedict Arnold

We're deserting the usual ham for fiber-rich artichoke hearts in this wonderful version of poached eggs on toast.

1 cup canned or frozen artichoke hearts, thawed if frozen	1 TB. white wine vinegar

1 cup prepared Hollandaise sauce (from jar or packet)

4 large eggs

Pinch salt

2 whole-wheat English muffins, split and toasted

2 tsp. finely chopped fresh parsley

Yield: 2 servings
Prep time: 20 minutes
Cook time: 3 minutes
Serving size: 2 eggs
Each serving has:
6 g fiber
250 calories
10 g fat
21 g carbohydrate
17 g protein

1. Pat dry artichoke hearts and slice in $^1/_2$.

2. In a medium saucepan over low heat, combine artichoke hearts and Hollandaise sauce, stirring occasionally. Set aside, cover, and keep warm.

3. Crack each egg into a small bowl or cup.

4. Fill a large skillet with 3 inches water, cover, and bring to a boil. When water has boiled, stir in white wine vinegar and salt. Carefully pour eggs into water, turn off heat, and cover. Allow to cook for about 3 minutes or until just firm. Remove eggs with a slotted spoon, and drain on paper towels.

5. To assemble, place 2 muffin halves on a serving plate, spoon $^1/_2$ of artichoke sauce mixture over, top each muffin $^1/_2$ with 1 poached egg, and sprinkle parsley over all.

 Grist for the Mill

Why add vinegar when poaching eggs? The acid helps keep the whites from dispersing into the water by lowering the pH level.

Super Southwest Omelet

Fully loaded with the fiber of meaty black beans and succulent corn, this delicious omelet with nacholike fixings will satisfy the biggest of appetites.

Yield: 2 servings
Prep time: 15 minutes
Cook time: 8 minutes
Serving size: ½ omelet
Each serving has:
9 g fiber
300 calories
15 g fat
30 g carbohydrate
10 g protein

1 cup canned black beans, drained and rinsed

½ cup canned corn kernels, drained

4 canned or fresh plum tomatoes, roughly chopped

½ green bell pepper, ribs and seeds removed, and thinly sliced

¼ tsp. chili powder

¼ tsp. ground cumin

Salt and pepper

4 large eggs

1 TB. vegetable oil

1 TB. unsalted butter

1 cup shredded cheddar or Colby cheese

2 TB. sour cream

2 green onions, chopped

1. In a small saucepan over medium heat, combine black beans, corn, tomatoes, green bell pepper, chili powder, cumin, salt, and pepper. Cook, stirring often, for 5 minutes. Set aside.

2. In a medium mixing bowl, whisk together eggs and season with salt and pepper.

3. In a large, nonstick skillet over medium heat, melt vegetable oil and butter. Pour in eggs. As eggs begin to set, use a rubber spatula to pull cooked edges to the middle and spread uncooked egg to the edge. Cover, reduce heat to low, and cook for about 1 minute or until eggs are firm on top.

4. Reduce heat to low. Spread bean mixture evenly over eggs, top with shredded cheese, and continue to cook, covered, for about 1 more minute or until cheese has melted.

5. Loosen omelet with a spatula around the edges and bottom of the pan, and slide it onto a heated platter, tipping the pan to fold over. Dollop sour cream and sprinkle onions on top to serve.

Smooth Move

For a brunch omelet, serve this with guacamole and a side of roasted potatoes for extra fiber.

Puffy Fruit Omelet

Fiber-rich, sweet, and juicy strawberries star in this delicate soufflé-like omelet topped off by a dusting of confectioners' sugar for extra sweetness.

1½ cups fresh strawberries, stemmed and quartered

1 TB. plus 2 tsp. sugar

2 large eggs, separated

¼ tsp. vanilla extract

Pinch salt

1 TB. unsalted butter

Confectioners' sugar

Yield: 2 servings
Prep time: 20 minutes
Cook time: 5 minutes
Serving size: ½ omelet
Each serving has:
2 g fiber
175 calories
11 g fat
13 g carbohydrate
7 g protein

1. In a small bowl, combine strawberries and 1 tablespoon sugar. Stir gently, and set aside for 10 minutes.

2. In a medium bowl, whisk together egg yolks and vanilla extract until pale yellow. In another medium bowl, beat egg whites with salt until soft peaks form. Fold beaten egg whites into yolks.

3. In a large, nonstick skillet over medium heat, melt butter. Pour in eggs, and spread evenly in pan. Cover, reduce heat to low, and cook for 3 or 4 minutes or until eggs are golden on bottom and set on top.

4. Spoon strawberries down center of omelet and use a spatula to fold in half. Transfer to a heated platter, dust with confectioners' sugar, and serve immediately.

Variation: Any seasonal fruit is perfect to substitute for the strawberries. Try other berries, sliced peaches, or diced mango. For crispier fruits like apples and pears, dice and cook briefly with sugar in a small pan to soften before adding to omelet.

 Smooth Move

Egg-sential tips: in some recipes, egg yolks need to be separated from their whites. Simply crack the egg in half over a bowl and allow the white to run down while keeping the yolk intact. To fold beaten egg whites into a batter, use a rubber spatula and cut down vertically through the two mixtures and then "fold" up. Shift the bowl a quarter turn and repeat until combined.

Spinach and 'Shroom Frittata

There's no flipping required with this hearty, open-faced vegetable omelet featuring crisp-fried potatoes and a flavorful sauté of seasoned spinach and mushrooms.

Yield: 4 servings
Prep time: 15 minutes
Cook time: 20 minutes
Serving size: ¼ frittata
Each serving has:
2 g fiber
320 calories
21 g fat
15 g carbohydrate
16 g protein

3 TB. olive oil

3 small red-skinned potatoes, cooked, skin on, and sliced

Salt and pepper

2 cups fresh baby spinach

1 cup thinly sliced white mushrooms

6 large eggs

¼ cup grated Pecorino Romano cheese

1 tsp. dried thyme

2 tsp. chopped fresh parsley

1. In a heavy, 12-inch skillet over medium-high heat, heat olive oil. Layer sliced potatoes in the skillet, and sprinkle with salt and pepper. Fry for 4 minutes or until lightly browned, turning slices over once.

2. Add spinach and mushrooms, stir to combine, reduce heat to low, and cook, covered, for about 3 minutes or until spinach has wilted.

3. In a medium bowl, whisk together eggs, cheese, thyme, and parsley. Season with salt and pepper. Pour egg mixture into skillet, use a spatula to distribute vegetables evenly, and cook, covered, over medium-low heat for 10 to 12 minutes or until bottom is browned and eggs are almost set.

4. While eggs are cooking, preheat the broiler.

5. Place the skillet under the broiler for about 2 minutes to finish cooking top of frittata.

6. Use a metal spatula to loosen the sides and bottom, and slide onto a warm platter. Serve immediately.

Grist for the Mill

Spinach as a great source of iron was debunked in the 1930s when researchers discovered a misplaced decimal point in an earlier nutritional analysis. Oops—maybe it was fiber that fortified Popeye.

Easiest Baked Asparagus Frittata

Your oven does all the work in this colorful and delicious frittata dotted with tender asparagus pieces and smoky-flavored roasted peppers.

10 large eggs

½ cup light cream

Salt and pepper

1 lb. asparagus, cooked and cut into 1-in. pieces

1½ cups prepared roasted bell pepper slices, roughly chopped

5 green onions, chopped

4 oz. diced cooked ham (about 1 cup)

Yield: 6 servings
Prep time: 20 minutes
Cook time: 35 minutes
Serving size: ⅙ frittata
Each serving has:
2 g fiber
235 calories
14 g fat
8 g carbohydrate
18 g protein

1. Preheat the oven to 350°F. Butter a 13×9-inch glass baking dish.

2. In a large mixing bowl, whisk together eggs, cream, salt, and pepper. Stir in asparagus, roasted peppers, green onions, and ham.

3. Pour mixture into the baking dish, distribute evenly with a fork, and bake for about 35 minutes or until lightly golden and firm.

4. Cut into 6 pieces and serve.

Variation: Replace asparagus with 2 cups cooked broccoli or cauliflower florets, or diced cooked red-skinned potatoes.

 Smooth Move

Frittatas reheat beautifully in the microwave or oven, so save any leftover slices in the fridge and enjoy as a light supper with a salad and bread.

Part 3

Fiberful Snacks and Beverages

Ah yes, America's favorite pastime—snacking. Did you know we spend more time nibbling, dipping, and munching than the rest of the world combined? Hey—its not a bad thing, you know. Experts say eating throughout the day is better for us health-wise than devouring one or two gargantuan meals. What matters is exactly what we're nibbling on. And that's where fiber-rich munchies can make a huge difference, helping us tally up those fiber grams in the process. In Part 3, you'll find a multitude of munchables that will keep you on track during the day and satisfy those nibbling urges at night.

Creamy, rich smoothies and shakes also fit into a fiber-conscious plan. Loaded with vital nutrients as well, they'll be great for a quick fix in between meals or as a beverage accompaniment for breakfast or lunch. You'll soon find that slurping your way to high fiber is a definite option, and a delicious one at that.

Chapter 6

Dips and Spreads

In This Chapter

- The skinny on dips
- Little dippers with big dipper results
- Spreading the wealth of fiber-rich ingredients

Dietary fiber can make an appearance in any number of forms when you create dips and spreads. It can be the star of the dip itself, such as in a bean dip, or it can be the dipper, as in fibrous vegetables. Spreads based on cheese can have healthful ingredients added to make them fiber rich and flavorful, and pairing whole-grain crackers with spreads can boost the fiber as well.

Dippideedoodah

As a nation of dippers, we've come a long way from the basic potato chip and onion dip. Varieties of beans now take center stage in everything from hummus to salsa, while healthful, multigrain dippers such as sweet potato chips and flatbreads are reached for more often than not.

The dilemma lies in what to choose and how to put it all together for the tastiest and most nutritious outcome. Here you'll find the best of the bunch.

A Widespread Selection

Fruit and nuts have always been delicious partners for cheese, so combining them into spreads is a natural upshot of our predilection for cheese and crackers. If saltines and Cheez Whiz is your only experience in this genre, you're in for a delightful surprise.

As a prelude to dinner or an accompaniment for drinks, snacks like these can't be beat, so why not tally up a bit of fiber in the process, and savor the diversity of dips and spreads.

Tuscan Bean Dip

Fiber-rich beans provide the base for this delicious pre-dinner dip that echoes the flavors of Tuscany with bold garlic, fragrant rosemary, and fruity olive oil.

1 (15-oz.) can cannellini beans, drained and rinsed

1 garlic clove, peeled

1 TB. fresh lemon juice

½ tsp. dried rosemary

2 tsp. extra-virgin olive oil plus more for drizzling

Salt and pepper

Raw vegetables for dipping (fennel quarters, carrot sticks, endive leaves, baby zucchini, etc.)

Yield: 3 servings
Prep time: 10 minutes
Serving size: ¹/₃ cup
Each serving has:
5 g fiber
200 calories
9 g fat
21 g carbohydrate
8 g protein

1. In a food processor fitted with a steel blade, purée beans, garlic, lemon juice, rosemary, and 2 teaspoons olive oil until smooth. Season with salt and pepper, and transfer to a bowl.

2. Drizzle top of dip with olive oil, and serve with raw vegetables. Store leftovers in the refrigerator for up to 1 week.

 Grist for the Mill _____

Cannellini beans are actually white kidney beans, a relative of red kidney beans, named for their resemblance to the shape of the kidney.

Sun-Dried Tomato Hummus

The flavorful addition of sun-dried tomatoes really kicks up the fiber in this popular Middle Eastern dip made with tahini.

Yield: 3 servings
Prep time: 10 minutes
Serving size: 1/3 cup
Each serving has:
8 g fiber
289 calories
20 g fat
37 g carbohydrate
8 g protein

1 (15-oz.) can chickpeas, drained and rinsed

2 garlic cloves, peeled

½ cup sun-dried tomatoes packed in oil, drained

¼ cup *tahini*

1 TB. fresh lemon juice

Salt and pepper

Extra-virgin olive oil

3 whole-wheat pita breads, cut into triangles

1. In a food processor fitted with a steel blade, purée chickpeas, garlic, sun-dried tomatoes, tahini, and lemon juice until smooth. Season with salt and pepper, and transfer to a bowl.

2. Drizzle top of hummus with olive oil, and serve with pita triangles for dipping. Store leftovers in the refrigerator for up to 1 week.

Fiber Optics

Tahini is a paste made from ground sesame seeds and is what gives hummus its characteristic flavor as well as a bit of fiber. Look for it in the condiment or deli section of your supermarket.

Black Bean and Corn Salsa

Two fiber giants—black beans and corn—team up for this spicy salsa that's the perfect prelude or accompaniment to a Mexican meal.

1 (15-oz.) can black beans, drained and rinsed

1 (3-oz.) can corn kernels, drained

½ medium red bell pepper, ribs and seeds removed, and diced

1 medium jalapeño pepper, seeds removed, and diced

3 green onions, chopped

1 TB. fresh lime juice

1 tsp. red wine vinegar

1 TB. olive oil

½ tsp. ground cumin

1 TB. chopped fresh cilantro

Salt and pepper

Multigrain tortilla chips

Yield: 4 servings
Prep time: 15 minutes
Serving size: ½ cup
Each serving has:
10 g fiber
200 calories
4 g fat
30 g carbohydrate
11 g protein

1. In a medium bowl, combine black beans, corn, bell pepper, jalapeño pepper, and green onions.

2. In a small bowl, whisk together lime juice, vinegar, olive oil, and cumin. Add to bean mixture, and stir well to coat.

3. Stir in cilantro, season with salt and pepper, and serve with tortilla chips for dipping. Store leftovers in the refrigerator up to 1 week.

Smooth Move

Combine this Black Bean and Corn Salsa with rice to make a vegetarian main course that's quick and full of fiber.

Chunky Guacamole

Avocado packs a powerful punch in a high-fiber diet and is irresistibly delicious in this easy version of the ever-popular dip.

Yield: 4 servings
Prep time: 12 minutes
Serving size: ¹/₂ cup
Each serving has:
5 g fiber
175 calories
15 g fat
7 g carbohydrate
2 g protein

2 ripe Hass avocados

1 TB. fresh lime juice

2 heaping TB. prepared salsa, mild or hot

1 TB. sour cream

Tortilla chips

1. Cut each avocado in ¹/₂ lengthwise and twist apart. Discard seed, and scoop out flesh into a medium bowl. Add lime juice, and mash, using the back of a fork, until smooth yet slightly chunky.

2. Stir in salsa and sour cream, transfer to a clean bowl, and serve immediately with tortilla chips. Cover the surface of leftovers with plastic wrap and refrigerate up to 1 day.

 Grist for the Mill

Not all avocados are created equal. The Hass variety from California is smaller, bumpier, and darker skinned than the Florida Fuerte, and is more flavorful as well. It also provides slightly more fiber despite its size.

Best-Ever Spinach-Artichoke Dip

Perfect for dipping or spreading, here's a thick, healthful, and delicious version of the restaurant favorite brimming with tangy garlic and sweetly fragrant Parmesan cheese.

1 TB. olive oil

1 medium red onion, chopped

3 garlic cloves, minced

Salt and pepper

1 (9-oz.) pkg. frozen spinach, thawed and squeezed dry

1 (10-oz.) pkg. frozen artichoke hearts, thawed and patted dry

1 cup grated Parmesan cheese

1 (3-oz.) pkg. cream cheese

½ cup mayonnaise

Woven wheat crackers, such as Triscuits

Yield: 6 servings
Prep time: 10 minutes
Cook time: 25 minutes
Serving size: ¹/₂ cup
Each serving has:
3 g fiber
295 calories
30 g fat
4 g carbohydrate
10 g protein

1. Preheat the oven to 375°F. Coat a glass or ceramic pie dish with cooking spray.

2. In a skillet over medium-high heat, heat olive oil. Add onion and cook, stirring often, for about 5 minutes or until onion is soft and lightly brown. Stir in garlic, season with salt and pepper, and cook for 1 more minute. Remove from heat.

3. In a food processor fitted with a steel blade, combine spinach, artichoke hearts, ¹/₂ cup Parmesan cheese, cream cheese, mayonnaise, and onion mixture, and pulse until well combined but still somewhat chunky. Season with salt and pepper, and transfer to the prepared pie dish.

4. Sprinkle remaining ¹/₂ cup Parmesan cheese over top, and bake for 15 to 20 minutes or until heated through and golden on top. Serve immediately with crackers.

 Grist for the Mill

Artichokes are a source of the prebiotic insulin, which is a fiberlike substance that acts as food for probiotics (beneficial bacteria in the colon) so they can grow and proliferate.

Baked Brie with Apples and Almonds

Here, fiber-filled apples and almonds combine with gooey, buttery Brie for a warm and wonderful spread.

Yield: 4 servings
Prep time: 15 minutes
Cook time: 15 minutes
Serving size: ¼ Brie wheel
Each serving has:
2 g fiber
275 calories
21 g fat
7 g carbohydrate
13 g protein

1 medium crisp apple such as Macintosh or Gala, cored and diced

⅓ cup sliced almonds

1 TB. firmly packed brown sugar

1 TB. unsalted butter, softened

1 (8-oz.) round Brie cheese

½ whole-wheat baguette, cut into ½-in. slices

1. Preheat the oven to 350°F. Line a baking sheet with parchment paper.

2. In a medium bowl, combine apple, almonds, brown sugar, and butter.

3. Slice Brie horizontally into 2 even rounds. Place bottom ½, rind side down, on the baking sheet, and top with ½ of apple mixture. Place remaining ½ of Brie on top, rind side up, and spoon remaining apple mixture over.

4. Bake for about 15 minutes or until filling and topping are bubbly and cheese begins to melt. Transfer to a platter and serve immediately with bread slices.

 Smooth Move _____

Is your brown sugar hard as a rock? Add a few apple slices to it, place in an airtight container, and by the next day, your sugar will have softened nicely.

Pesto Cheese Spread with Toasted Pine Nuts

Hidden wheat germ provides extra fiber and crunch in this delectable, creamy spread that features aromatic basil pesto and rich-tasting pine nuts.

1 (8-oz.) pkg. whipped cream cheese, softened

1 (7-oz.) pkg. prepared pesto sauce

2 TB. toasted wheat germ

¼ cup pine nuts

Seeded flatbread crackers

Yield: 6 servings
Prep time: 5 minutes
Cook time: 2 minutes
Serving size: ¹/₄ cup
Each serving has:
4 g fiber
200 calories
13 g fat
30 g carbohydrate
4 g protein

1. In a medium bowl, beat together cream cheese, pesto sauce, and wheat germ. Transfer to a serving bowl, cover, and chill.

2. In a small skillet over high heat, toast pine nuts for about 2 minutes, shaking the pan to evenly brown. Set aside to cool.

3. To serve, sprinkle pine nuts on top of spread and surround with flatbread crackers.

Grist for the Mill

Wheat germ is a popular addition to the diets of body builders as its high concentration of complex carbs and protein help gain muscle.

Cranberry Pecan Cheese Log

The creamy richness of goat cheese is complemented by a sweet and satisfying coating of dried cranberries and tasty pecans in this show-stopper of spreads.

Yield: 6 servings
Prep time: 12 minutes
Serving size: 2 table-spoons
Each serving has:
4 g fiber
380 calories
25 g fat
32 g carbohydrate
12 g protein

½ cup dried cranberries

½ cup pecan pieces

¼ tsp. ground cinnamon

1 (11-oz.) log *goat cheese*

1½ TB. honey

Stoned wheat crackers

1. In a small bowl, combine cranberries, pecans, and cinnamon. Spread out on a 12-inch-long piece of parchment paper.

2. Place whole goat cheese log on nut mixture, and gently press and roll until log is completely covered.

3. Transfer to a platter, drizzle with honey, and serve with crackers.

Fiber Optics

Goat cheese, also called *chèvre* (French for "goat"), is generally sold in logs. Its flavor is slightly tarter than cow or sheep milk cheeses.

Hors d'Oeuvres and Appetizers

In This Chapter

◆ Smart choices for predinner fare

◆ Kicking up favorite menu selections

◆ Enticing ingredients await

You probably already get in host mode and prepare some hors d'oeuvres and appetizers with your family and guests when entertaining. Now you can make them fiberlicious!

Whether it's exotic stuffed dates or the ever-popular nacho platter, fiber can find its way quite naturally into a variety of offerings. In fact, some of our most beloved finger foods, like potato skins and bruschetta, already provide a great jumping-off point and encourage the addition of some tasty, fiber-rich ingredients.

Goal Assistance

Meal starters like these can be particularly helpful when you're trying to reach your daily 35 grams fiber, especially when dinner itself may not provide as high a number as you'd like. Sneaking in a few grams before your main meal will not only bring you closer to your goal, but may lessen the amount of fiberless calories you consume later on because of the satiating quality dietary fiber possesses.

Not Guilty!

Quickly made appetizers can also serve as accompaniments to a bowl of soup at lunch, a light salad at supper, or a close-to-midnight snack. So always keep good-quality ingredients on hand to encourage you to create more healthful selections.

Shop wisely, too, and snatch up those fresh figs or broccoli crowns when they're on sale. They'll be more likely to tempt you to use them when they look you in the eye every time you open the fridge. They're also very good at playing the guilt card when you think about reaching for those leftover chicken wings from last night's bar visit!

Sweet and Savory Stuffed Dates

These tasty, fiber-rich date hors d'oeuvres stuffed with sweet Parmesan and almonds, all wrapped up in crisp, savory bacon will disappear faster than you can make them!

18 *Medjool dates*	6 thin bacon slices, cut into thirds
¼ lb. Parmesan cheese	
18 whole blanched almonds	Wooden toothpicks

1. Preheat the oven to 425°F. Line a rimmed baking sheet with parchment paper.

2. Using a sharp paring knife, cut a slit down each date to remove pit. Cut Parmesan into 18 thin 1-inch-long pieces.

3. Stuff each date with 1 Parmesan slice and 1 almond, and press to close. Wrap each date in a piece of bacon, secure with a toothpick, and place on the baking sheet.

4. Bake for 8 to 10 minutes or until bacon is crisp, turning over once. Drain on paper towels before serving, with the toothpicks intact.

Yield: 6 servings
Prep time: 15 minutes
Cook time: 8 to 10 minutes
Serving size: 3 dates
Each serving has:
3 g fiber
199 calories
5 g fat
20 g carbohydrate
10 g protein

Fiber Optics

Medjool dates are the elite of all date varieties. Hailing from Morocco and high in fiber, they're larger, sweeter, and more succulent than the average supermarket date.

Fig and Prosciutto Bruschetta

A pair made in appetizer heaven, sweet fresh figs and flavorful Italian prosciutto make for an extraordinarily delicious start to any meal.

Yield: 4 servings
Prep time: 15 minutes
Serving size: 2 bruschetta slices
Each serving has:
3 g fiber
247 calories
10 g fat
31 g carbohydrate
9 g protein

8 medium fresh figs, quartered

2 cups arugula leaves, roughly chopped

2 TB. extra-virgin olive oil

1 TB. balsamic vinegar

Pinch salt

8 (½-in.-thick) slices multi-grain Italian bread, toasted

8 thin slices prosciutto

Freshly ground black pepper

1. In a medium bowl, toss together figs, arugula, olive oil, vinegar, and salt until evenly coated.

2. Distribute fig mixture evenly over bread slices, drape 1 slice prosciutto over each, top with a grinding of black pepper, and serve immediately.

 Grist for the Mill _____

Go *fig*-ure! Figs have been grown since ancient times for ailments ranging from constipation to warts. Their natural emollients soften body tissue and balance dryness.

Smoked Salmon on Rye Bites

Chewy and delicious whole rye bread provides the base for this easy yet elegant treat featuring a healthful vegetable cream cheese and succulent smoked salmon.

4 slices *whole rye bread*

4 TB. vegetable cream cheese

1 (4-oz.) pkg. sliced smoked salmon

Juice of ½ lemon

¼ cup capers

Yield: 4 servings	
Prep time: 5 minutes	
Serving size: 4 rye bites	
Each serving has:	
2 g fiber	
157 calories	
8 g fat	
13 g carbohydrate	
8 g protein	

1. Place bread slices on a work surface, and spread 1 tablespoon cream cheese evenly over each.

2. Drape smoked salmon slices over each bread slice, and drizzle lemon juice over top.

3. Using a serrated knife, cut each topped bread slice into 4 rectangles, and top with capers. Serve immediately.

Fiber Optics

Dense and dark **whole rye bread** is the original pumpernickel bread of Westphalia, Germany. Once relegated to health food stores, it's now readily available in supermarkets and is prized for its high-fiber content.

Broccoli and Cheddar Baked Potato Skins

Who knew our favorite appetizer could be fiber friendly? Feel free to load up on these crispy, flavorful skins topped with tender broccoli and melted cheese.

Yield: 4 servings
Prep time: 1 hour
Cook time: 25 minutes
Serving size: 2 potato skins
Each serving has:
3 g fiber
250 calories
15 g fat
18 g carbohydrate
7 g protein

4 medium Idaho or russet potatoes

2 TB. vegetable oil

Salt and pepper

1½ cups broccoli florets, cooked crisp-tender

1 cup shredded cheddar cheese

Sour cream

1. Preheat the oven to 400°F.

2. Bake potatoes directly on the upper oven rack for about 45 minutes or until fork-tender.

3. When potatoes are cool enough to handle, cut each in ½ lengthwise and scoop out all but ¼-inch potato next to skin. Lightly brush both sides with vegetable oil, season with salt and pepper, and place cut side down on a baking sheet.

4. Increase the oven temperature to 450°F, and bake potato halves for about 15 minutes or until golden and crispy.

5. Turn potatoes cut side up, fill each with broccoli, sprinkle cheese over, and return to oven for 5 to 8 minutes or until cheese is melted. Serve immediately with sour cream.

 Smooth Move

When making baked potatoes for dinner, throw in a few extra to have on hand for quick potato-skin appetizer production. Save your scooped-out flesh for a quick mashed potato side dish.

Microwave Nachos Supreme

Easy to make but hard to resist, fiber-rich pinto beans highlight this ever-popular Tex-Mex treat, topped with spicy jalapeño for added zip.

18 tortilla chips

½ cup canned pinto beans, drained and rinsed

⅔ cup shredded cheddar or Monterey Jack cheese

3 TB. canned jalapeño slices

2 TB. sliced black olives

2 green onions, chopped

Sour cream or guacamole

Yield: 2 servings
Prep time: 10 minutes
Cook time: 3 minutes
Serving size: ¹/₂ nacho platter
Each serving has:
3 g fiber
271 calories
15 g fat
20 g carbohydrate
11 g protein

1. Arrange tortilla chips on a microwave-safe plate, overlapping as necessary. Distribute beans over chips, and top with cheese and jalapeño slices.

2. Microwave on high for 2 or 3 minutes or until cheese is melted and beans are heated through.

3. Sprinkle with olives and green onions, and serve immediately with sour cream or guacamole.

 Smooth Move _____

Keep leftover canned beans in the fridge for up to 5 days. Add them to stews, soups, and salads for extra fiber.

Greek Eggplant Rounds

The irresistible flavors of the Greek Mediterranean combine in this fabulous appetizer that includes creamy, rich feta; pungent oregano; and smoky roasted peppers.

Yield: 4 servings
Prep time: 15 minutes
Cook time: 30 to 35 minutes
Serving size: 2 rounds
Each serving has:
2 g fiber
122 calories
9 g fat
4 g carbohydrate
5 g protein

1 large eggplant, unpeeled

Olive oil

Salt and pepper

1 cup crumbled feta cheese

2 tsp. dried oregano

½ cup prepared roasted red bell peppers, chopped

½ cup pitted kalamata olives, roughly chopped

8 sprigs basil

1. Preheat the oven to 350°F.

2. Trim ends of eggplant, and slice into 8 ($^3/_4$-inch) rounds. Place eggplant on a large baking sheet, brush both sides of slices with olive oil, and season with salt and pepper. Bake, turning over once, for 20 to 25 minutes or until softened and lightly browned. Brush with more oil as necessary to keep moist but not greasy.

3. Top each round with feta cheese, oregano, roasted red peppers, and olives. Return to the oven, and bake for about 8 minutes or until cheese begins to melt.

4. Transfer to a platter or individual plates, and garnish each round with 1 sprig basil. Serve immediately.

 Smooth Move _____

Roast your own bell peppers by placing them under the broiler or on an open grill flame until blackened. Remove burnt skin with a paper towel, slice into strips, and keep in an airtight container in the fridge for up to 1 week.

Chapter 8

Nibbles and Trail Mixes

In This Chapter

◆ Simple and satisfying munchies

◆ Nibbles with a twist

◆ Trail mix as super food

One of the best ways to increase your fiber intake is by nibbling on nuts. From almonds to pistachios, all types of nuts are high in fiber and loaded with many vitamins and minerals.

Unfortunately, they're also high in fat, so it's a good idea to mix them, when possible, with low-fat ingredients such as grain cereals and dried fruit. Hello, trail mix, your nutritional-minded answer to healthy snacking!

Creating your own versions of trail mixes can be fun as well as satisfying, so use the recipes in this chapter to spur you on to great trail-mix blazing!

Eat Like a Bird

Just like nuts, seeds are extremely good sources of fiber and can satisfy a nibble urge in no time. They are energy powerhouses, and their fiber can keep you going at full speed. Look at birds—apart from the occasional flying insect or worm, seeds account for the bulk of most birds' diets, and they always seem to be zipping along pretty quickly.

The high level of insoluble fiber in seeds is also helpful in keeping digestive tracts moving along.

All Dried Up

Years ago, the dried fruit in trail mixes was usually only raisins, but today we're fortunate to have a cornucopia of dried fruit and berries at our fingertips. From dried blueberries to dehydrated papaya, our choices are truly exceptional.

As a bonus, the removal of moisture from these fruits increases their shelf life, making them great stand-ins when fresh fruit choices are limited. Try using them on cereal, in yogurt, in baking, or any other place you might find their fresh counterparts. You'll be *berry* glad you did!

Cereal and Nut Blend Nibblers

Both salty and sweet, this snack will keep nibblers satisfied in between meals while chalking up some good fiber.

2 TB. unsalted butter

2 TB. sugar

1 tsp. chili powder

2 cups Wheat Chex cereal

1 cup Multigrain Cheerios cereal

1 cup salted mixed nuts

Yield: 8 servings
Prep time: 10 minutes
Cook time: 20 minutes
Serving size: ¹/₂ cup
Each serving has:
2 g fiber
82 calories
3 g fat
13 g carbohydrate
1 g protein

1. Preheat the oven to 325°F.

2. In a small saucepan, melt butter with sugar and chili powder. Set aside.

3. In a large roasting pan or rimmed baking sheet, combine Wheat Chex, Multigrain Cheerios, and mixed nuts. Pour butter mixture over top, and toss well to combine.

4. Bake, stirring occasionally, for about 20 minutes or until mixture begins to brown. Cool completely, transfer to an airtight container, and keep for up to 2 weeks.

Smooth Move

Save and combine the last bits in each near-empty cereal box to use as a base for a quick trail mix. Then, all you have to do is add your favorite nuts and dried fruit.

Asian Crunch Mix

Fans of Asian flavors will gobble up this yummy snack filled with crunchy and savory ingredients.

Yield: 8 servings
Prep time: 10 minutes
Cook time: 15 minutes
Serving size: ½ cup
Each serving has:
2 g fiber
244 calories
16 g fat
19 g carbohydrate
6 g protein

2 TB. unsalted butter

1 TB. sugar

1 TB. soy sauce

¼ tsp. garlic powder

¼ tsp. onion powder

1 cup chow mein noodles

1 cup sesame rice crackers, broken into bite-size pieces

½ cup cashew halves

½ cup salted dry-roasted peanuts

½ cup nori maki arare

½ cup wasabi peas

1. Preheat the oven to 325°F.

2. In a small saucepan, melt butter with sugar, soy sauce, garlic powder, and onion powder. Set aside.

3. In a large roasting pan, combine chow mein noodles, sesame rice crackers, cashews, and peanuts. Pour butter mixture over, and toss well to combine.

4. Bake, stirring occasionally, for about 15 minutes or until mixture begins to brown. Remove from the oven, and stir in nori maki arare and wasabi peas. Cool completely, transfer to an airtight container, and keep for up to 2 weeks.

 Smooth Move

Check out Asian markets and health food stores for different flavors of nori maki arare, or rice crackers wrapped in seaweed, as well as dried peas and other crunchy legumes.

Nutty Chocolate Popcorn

The chocolate lover's answer to high-fiber snacking, it'll be hard to resist this combo of sweet, salty, and crunchy.

6 cups plain popped popcorn

1½ cups sweet and salty glazed peanuts, such as Beer Nuts

⅔ cup whole, salted almonds

1 cup semisweet chocolate chips

½ cup light corn syrup

⅓ cup chunky peanut butter

2 TB. unsalted butter

Yield: 8 servings
Prep time: 10 minutes
Cook time: 30 minutes
Serving size: 1 cup
Each serving has:
6 g fiber
460 calories
31 g fat
44 g carbohydrate
10 g protein

1. Preheat the oven to 300°F. Cover a large, rimmed baking sheet with foil and coat with cooking spray. Coat a large roasting pan with cooking spray.

2. In the prepared roasting pan, combine popcorn, peanuts, and almonds.

3. In a medium saucepan, over medium-high heat, combine chocolate chips, corn syrup, peanut butter, and butter. Cook, stirring often, for about 10 minutes or until bubbly. Carefully pour over popcorn mixture, and stir to coat.

4. Bake, stirring every 10 minutes, for about 30 minutes or until entire mixture bubbles. Immediately pour onto prepared baking sheet and spread out evenly.

5. Cool completely and break into small chunks. Store in an airtight container for up to 1 week.

 Grist for the Mill

In 1946, popcorn became the first food to be microwaved. Today, Americans consume 17 billion quarts of this high-fiber snack every year.

White Chocolate–Pistachio Bark

Fiber-rich nuts, seeds, and dried fruit speckle this easy, delicious snack featuring creamy white chocolate.

Yield: 8 servings
Prep time: 25 minutes
Serving size: 4 ounces, 1 medium piece
Each serving has:
3 g fiber
446 calories
28 g fat
45 g carbohydrate
8 g protein

1 lb. white chocolate, roughly chopped

1 cup shelled pistachio nuts

⅓ **cup sunflower seeds**

⅔ **cup chopped dried apricots**

1. Line a large, rimmed baking sheet with parchment paper.

2. In the top of a double boiler over gently simmering water, melt white chocolate, stirring occasionally, until smooth. Remove from heat and allow to cool for about 15 minutes or until no longer hot to the touch.

3. Stir in pistachio nuts, sunflower seeds, and dried apricots. Pour onto prepared baking sheet, and spread out evenly. Place another piece of parchment paper on top of mixture, and press down gently.

4. Transfer baking sheet to the refrigerator and chill for at least 1 hour or until set. Remove paper, cut or break bark into pieces, and store in an airtight container for up to 1 week.

 Smooth Move _____

Chocolate of all types can be melted in the microwave. Roughly chop, place in a microwave-safe bowl, and cook at 15-second intervals, stirring each time, until smooth.

Honey-Sesame Seed Brittle

Itty-bitty sesame seeds and pepitas pack a powerful fiber punch in this delectable crunchy snack based on a popular Middle Eastern candy.

2 cups sesame seeds

1⅓ cups honey

2 cups sugar

1 tsp. baking soda

2 TB. unsalted butter

½ cup *pepitas*

Yield: 8 servings
Prep time: 10 minutes
Cook time: 10 minutes
Serving size: 2 medium pieces
Each serving has:
5 g fiber
470 calories
27 g fat
97 g carbohydrate
11 g protein

1. Preheat the oven to 350°F. Coat a baking sheet with cooking spray.

2. Place sesame seeds on a large, rimmed baking sheet and toast in the oven, shaking the pan occasionally, for 5 to 8 minutes or until lightly browned.

3. In a large, nonstick skillet over medium heat, bring honey to a boil, stirring constantly, and cook gently for 3 minutes. Add sugar and continue to stir until sugar has dissolved and mixture is thick.

4. Remove from heat and whisk in baking soda and butter. Stir in toasted sesame seeds and pepitas. Pour onto the prepared baking sheet and spread out evenly.

5. When candy has set, crack into 2-inch pieces and store in an airtight container for up to 2 weeks.

Fiber Optics

Pepitas is Spanish for "pumpkin seeds," but the term is commonly used when describing trail mix and Mexican recipe ingredients. Pepitas are almost always found already shelled and roasted in grocery and health food stores.

Very Berry Trail Mix

Sweet, dried berries are superstars when it comes to fiber as well as antioxidants, with goji berries being the latest starlet on the scene and featured in this flavorful combo.

Yield: 8 servings
Prep time: 5 minutes
Serving size: ¹/₂ cup
Each serving has:
3 g fiber
233 calories
17 g fat
22 g carbohydrate
3 g protein

1½ cups mixed dried berries, such as *goji berries*, cranberries, blueberries, and strawberries

½ cup dried cherries

½ cup flaked coconut

½ cup macadamia nut pieces

½ cup Brazil nut pieces

½ cup mini chocolate chips

1. In a large mixing bowl, combine dried berries, dried cherries, coconut, macadamia nuts, Brazil nuts, and chocolate chips.

2. Transfer to an airtight container, and store for up to 1 month.

Fiber Optics

Goji berries have been used medicinally in China for thousands of years, and unlike other berries, they're almost always found dried. They look like red raisins and taste both sweet and sour like cranberries.

Ultimate Fiber Trail Mix

A far cry from traditional GORP, or "good old raisins and pea-nuts," this medley of all things fiber will keep your energy level high as you trek through the day.

1 cup roasted soy nuts

1 cup dried apple chips

1 cup purchased granola cereal

½ cup raisins

½ cup sunflower seeds

Yield: 8 servings
Prep time: 5 minutes
Serving size: ½ cup
Each serving has:
5 g fiber
200 calories
9 g fat
26 g carbohydrate
7 g protein

1. In a large mixing bowl, combine soy nuts, apple chips, granola, raisins, and sunflower seeds.

2. Transfer to an airtight container, and store for up to 3 weeks.

Grist for the Mill

GORP is the original trail mix hikers and backpackers eat for sustained energy. Good for mental energy as well, it's no surprise that GORP is called "student food" in Germany.

Chapter 9

Smoothies and Shakes

In This Chapter

- ◆ Drinking to good health
- ◆ Great blended fruit smoothies
- ◆ Shaking up a bit of fiber

Trying to get dietary fiber into a glass is a lot easier than you think. Thanks to smoothies, many fiber-rich berries and fruits can be quickly blended into super-delicious, drinkable treats. All you need is a blender and a finger to press the button.

You also need some easy recipes to guide you, of course. You'll find them in this chapter.

The Benefits of Blending

One of the great things about blended fruit drinks is that they enable you to include all the fibrous membranes and skins you might not normally eat when enjoying fruit out of hand. Citrus pulp, peach skins, and those annoying berry seeds all become puréed into an easy-to-ingest drink, making it possible to gain the benefits of these often-discarded bits of fiber.

Unlike purchased fruit juices that usually contain no fiber at all, your smoothies will have the best of everything fruit has to offer.

Roughly Speaking

Smoothies and shakes are also perfect for supplementing your fiber intake when necessary by adding a little bit of roughage in the form of psyllium husk, wheat germ, or flaxseed meal. Provided you don't supplement with abandon, the presence of these additions will be hard to detect while the health benefits will do a body good.

You can also add nuts and seeds, which will increase the fiber content as well as contribute to the drink's richness.

Citrus Medley Smoothie

Whole fruit provides the fiber in this flavorful and refreshing any-time smoothie with the tang of citrus and the richness of yogurt.

1 medium orange, peeled, seeded, and roughly chopped

½ medium grapefruit, peeled, seeded, and roughly chopped

¼ cup lemonade or limeade

1 cup vanilla low-fat yogurt

½ cup water

2 TB. sugar

6 ice cubes

Yield: 2 servings
Prep time: 15 minutes
Serving size: 1 cup
Each serving has:
7 g fiber
265 calories
2 g fat
55 g carbohydrate
8 g protein

1. Place orange and grapefruit pieces in a blender, and purée thoroughly on high speed.

2. Add lemonade, yogurt, water, sugar, and ice cubes, and blend until smooth.

3. Pour into glasses, and serve immediately.

Smooth Move

Add 1 tablespoon psyllium husk powder to any smoothie or shake, for a 4-gram boost of fiber.

Pineapple-Mango Smoothie

Sweet, tropical fruit makes this rich and flavor-packed smoothie a real treat, while wheat germ kicks up the fiber.

Yield: 2 servings
Prep time: 10 minutes
Serving size: 1 cup
Each serving has:
7 g fiber
355 calories
2 g fat
72 g carbohydrate
6 g protein

1 cup fresh or frozen mango pieces

1 cup fresh or canned pineapple pieces

½ cup mango nectar

½ cup pineapple juice

¼ cup vanilla soy milk

2 TB. wheat germ

6 ice cubes

1. Place mango, pineapple, mango nectar, pineapple juice, soy milk, wheat germ, and ice cubes in a blender, and purée until smooth.

2. Pour into glasses, and serve immediately.

 Smooth Move

Store peeled, diced, ready-to-go, fresh fruit in zipper-lock bags in the freezer for spontaneous smoothie making. (You still need the ice cubes, though, for the balance of liquid.)

Kiwi and Strawberry Yogurt Smoothie

The kiwi's tartness brings out the best in the sweetheart of berries, the strawberry.

2 medium *kiwi*, peeled and diced

1 cup frozen strawberries

1 cup strawberry low-fat yogurt

½ cup vanilla soy milk

1. Place kiwi, strawberries, yogurt, and soy milk in a blender, and purée until smooth.

2. Pour into glasses, and serve immediately.

Yield: 2 servings
Prep time: 10 minutes
Serving size: 1 cup
Each serving has:
5 g fiber
185 calories
3 g fat
28 g carbohydrate
9 g protein

Fiber Optics

Kiwi fruit, also called the Chinese gooseberry, became a popular New Zealand export in the 1950s. It's now readily grown and eaten worldwide, and valued for not only its high-fiber content but also as an excellent source of vitamin C.

Creamiest Mixed-Berry Smoothie

The berries have it in this super smoothie that's both healthful and dessertlike decadent.

Yield: 2 servings	
Prep time: 5 minutes	
Serving size: 1 cup	
Each serving has:	
5 g fiber	
240 calories	
4 g fat	
45 g carbohydrate	
6 g protein	

2 cups frozen mixed berries

1 cup blueberry low-fat yogurt

½ cup vanilla bean ice cream

1. Place berries, yogurt, and ice cream in a blender, and purée until smooth.

2. Pour into glasses, and serve immediately.

Grist for the Mill

Will the real berry please stand up? Unless derived entirely from the plant's ovary, what we commonly call berries are actually "false" berries, or at best, "accessory" berries. The only "true" berries in the fruit world are blackcurrants, redcurrants, and gooseberries.

Triple Chocolate–Almond Shake

Chocolate lovers will flip over this luxurious shake made with creamy soy milk and ice cream. Cocoa powder adds the final punch of flavor and fiber.

1½ cups chocolate almond or rocky road ice cream

1 cup chocolate soy milk

2 TB. unsweetened cocoa powder

2 TB. honey

1 TB. toasted wheat germ

½ tsp. almond extract

Yield: 2 servings
Prep time: 5 minutes
Serving size: 1 cup
Each serving has:
3 g fiber
230 calories
7 g fat
40 g carbohydrate
6 g protein

1. Place ice cream, soy milk, cocoa powder, honey, wheat germ, and almond extract in a blender, and purée until smooth.

2. Pour into glasses, and serve immediately.

Grist for the Mill

Yet another reason to love chocolate: cocoa powder is made from ground cocoa beans, so it actually contains about 1 gram fiber per tablespoon.

Peaches and Ice Cream Shake

Succulent, sweet peaches bring just the thing to this satisfying shake with hidden fiber.

Yield: 2 servings	
Prep time: 10 minutes	
Serving size: 1 cup	
Each serving has:	
5 g fiber	
410 calories	
14 g fat	
65 g carbohydrate	
7 g protein	

2 medium peaches, skin on, pitted, and diced

½ cup peach nectar

1½ cups vanilla ice cream

¼ cup light cream

2 TB. toasted wheat germ

2 TB. honey

1. Place peaches and peach nectar in a blender, and purée thoroughly on high speed.

2. Add ice cream, light cream, wheat germ, and honey, and blend until smooth.

3. Pour into glasses, and serve immediately.

 Smooth Move

Use frozen yogurt and low-fat milk for a slimmer version of any smoothie or shake.

Banana-Date-Nut Shake

Fiber-rich dates add silky sweetness to this quick and healthful shake featuring the flavors of walnuts and bananas.

1 cup frozen banana pieces

1 cup pitted dates

½ cup vanilla low-fat yogurt

¼ cup low-fat milk

¼ cup walnut pieces

6 ice cubes

Yield: 2 servings	
Prep time: 10 minutes	
Serving size: 1 cup	
Each serving has:	
8 g fiber	
310 calories	
9 g fat	
51 g carbohydrate	
8 g protein	

1. Place banana, dates, yogurt, milk, walnuts, and ice cubes in a blender, and purée until smooth.

2. Pour into glasses, and serve immediately.

Grist for the Mill

Don't forget! Walnuts may reduce the risk or delay the onset of Alzheimer's disease by maintaining important proteins in the brain involved with memory.

Part 4

The Lunch Menu

When midday rolls around, stomachs begin to grumble. Often with limited time to spare, many of us reach for the fast solution that doesn't provide much nutrition, never mind fiber. And before we know it, we're hungry again. Not so for the high-fiber lunch bunch. Healthy and delicious soups, salads, and sandwiches can be the difference between mindless eating of empty calories mid-afternoon and a physically satisfied and mentally alert outlook an hour later.

Here, all types of fiber-rich ingredients have a chance to star, whether they're beans, grains, variety vegetables, or fibrous fruits. Each selection is more tantalizing than the last, and every choice will put you in good stead as you continue your day. No matter what your preference, there's something for everyone on the fiber-friendly lunch menu.

10

Soups of Substance

In This Chapter

- ◆ Hearty, beany soups
- ◆ Veggies + grains = maximum impact
- ◆ Easy creamed soup selections

The majority agrees that sometimes there's nothing more soothing and satisfying than a good bowl of soup. From chicken to split pea, and chowder to bisque, who can resist this ultimate comfort food?

Happily, many familiar soups contain a good amount of fiber in the form of beans, vegetables, and grains. But you do have a few tricks up your sleeve that can hike up your fiber intake even more, and you'll be learning them in this chapter.

To Can or Not to Can?

When making homemade soups, a few inevitable questions arise.

When broth is called for, is it better to use a stock from scratch, a simple bouillon cube, or canned broth? The answer is: whatever's better for you. If you're an aspiring chef who enjoys nurturing a gigantic stockpot of simmering chicken bones and vegetable scraps on the back burner, then surely home-made is the way to go. But for the most part, dissolving a cube in some boiling water or opening a can of broth is the easiest solution and will not detract from your soup making.

Ditto on whether to use canned beans or those that have been soaked and patiently simmered for hours. The choice is really up to you and how much time you're willing to spend in the kitchen.

Blending In

One of the great things about fiber-rich soups is that, when cooked or blended, they become thick and rich just by the nature of their ingredients. Bean-based soups are classic in this regard, as are those that contain grains like barley or rice. In many ways, the fiber is doing the work for you, and the result couldn't be better.

Similarly, blended soups made from vegetables like butternut squash result in a luxurious texture even before the addition of cream. So if you'd like to omit excess fat from your soups, it's usually okay to leave out the cream. Again, the choice is yours.

Get Creative!

Remember that soup making is one of those rare pleasures in the kitchen that doesn't necessarily insist on strict recipe adherence. If that little container of cooked broccoli florets needs a home, add it to your vegetable soup. Same with the leftover peas or half can of cannelloni beans. Who knows? It may eventually end up as part of your very own signature soup.

So start cooking some fabulous creations in your soup kitchen, and watch as your hungry troops start anxiously filing in. Is it soup yet?

Hearty Split Pea Soup

Extra veggies make this already-fiberful soup thick, rich, and even more flavorful.

2 TB. olive oil

1 medium onion, diced

2 medium celery stalks, diced

2 medium carrots, peeled and diced

8 cups low-sodium chicken or vegetable broth

1 (16-oz.) pkg. dried green split peas, picked over and rinsed

2 medium red-skinned potatoes, skin on and diced

Salt and pepper

Whole-Grain Croutons (recipe in Chapter 21)

Yield: 6 servings
Prep time: 15 minutes
Cook time: 55 minutes
Serving size: 1½ cups
Each serving has:
14 g fiber
250 calories
4 g fat
39 g carbohydrate
15 g protein

1. In a soup pot over medium heat, heat olive oil. Add onion, celery, and carrots, and cook, stirring often, for 8 to 10 minutes or until softened.

2. Stir in broth and split peas, increase heat to high, and bring to a boil. Reduce heat to medium-low and cook at a simmer, stirring occasionally, for about 30 minutes or until peas are nearly tender.

3. Add potatoes and cook for 15 to 20 more minutes. Season with salt and pepper and serve with Whole-Grain Croutons.

Variation: Ham it up by adding a smoked ham hock or ham bone with the split peas. Substitute ½ of broth with water, and add diced cooked ham before serving.

 Smooth Move

Always pick over dried beans and legumes before cooking them to remove any tiny pebbles and discolored bits that may be lurking in the bag.

White Bean and Escarole Soup

Canned cannellini beans make this a snap to prepare, while delicious garlic-sautéed escarole steals the show.

Yield: 6 servings
Prep time: 20 minutes
Cook time: 40 minutes
Serving size: 1½ cups
Each serving has:
5 g fiber
170 calories
7 g fat
18 g carbohydrate
7 g protein

3 TB. olive oil

1 small onion, diced

2 medium carrots, peeled and diced

1 medium celery stalk, diced

4 garlic cloves, minced

1 medium head escarole, cored, rinsed, and roughly chopped

8 cups low-sodium chicken or vegetable broth

1 bay leaf

2 (15-oz.) cans cannellini beans, drained and rinsed

Salt and pepper

1. In a soup pot over medium heat, heat 2 tablespoons olive oil. Add onion, carrots, and celery, and cook, stirring often, for 6 to 8 minutes or until softened.

2. Add garlic and cook 1 more minute. Stir in remaining 1 tablespoon olive oil. Add escarole and cook, stirring often, for about 4 minutes or until leaves begin to wilt.

3. Add broth and bay leaf, increase heat to high, and bring to a boil. Reduce heat to medium-low and cook at a simmer, stirring occasionally, for about 20 minutes or until escarole is tender.

4. Stir in beans, and continue cooking for 8 minutes. Season with salt and pepper, and remove from heat. Discard bay leaf. Using a potato masher, break down some beans to thicken soup. Stir well and serve immediately.

Grist for the Mill

Eat up! The word *escarole* derives from the Latin *esca,* meaning "food." It's also the root of the words *edible* and *eat.*

Havana Black Bean Soup

Enjoy the flavors of Cuba in this quick version of the classic bean soup featuring spicy jalapeño pepper, garlic, and aromatic ground cumin.

2 TB. olive oil

1 medium onion, diced

1 medium celery stalk, diced

1 green bell pepper, ribs and seeds removed, and diced

1 jalapeño pepper, seeded and chopped

2 garlic cloves, minced

1 bay leaf

1½ tsp. ground cumin

6 cups low-sodium beef or vegetable broth

3 (15-oz.) cans black beans, drained and rinsed

1 tsp. fresh lime juice

Salt and pepper

Sour cream

Chopped cilantro

Yield: 6 servings
Prep time: 15 minutes
Cook time: 25 minutes
Serving size: 1½ cups
Each serving has:
9 g fiber
170 calories
5 g fat
22 g carbohydrate
8 g protein

1. In a soup pot over medium heat, heat olive oil. Add onion, celery, green bell pepper, and jalapeño pepper. Cook, stirring often, for 6 to 8 minutes or until veggies are softened.

2. Stir in garlic, bay leaf, and cumin, and cook 1 more minute. Add broth and beans, increase heat to high, and bring to a boil. Reduce heat to medium-low, and cook at a simmer, stirring occasionally, for 10 minutes.

3. Transfer 2 cups soup to a blender and purée. Return puréed soup to the pot, add lime juice, season with salt and pepper, and serve with a dollop of sour cream and a sprinkling of cilantro.

 Smooth Move

Serve your black bean soup the Cuban way by ladling it over a mound of rice (try brown) and topping it with diced red onion, avocado, and tomato for lots of extra fiber.

Mom's Lentil Soup

A hint of curry is the magic ingredient in this delicious soup featuring lentils, the queen of legumes.

Yield: 6 servings
Prep time: 15 minutes
Cook time: 40 minutes
Serving size: 1½ cups
Each serving has:
9 g fiber
285 calories
5 g fat
45 g carbohydrate
17 g protein

2 TB. olive oil

1 medium onion, diced

1 medium celery stalk, diced

2 medium carrots, peeled and diced

1 garlic clove, minced

8 cups low-sodium chicken or vegetable stock

1 (16-oz.) pkg. dried brown lentils, picked over and rinsed

1½ tsp. curry powder

Salt and pepper

1. In a soup pot over medium heat, heat olive oil. Add onion, celery, and carrots, and cook, stirring often, for 8 to 10 minutes or until softened. Stir in garlic, and cook 1 more minute.

2. Stir in broth, lentils, and curry powder. Increase heat to high and bring to a boil. Reduce heat to medium-low and cook at a simmer, stirring occasionally, for about 25 minutes or until lentils are soft but firm to the bite.

3. Transfer 2 cups soup to a blender and purée. Return puréed soup to the pot, season with salt and pepper, and serve immediately.

 Grist for the Mill

The history of legumes is closely connected to successful early civilizations. Those who were able to utilize legumes such as lentils and beans as a protein source were more likely to survive when animal protein was scarce.

Garden Vegetable–Barley Soup

Nutritious barley is the base for this hearty soup that features the flavors of fresh summer garden vegetables.

1 TB. unsalted butter	1 large potato, peeled and cubed
1 TB. olive oil	1 cup fresh or canned plum tomatoes, diced
1 medium leek, trimmed and thinly sliced	½ cup fresh or frozen corn kernels
1 large celery stalk, sliced	½ cup fresh or frozen peas
2 large carrots, peeled and sliced	½ cup fresh or frozen lima beans
8 cups low-sodium chicken or vegetable broth	Salt and pepper
1 cup pearl barley	2 TB. chopped fresh parsley leaves
1 medium zucchini, sliced	

Yield: 6 servings	
Prep time: 15 minutes	
Cook time: 50 minutes	
Serving size: 1½ cups	
Each serving has:	
10 g fiber	
290 calories	
5 g fat	
50 g carbohydrate	
9 g protein	

1. In a soup pot over medium heat, melt butter with olive oil. Add leek, celery, and carrots, and cook over low heat, stirring often, for 8 to 10 minutes or until softened but not browned.

2. Add broth and barley, increase heat to high, and bring to a boil. Reduce heat to medium-low, and cook at a simmer, stirring occasionally, for 20 minutes.

3. Add zucchini, potato, tomatoes, corn, peas, and lima beans, and continue cooking, stirring occasionally, for about 20 more minutes or until vegetables and barley are tender.

4. Season with salt and pepper, stir in parsley, and serve immediately.

Grist for the Mill

Barley was a staple grain in ancient Egypt, where it was used to make bread and beer—a combination that, at the time, was considered a complete diet.

Chicken Tortilla Gumbo

Two tasty soups—spicy chicken tortilla and intensely flavorful gumbo—come together for a burst of flavor and fiber.

Yield: 6 servings
Prep time: 10 minutes
Cook time: 40 minutes
Serving size: 1½ cups
Each serving has:
7 g fiber
275 calories
9 g fat
35 g carbohydrate
14 g protein

3 TB. vegetable oil

3 TB. all-purpose flour

1 medium onion, diced

1 medium celery stalk, diced

1 medium green bell pepper, ribs and seeds removed, and diced

1 garlic clove, minced

1½ cups frozen cut okra

1 (15-oz.) can stewed tomatoes, chopped

6 cups low-sodium chicken broth

1 TB. chili powder

¼ tsp. cayenne or to taste

1 cup cooked diced chicken

1 cup canned black beans, drained and rinsed

1½ cups coarsely broken multigrain or corn tortilla chips

Grist for the Mill

Glory be! All gumbos, whether Cajun or Creole, contain the "holy trinity": diced onion, celery, and green bell pepper.

1. In a soup pot over medium-high heat, whisk together vegetable oil and flour for about 5 minutes or until dark and smooth.

2. Stir in onion, celery, and green bell pepper, and cook, stirring often, for 4 to 6 minutes or until softened. Add garlic, okra, and tomatoes. Stir well to combine, and cook 1 more minute.

3. Add broth, chili powder, and cayenne. Increase heat to high, and bring to a boil. Reduce heat to medium-low, and cook at a simmer, stirring occasionally, for 20 minutes.

4. Add chicken, black beans, and ½ of tortilla chips, and cook 10 more minutes. Ladle into soup bowls, and top with remaining chips before serving.

Granny Smith Butternut Creamed Soup

Tart apple and sweet cider enhance this creamy and satisfying blended soup featuring creamy butternut squash.

3 TB. unsalted butter

1 small onion, diced

2 Granny Smith or other tart apples, cored and diced

1 medium carrot, peeled and diced

1 (2½-lb.) butternut squash, peeled, seeded, and cubed

6 cups low-sodium chicken or vegetable broth

1 cup apple cider

Salt and pepper

Sour cream or crème fraîche

Yield: 6 servings
Prep time: 20 minutes
Cook time: 30 minutes
Serving size: 1½ cups
Each serving has:
6 g fiber
235 calories
6 g fat
40 g carbohydrate
5 g protein

1. In a soup pot over medium heat, melt butter. Add onion, ½ of diced apples, and carrot, and stir well to combine. Reduce heat to medium-low, and cook for about 4 minutes or until apple is softened.

2. Stir in squash, broth, and cider. Increase heat to high, and bring to a boil. Reduce heat to medium-low, and simmer, stirring occasionally, for 20 to 25 minutes or until squash is fork-tender.

3. Working in batches, purée soup in a blender. Return puréed soup to the pot, season with salt and pepper, and serve topped with sour cream and remaining diced apple.

Grist for the Mill

Who's Granny Smith? She's an old Australian lady who, in 1868, propagated a chance seedling that became her famous namesake apple. She had nine children and a bushel of grandkids.

Creamy Turkey and Wild Rice Chowder

Wild rice and hominy provide the fiber in this thick and soothing meal-in-a-bowl soup with the rich flavor of turkey.

Yield: 6 servings
Prep time: 10 minutes
Cook time: 35 minutes
Serving size: 1½ cups
Each serving has:
12 g fiber
310 calories
12 g fat
31 g carbohydrate
15 g protein

2 TB. unsalted butter

1 medium onion, finely chopped

6 cups low-sodium chicken broth

1 large russet or Idaho potato, peeled and diced

1 cup heavy cream

1½ cups cooked, diced turkey breast

1 cup cooked wild rice

1 (15-oz.) can white *hominy*, drained

1 (8-oz.) can cream-style corn

Dash paprika

Salt and pepper

1. In a soup pot over medium heat, melt butter. Add onion and cook, stirring often, for about 3 minutes or until onion is softened.

2. Add broth and potato, increase heat to high, and bring to a boil. Reduce heat to medium-low, and cook at a simmer, stirring occasionally, for about 20 minutes or until potato is fork-tender. Stir in heavy cream, and cook 1 more minute.

3. Transfer ½ of soup to a blender and purée. Return puréed soup to the pot, and stir in turkey, wild rice, hominy, corn, and paprika. Cook over medium-low heat, stirring often, for about 10 minutes or until thick and piping hot. Season with salt and pepper, and serve immediately.

Fiber Optics

Hominy is dried maize, or corn kernels, that have been soaked in an alkali solution to remove the hull. Despite this process, it has a high-fiber content—4 grams per ½ cup. When left whole, they're used in soups and stews; when ground, they become hominy grits.

Asian Beef Noodle Soup

Japanese soba noodles and crisp-tender Asian vegetables combine with lean beef for a quick and healthful soup.

4 oz. *soba noodles* or whole-wheat spaghetti

4 cups beef broth

1 TB. minced peeled fresh ginger

1 cup fresh snow peas, cut into thin strips

½ medium red bell pepper, ribs and seeds removed, and cut into thin strips

⅓ cup peeled and shredded carrots

1 cup shredded bok choy

1½ TB. rice vinegar

1 TB. toasted sesame oil

Freshly ground pepper

½ lb. thinly sliced deli roast beef, cut into strips

Yield: 4 servings
Prep time: 15 minutes
Cook time: 5 minutes
Serving size: 2 cups
Each serving has:
7 g fiber
150 calories
5 g fat
17 g carbohydrate
7 g protein

1. Cook soba noodles according to package directions.

2. Meanwhile, in a medium saucepan over medium heat, bring broth just to a boil. Add ginger, snow peas, red bell pepper, carrots, and bok choy. Reduce heat to low, and cook for 2 minutes.

3. Remove from heat and stir in vinegar, sesame oil, and pepper.

4. Mound noodles and beef in center of 4 deep soup bowls, and ladle broth mixture evenly over each. Serve immediately.

Fiber Optics

Soba noodles are Japanese noodles made from buck wheat flour, usually with the addition of wheat flour. They are a popular fast food in Japan.

Silky Shrimp Bisque

Smooth as silk but full of hidden fiber, this elegant soup made from succulent shrimp with a hint of anise will impress even the toughest customer at your table.

Yield: 4 servings
Prep time: 25 minutes
Cook time: 50 minutes
Serving size: 1½ cups
Each serving has:
7 g fiber
310 calories
15 g fat
25 g carbohydrate
18 g protein

2 TB. unsalted butter

1 lb. large, uncooked shrimp, (21 to 25 count) peeled and deveined

1 TB. olive oil

1 medium leek, white part only, roughly chopped

1 medium fennel bulb, trimmed and roughly chopped

1 medium carrot, peeled and roughly chopped

2 (8-oz.) bottles clam juice

3 cups water

3 TB. uncooked brown rice

2 TB. tomato paste

½ cup heavy cream

1 TB. fresh lemon juice

Salt and pepper

1. In a soup pot over medium heat, melt butter. Add shrimp and cook, stirring, for about 3 minutes or until shrimp are no longer pink. With a slotted spoon, remove shrimp to a bowl and set aside.

2. Add olive oil, leek, fennel, and carrot to the pot, and cook, stirring occasionally, for 5 minutes.

3. Stir in clam juice, water, rice, tomato paste, and shrimp. Reduce heat to medium-low, and cook, covered, at a simmer, stirring occasionally, for 35 minutes. Stir in heavy cream, and cook, uncovered, 5 more minutes.

4. Working in batches, purée bisque and return puréed soup to the pot. Add lemon juice, season with salt and pepper, and serve immediately.

Smooth Move

Soups made with cream are not recommended for freezing because the cream will separate. To freeze a bisque, omit the cream and wait to add it after you defrost the soup. Whisk while reheating.

11

The Salad Bar

In This Chapter

◆ Quick-and-easy side salads

◆ Familiar yet fiberful recipes

◆ Broadening your salad horizons

Not surprisingly, when most people think of fiber, visions of chomping on raw vegetables and salads usually appear. Ironically, lettuce itself has little fiber to offer, and more often than not, it's the other selections at the salad bar that provide the fiber you're after.

Having said that, tossed green salads are only the tip of the iceberg when talking about salad. Potatoes, pasta, grains, and even fruit can all provide the foundation for a salad that's part of a lunch or even the main course. How it fits in with a goal of high fiber depends on the entire gamut of ingredients that end up on your plate. There are loads of delicious combinations and assortments in this chapter that will please every palate.

Not Your Usual Suspects

Often, the addition of some unusual players such as wheat berries or Japanese noodles result in the tastiest salads around. Learning to cook these fiber-rich gems and including them in different courses is a great way to expand your cooking repertoire while also increasing your fiber intake. Before you know it, you'll be creating terrific, healthy salads from even a greater selection of ingredients than your local restaurant salad bar has to offer.

Don't discount a sprinkle here or there of nuts or seeds, or the addition of fibrous fruits, fresh or dried. These enhancements can quickly tote up your fiber grams in no time, not to mention heighten your enjoyment. So toss out any old beliefs you may have about salads being boring, and introduce yourself to the many splendors of sensational salad making!

Quickie Coleslaw

This coleslaw is a super solution for a fiberful side salad even the kids will love, sweetened up with apple and raisins.

1 (16-oz.) pkg. shredded coleslaw cabbage

2 TB. apple cider vinegar

1 tsp. sugar

½ cup mayonnaise

2 TB. milk

1 TB. honey

1 red delicious apple, cored and coarsely shredded

½ cup golden raisins

Salt and pepper

Yield: 6 servings
Prep time: 10 minutes
Serving size: 1 cup
Each serving has:
2 g fiber
197 calories
1 g fat
17 g carbohydrate
1 g protein

1. In a medium bowl, toss together cabbage, apple cider vinegar, and sugar.

2. In a small bowl, whisk together mayonnaise, milk, and honey. Pour over cabbage mixture, and toss well to coat.

3. Stir in apple and raisins, season with salt and pepper, and refrigerate for 30 minutes before serving.

Grist for the Mill

Coleslaw gets its name from *koolsla,* the eighteenth-century Dutch term for "cabbage salad." In addition to a high-fiber content, cabbage is a great source of vitamin C.

Napa Sunshine Slaw

Light and refreshing with a hint of dill and the crunch of nutty sunflower seeds, this slaw is the perfect salad for a sunny day.

Yield: 6 servings
Prep time: 30 minutes
Serving size: 1 cup
Each serving has:
3 g fiber
134 calories
10 g fat
9 g carbohydrate
2 g protein

4 cups thinly sliced napa cabbage (about 1 lb.)

1 large carrot, peeled and coarsely grated

1 TB. chopped fresh dill

3 TB. olive oil

1 TB. white wine vinegar

½ tsp. sugar

¼ tsp. salt

2 clementines or mandarin oranges, peeled and segmented

¼ cup shelled sunflower seeds

1. In a medium bowl, toss together cabbage, carrot, and dill.

2. In a small bowl, whisk together olive oil, white wine vinegar, sugar, and salt. Pour over cabbage mixture, and toss well to coat.

3. Stir in orange segments and sunflower seeds, and set aside at room temperature for 15 minutes before serving.

 Smooth Move _____

Save leftover napa cabbage, also referred to as Chinese cabbage, to add fiber to stir-fries.

Baby Potato Salad with Mint and Peas

Aromatic mint brings tender little potatoes and sweet peas together in this delicious side salad.

3 lb. baby red or white-skinned potatoes, skin on

1 shallot, minced

3 TB. red wine vinegar

Salt and pepper

¼ cup olive oil

1 cup frozen peas, thawed

½ cup fresh mint leaves, roughly chopped

Yield: 6 servings
Prep time: 10 minutes
Cook time: 30 minutes
Serving size: ³/₄ cup
Each serving has:
3 g fiber
140 calories
9 g fat
9 g carbohydrate
2 g protein

1. Place potatoes in a large pot, cover with cold, salted water, and bring to a boil over high heat. Reduce heat to medium-low, and cook at a simmer for 12 to 15 minutes or until tender.

2. Meanwhile, in a small bowl, whisk together shallot, vinegar, salt, and pepper. Drain potatoes, cut in ¹/₂, and transfer to a medium bowl. While still warm, add vinegar mixture and toss gently to coat.

3. When potatoes are cooled, add olive oil, peas, and mint, and toss gently. Season with salt and pepper, and serve at room temperature.

 Grist for the Mill

Baby potatoes are actually a misnomer. They're not young versions of their elders, but simply a different variety that matures to a smaller size.

Rotini Primavera Salad

A fiber-rich alternative to the average macaroni salad, crisp and flavorful *al dente* vegetables highlight this terrific whole-wheat version suitable for a side dish or main course lunch.

Yield: 4 servings
Prep time: 15 minutes
Cook time: 20 minutes
Serving size: 1½ cups
Each serving has:
5 g fiber
324 calories
1 g fat
42 g carbohydrate
8 g protein

½ lb. whole-wheat rotini pasta

1 cup broccoli florets, cooked to crisp-tender

½ medium red bell pepper, ribs and seeds removed, and thinly sliced

½ cup peeled and shredded carrots

½ medium red onion, cut into thin circles

1 cup grape tomatoes, halved

¼ cup extra-virgin olive oil

2 TB. balsamic vinegar

1 tsp. prepared mustard

1 small garlic clove, minced

1 TB. finely chopped fresh basil leaves

Salt and pepper

1. Cook rotini according to package directions, drain, and rinse under cold water. Transfer to a large bowl.

2. Stir in broccoli, bell pepper, carrots, red onion, and tomatoes.

3. In a small bowl, whisk together olive oil, balsamic vinegar, mustard, and garlic. Pour over rotini mixture, and toss well to coat.

4. Stir in basil, and season with salt and pepper. Serve at room temperature.

Fiber Optics

Al dente is the Italian term, most commonly used in describing pasta, for "crisp-tender" or literally, "to the tooth," meaning cooked through but still firm to the bite.

Sesame Peanut Noodle Salad

Better than take-out, this version of the popular Chinese dish gets an extra fiber boost from crunchy peanuts and sweet sugar snap peas.

½ lb. Chinese egg noodles

3 green onions, thinly sliced

½ yellow or orange bell pepper, ribs and seeds removed, and thinly sliced

⅔ cup fresh sugar snap peas, trimmed

⅔ cup fresh bean sprouts

½ cup chunky peanut butter

¼ cup soy sauce

¼ cup warm water

2 TB. rice vinegar

2 TB. toasted sesame oil

1 TB. honey

¼ tsp. dried red pepper flakes or to taste

½ cup dry-roasted peanuts

Yield: 4 servings
Prep time: 15 minutes
Serving size: 1½ cups
Each serving has:
6 g fiber
426 calories
35 g fat
13 g carbohydrate
13 g protein

1. Cook Chinese egg noodles according to package directions.

2. In a large bowl, toss together cooked noodles, green onions, bell pepper, sugar snap peas, and bean sprouts.

3. In a small bowl, whisk together peanut butter, soy sauce, water, vinegar, sesame oil, honey, and red pepper flakes. Pour over noodle mixture, and toss well to coat. Sprinkle with peanuts before serving.

 Smooth Move

Keep sesame oil, as well as other oils made from nuts and seeds, in the refrigerator, as they're highly perishable and can quickly become rancid at room temperature.

Turkish Bulgur Wheat Salad

Bulgur cooks in no time at all and happily absorbs the exotic spices and flavors of the Middle East featured in this salad.

Yield: 6 servings
Prep time: 10 minutes
Cook time: 20 minutes
Serving size: 1 cup
Each serving has:
6 g fiber
331 calories
14 g fat
33 g carbohydrate
7 g protein

1½ cups *bulgur wheat*

2 cups boiling water

1 cup cooked fava or lima beans

1 cup red seedless grapes, halved

3 green onions, chopped

½ cup walnut pieces

Juice of 2 lemons

3 TB. olive oil

¼ tsp. ground coriander

¼ tsp. cumin

¼ tsp. paprika

Salt and pepper

¼ cup pomegranate seeds

1. Place bulgur wheat in a medium bowl, pour boiling water over, stir well, cover, and let stand for 15 to 20 minutes or until water is absorbed.

2. Add fava beans, grapes, green onions, and walnuts, and stir to combine.

3. In a small bowl, whisk together lemon juice, olive oil, coriander, cumin, and paprika. Pour over bulgur mixture, and toss well to coat. Season with salt and pepper, sprinkle pomegranate seeds over top, and serve.

Fiber Optics

Bulgur wheat, often confused with cracked wheat, is actually whole wheat that's been parboiled, dried, ground, and made into small grain shapes. It's the main ingredient in Lebanese tabbouleh, a bulgur dish made with tomatoes and fresh herbs.

Wheat Berry–Nut Salad

Although they take a bit longer to cook, wheat berries are well worth the wait. They have a chewy, nutty character that pairs deliciously with the citrus and nuts in this salad.

2 cups *wheat berries*	4 green onions, finely sliced
7 cups water	½ cup hazelnuts, roughly chopped
1 tsp. salt	3 TB. red wine vinegar
⅓ cup orange juice	3 TB. vegetable oil
⅓ cup golden raisins	1 TB. honey
1 small cucumber, skin on and cut into small dice	½ tsp. grated orange zest
½ medium red bell pepper, ribs and seeds removed, and cut into small dice	Salt and pepper
½ medium green bell pepper, ribs and seeds removed, and cut into small dice	

Yield: 6 servings
Prep time: 30 minutes
Cook time: 1 hour
Serving size: 1 cup
Each serving has:
8 g fiber
170 calories
2 g fat
19 g carbohydrate
4 g protein

1. Rinse wheat berries under cold water. Place in a large saucepan, add water and salt, and bring to a boil over high heat. Reduce heat to low, cover, and cook for 1 hour, stirring occasionally, until tender yet chewy. Drain, rinse, and set aside.

2. Meanwhile, in a small bowl, combine orange juice and raisins. Set aside to soak for 20 minutes. Drain raisins and reserve juice.

3. In a large bowl, combine cooked wheat berries, drained raisins, cucumber, red bell pepper, green bell pepper, green onions, and hazelnuts.

4. In another small bowl, whisk together reserved orange juice, red wine vinegar, vegetable oil, honey, and orange peel. Pour over wheat berry mixture, and toss to coat. Season with salt and pepper, and refrigerate for 30 minutes before serving.

Fiber Optics

Wheat berries are whole, unprocessed wheat kernels. They contain a high level of fiber and come in winter and spring varieties. Hard winter wheat berries may require an overnight soak before cooking, unlike their softer spring cousins.

Spinach Salad with Blackberries and Almonds

This unusual combination of sweet blackberries, crunchy almonds, and rich goat cheese will have you hooked on the first bite—and provide a good dose of fiber to boot.

Yield: 4 servings
Prep time: 10 minutes
Serving size: 2 cups
Each serving has:
5 g fiber
313 calories
27 g fat
12 g carbohydrate
10 g protein

¼ **cup olive oil**

3 **TB. raspberry vinegar**

Salt and pepper

8 **cups baby spinach, washed and dried**

1 **pt. fresh blackberries**

½ **cup sliced almonds**

½ **cup crumbled goat cheese**

1. In a small bowl, whisk together olive oil, raspberry vinegar, salt, and pepper.

2. Place spinach in a large bowl. Pour dressing over, toss well to coat, and transfer to a large platter or individual plates.

3. Distribute blackberries, almonds, and goat cheese evenly over spinach, and serve immediately.

 Smooth Move

If this salad will be sitting out for longer than a few minutes, avoid premature wilting by serving the dressing on the side for diners to add themselves.

La Grande Salade

A "big salad" full of fresh flavor and crunch for lunch is one of the best fiber choices you can make. Use these ingredients as inspiration for your own favorite rendition.

2 cups mixed salad greens

½ cup sliced red cabbage

1 medium tomato, quartered

½ medium carrot, peeled and thinly sliced

½ cup broccoli florets

¼ cup sliced cucumber

¼ cup canned sliced beets

¼ cup canned chickpeas

1 TB. sunflower seeds

½ cup Whole-Grain Croutons (recipe in Chapter 21)

Dressing of choice

Yield: 1 serving
Prep time: 5 to 10 minutes
Serving size: 4 cups
Each serving has:
18 g fiber
343 calories
4 g fat
15 g carbohydrate
6 g protein

1. In a large serving bowl, toss together salad greens and cabbage.

2. Add tomato, carrot, broccoli florets, cucumber, beets, and chickpeas, and toss gently.

3. Sprinkle sunflower seeds and croutons over top, and serve with your choice of salad dressing.

Smooth Move

Make use of prewashed packaged salad greens as your base to save time, especially when you have other ingredients to chop and slice.

Chapter 12

The Sandwich Counter

In This Chapter

◆ Choosing the right sandwich foundation

◆ Fabulous fiberful fillings

◆ Wraps and pockets to go

I know what you're thinking. As long as you choose whole-wheat bread over white, you're being fiber conscious in the sandwich department. But that's only the beginning of the story, and in this chapter you find some particularly tasty ways to kick up your fiber intake that have more to do with the filling and less to do with the bread.

How so? Sandwiches are great receptacles for a variety of fiber-rich ingredients, from grilled vegetables to chunky peanut butter. Putting it all together in the right combination ensures a good dose of fiber at lunchtime and goes a long way in satisfying those hunger pangs until dinner.

Building Your Sandwich Empire

Most certainly your choice of bread is an important aspect fiber-wise. Choosing commercial sliced breads (and there are many to choose from) with at least 2 or 3 grams fiber per slice is a good place to start. Opting for whole-wheat rolls and buns over traditional white wheat is also a good habit to get into.

Fortunately, there are also numerous varieties of wraps, tortillas, and pitas to be had, so take advantage of these healthier choices when shopping for lunch-making supplies. You'll be glad you have them on hand when a craving for a sandwich strikes!

Not by Bread Alone

What you put inside your sandwiches is the next big decision, and having a choice on hand makes a fiberful life easier. Avocadoes, tomatoes, salad sprouts, jars of marinated artichoke hearts—and of course chunky peanut butter—all add a little punch to your creation, fiber-wise as well as taste-wise.

And don't hesitate to create your sandwiches from seemingly "nonsandwichable" ingredients. Hummus and bean spreads, leftover coleslaw and salads, and even last night's eggplant Parmesan are better bets than baloney. After all, how do you think the Earl of Sandwich got started? He needed a free hand to play cards, so he folded up his entire meal in a big slice of bread. What a hero.

Health-Nut Whole-Grain Club

Start with a fiber-rich nutty grain bread, and you're well on your way to a healthful and delicious take on a classic sandwich that features creamy avocado, tangy sprouts, and lean turkey bacon.

3 slices whole-grain bread

2 TB. light mayonnaise

4 slices turkey bacon, fried crisp

1 medium tomato, thinly sliced

Salt and pepper

1 ripe avocado, peeled, seeded, and sliced

1 cup alfalfa sprouts

Yield: 2 servings
Prep time: 10 minutes
Serving size: ¹/₂ sandwich
Each serving has:
9 g fiber
333 calories
22 g fat
25 g carbohydrate
9 g protein

1. Toast bread slices and place on a cutting board. Spread each slice with mayonnaise.

2. Place 2 slices bacon, ¹/₂ of tomato, salt, pepper, ¹/₂ of avocado, and ¹/₂ of alfalfa sprouts on 1 bread slice. Top with another bread slice. Repeat with remaining ingredients for second sandwich.

3. Insert 4 toothpicks through sandwich at each corner and, using a serrated knife, cut into quarters. Serve immediately.

Grist for the Mill

The original club sandwich was invented in an exclusive New York state gambling club in Saratoga Springs, where the potato chip is said to have originated as well.

Tuna and Artichoke Panini

Tasty Italian ingredients come together in this hearty and healthy sandwich featuring tuna in olive oil, which compliments the salty capers and tart lemon juice.

Yield: 2 servings
Prep time: 15 minutes
Serving size: 1 panino
Each serving has:
6 g fiber
544 calories
22 g fat
25 g carbohydrate
9 g protein

¼ **cup pitted Sicilian, or large green olives, roughly chopped**

1 tsp. small capers

1 small garlic clove, minced

¼ **cup diced celery**

¼ **cup mayonnaise**

1 tsp. fresh lemon juice

1 (6-oz.) can tuna in olive oil, drained

1 (6-oz.) jar marinated artichokes, drained and roughly chopped

½ **cup canned cannellini beans, drained and rinsed**

1 TB. coarsely chopped Italian parsley

Freshly ground pepper

2 whole-wheat crusty rolls

1. In a small bowl, stir together olives, capers, garlic, celery, mayonnaise, and lemon juice.

2. In a medium bowl, toss together tuna, artichokes, cannellini beans, parsley, and pepper.

3. Slice open each roll horizontally. Spread mayonnaise mixture evenly on all cut sides, and fill with tuna mixture. Press closed and serve immediately.

 Smooth Move _____

Make extra of the delicious mayo mixture used in this recipe, and serve it in place of tartar sauce with fried fish fillets.

Curry Chicken Salad Pita Pockets

Almonds, pineapple, and curry add crunch and flavor to this delicious version of a chicken salad favorite served in a hearty, whole-wheat pita.

1½ cups cooked, diced chicken breast

¼ tsp. curry powder

Dash paprika

Salt and pepper

¼ cup coarsely chopped almonds

½ cup diced canned pineapple, drained and juices reserved

1 small celery stalk, diced

⅓ cup mayonnaise

1 TB. pineapple juice

2 whole-wheat pitas, cut in ½ and opened

Yield: 2 servings
Prep time: 10 minutes
Serving size: 1 pita
Each serving has:
5 g fiber
633 calories
28 g fat
33 g carbohydrate
34 g protein

1. In a medium bowl, combine chicken, curry powder, paprika, salt, pepper, almonds, pineapple, and celery, and toss to combine.

2. Add mayonnaise and pineapple juice, and gently stir to coat.

3. Stuff each pita ½ with chicken salad, and serve immediately.

 Grist for the Mill

Pineapples and their juice make terrific marinades due to the enzyme bromelain, which helps break down protein. Try it as a delicious flavor enhancer for chicken or pork.

Hummus and Greek Salad Wrap

Fiber-rich chickpea hummus stars in this Mediterranean salad wrap that's surprisingly hearty and flavorful with the addition of zesty olives and creamy feta.

Yield: 2 servings
Prep time: 12 minutes
Serving size: ½ wrap
Each serving has:
5 g fiber
343 calories
22 g fat
25 g carbohydrate
9 g protein

1 large (12-in.) multigrain or whole-wheat sandwich wrap

⅔ cup prepared hummus

2 TB. roughly chopped kalamata olives

½ medium tomato, diced

½ small green bell pepper, ribs and seeds removed, and sliced

½ small red onion, thinly sliced

2 TB. crumbled feta cheese

1 cup romaine lettuce, roughly chopped

1 TB. bottled olive oil and vinegar dressing

1. Place wrap on a cutting board, and spread hummus in center ⅓ to edges.

2. Top hummus evenly with olives, tomato, bell pepper, and onion. Sprinkle feta on top. Finish with lettuce, and drizzle dressing evenly over all.

3. Fold edges of wrap in 1 inch, and roll wrap up and away from you. Cut in ½ and serve immediately.

 Grist for the Mill _____

Wraps were invented in Boston at Sami's Wrap-N-Roll in 1979, where they were called "roll-up sandwiches."

Turkey in the Rye Reuben

A kicked-up slaw featuring sweet dried cranberries and a hearty rye bread are the keys to this quick and delectable toasted sandwich. A garnish of sweet potato chips finishes the dish with Thanksgiving style.

½ **cup prepared coleslaw**

1 TB. dried cranberries

1 tsp. caraway seeds

4 oz. thinly sliced turkey breast

2 oz. thinly sliced Swiss cheese

2 slices hearty rye bread

1 TB. Russian dressing

Sweet potato chips

Yield: 1 serving
Prep time: 10 minutes
Cook time: 3 minutes
Serving size: 1 sandwich
Each serving has:
2 g fiber
700 calories
34 g fat
54 g carbohydrate
42 g protein

1. In a small bowl, stir together coleslaw, cranberries, and caraway seeds.

2. Mound turkey on a plate, drape cheese over, and microwave for 1 minute.

3. Toast rye bread, and spread dressing on 1 slice.

4. Transfer turkey and cheese to bread slice with dressing, top evenly with coleslaw mixture, and press remaining bread slice on top. Cut in ½ with a serrated knife, and serve with chips.

Smooth Move

When serving prepared coleslaw, don't hesitate to add your own flair and fiber with ingredients like dried fruit, nuts, and seeds.

Grilled Eggplant and Mozzarella Burger

Uniquely grilled and full of Mediterranean flavor, this burger will earn you rave reviews from even the staunchest of meat eaters.

Yield: 4 servings
Prep time: 10 minutes
Cook time: 12 minutes
Serving size: 1 sandwich
Each serving has:
4 g fiber
196 calories
7 g fat
23 g carbohydrate
10 g protein

8 (½-in.-thick) eggplant slices

Salt and pepper

Olive oil

4 (¼-in.-thick) mozzarella slices

4 sun-dried tomatoes in oil, thinly sliced

4 large fresh basil leaves

4 whole-wheat burger buns, toasted

1. Heat an outdoor or indoor grill to medium-high, and coat lightly with olive oil. Add eggplant slices, season with salt and pepper, and brush with additional olive oil. Grill for about 10 minutes, turning occasionally, or until tender.

2. While still on the grill, top 4 eggplant slices with mozzarella, sun-dried tomatoes, and basil leaves, and place remaining eggplant slices on top. Press down gently with a spatula, and continue grilling for about 2 minutes or until cheese melts.

3. Transfer to toasted buns, and serve immediately.

 Grist for the Mill

Peeled or unpeeled, eggplant's fiber content is more or less the same. It's the seeds that provide the valuable insoluble fiber. White- and lavender-skinned eggplant, although less bitter than their dark-purple siblings, have fewer seeds and, consequently, fewer grams of fiber.

Twelve-Grain Peanut Butter– Chocolate Panini

Gooey and deliciously sweet, here's a peanut butter cup lover's dream come true.

2 thick slices 12-grain bread

3 TB. chunky peanut butter

1 TB. semisweet chocolate chips

2 tsp. unsalted butter

Yield: 1 serving	
Prep time: 5 minutes	
Cook time: 2 minutes	
Serving size: 1 panino	
Each serving has:	
6 g fiber	
484 calories	
22 g fat	
25 g carbohydrate	
9 g protein	

1. Toast bread slices until lightly golden. Spread peanut butter on 1 slice up to ½ inch on the sides. Sprinkle chocolate chips over peanut butter, and press remaining bread slice on top.

2. Melt butter in a heavy skillet over medium heat, and place sandwich in the middle, pressing down gently with a spatula. Cook, turning over once, for about 2 minutes or until peanut butter begins to melt.

3. Transfer to a plate, allow to rest for 1 minute, cut in ½, and serve.

Variation: Some folks love the combo of peanut butter and bananas. (Elvis did!) Try replacing the chocolate chips with ½ a sliced ripe banana for another delectable (and even more fiberful) sandwich.

 Smooth Move

Classic peanut butter and jelly sandwiches aren't bad fiber choices if you stick to a whole-grain bread and use preserves instead of jelly.

Part 5

What's for Dinner?

Getting a healthful dinner on the table can be a daunting prospect at the best of times. What's a fiber seeker to do? Can dinner prep be easy and quick and still result in a meal that suits your fiber goals? You bet. Putting it all together is the trick, and after trying your hand at these recipes, you'll see how truly simple it can be.

If you love chicken and poultry, you've come to the right place. If fish is more your favorite, you'll find incredible dishes that highlight all types while including fiberful, tasty ingredients that enhance flavor and health. The same goes for meat eaters or meat avoiders. From beef stew to vegetarian pizza, it's all here, brimming with healthful additions that will make you wonder if you're really eating high fiber at all. And let's not forget pasta, both whole-grain varieties and traditional versions. They, too, have a place at the dinner table.

Poultry a Plenty

In This Chapter

- ◆ Poultry meets fiber—with delicious results
- ◆ Cooped-up chicken gets creative
- ◆ Chicken classics with a fiber twist

Today, Americans eat more chicken than ever. In an attempt to be healthier, people often shun red meat and opt for poultry instead. As long as you don't overdo the fried chicken and buffalo wings, you're doing a pretty good job.

But what about the fiber? Because animal protein is naturally devoid of this essential nutrient, how do you be sure to include fiber at dinner time? Sure, a side salad and a baked potato help, but isn't there a better and tastier way?

Chicken Parts from the Norm

In this chapter, we explore the abundant possibilities of cooking with poultry in a fiber-conscious world. Roasting a chicken has a whole new meaning when you start adding ingredients that not only enhance the flavor of the chicken, but also benefit from the company of the bird. Such ingredient combinations illustrate the old adage that "the whole is more than the sum of the parts."

For example, when carrots have the opportunity to cook alongside a chicken, they inevitably become more scrumptious than cooked on their own. The same goes for stews and stir-fries, where flavors intermingle and the outcome is outstanding. The key is in choosing fiberful ingredients to mingle with, and, happily for us, there are many to choose from.

Tutti Frutti

As we've seen before, fruit, both fresh and dried, as well as nuts and seeds can be our best friends in a fiber-seeking kitchen, and in the case of poultry, can comprise some of the most delicious recipe ingredients. From pecan-crusted chicken breasts to turkey with a dried cranberry sauce, the unique flavor combinations you'll create are down-right unbeatable.

And as for fiber, that's the hidden added benefit! So quit your squawking, you skeptics, and enter the real world of healthful chicken and poultry dishes. Before you know it, old Colonel Sanders will be just a faint and distant memory in the cooped-up world of fast food.

Roast Chicken with Dried Plums

Dried plums, when cooked up plump and juicy, add a terrific sweetness while also serving as a great source of fiber.

1 whole chicken (about 3½ lb.)

1 TB. vegetable oil

Salt and pepper

½ tsp. dried thyme

1 medium onion, peeled and quartered

4 medium carrots, peeled and cut into 2-in. pieces

4 garlic cloves, peeled and left whole

16 pitted dried plums (prunes)

1 cup water

Yield: 4 servings	
Prep time: 15 minutes	
Cook time: 80 minutes	
Serving size: ¼ chicken	
Each serving has:	
9 g fiber	
640 calories	
20 g fat	
54 g carbohydrate	
36 g protein	

1. Preheat the oven to 375°F.

2. Remove excess fat, giblets, and neck from chicken cavity. Rinse chicken under cold water, and pat dry with paper towels. Place in a large roasting pan, and rub skin with vegetable oil. Season with salt and pepper, and sprinkle with thyme.

3. Scatter onion, carrots, garlic, and dried plums around chicken, and add water to the pan.

4. Roast in middle of the oven, occasionally stirring vegetables and basting chicken with juices, for 80 minutes or until an instant-read thermometer inserted into chicken thigh reads 175°F. Add a little water to the pan as needed to prevent sticking.

5. Using tongs, place chicken on a heated platter and allow to rest for 10 minutes. With a slotted spoon, transfer vegetables around chicken, and serve with pan juices.

Variation: Try substituting other fiber-rich dried fruit for the prunes such as apricots, figs, or dates.

 Grist for the Mill

In the 1990s, healthful prunes were commercially renamed "dried plums" in an attempt to market to a more youthful audience. Until then, the majority of prune consumers were primarily wrinkly old prunes themselves. Sorry, Granny!

Roasted Spiced Chicken Breasts

Exotically spiced and deliciously accompanied by roasted chickpeas, tender sweet potato, and plumped up raisins, this dish will quickly become a family favorite.

Yield: 4 servings
Prep time: 15 minutes
Cook time: 30 minutes
Serving size: 1 chicken breast
Each serving has:
8 g fiber
525 calories
17 g fat
52 g carbohydrate
40 g protein

¼ **cup olive oil**

1 tsp. ground cumin

1 tsp. ground cinnamon

½ **tsp. ground cardamom**

1 (15-oz.) can chickpeas, drained and rinsed

2 medium sweet potatoes, peeled and diced

½ **cup golden raisins**

4 split chicken breasts on the bone

Salt and pepper

1 cup plain Greek yogurt

1 TB. finely chopped fresh mint

Lemon wedges

1. Preheat the oven to 425°F.

2. In a small bowl, whisk together olive oil, cumin, cinnamon, and cardamom.

3. In a medium bowl, combine chickpeas, sweet potatoes, and raisins.

4. Season chicken with salt and pepper, and place chicken breasts skin side up in a large roasting pan. Drizzle ⅓ oil mixture over top, and pour remaining oil mixture in bowl with chickpeas, tossing well to coat. Sprinkle chickpea mixture with salt and pepper, and transfer to a roasting pan, spreading around chicken.

5. Roast 30 to 35 minutes or until chicken is cooked through, skin is browned, and vegetables are golden and tender. Occasionally stir to brown evenly.

6. Serve each breast surrounded by chickpea mixture and topped with a dollop of yogurt and a sprinkling of mint, with lemon wedges on the side.

Grist for the Mill

Popular in Middle Eastern as well as Scandinavian cuisine, cardamom is a member of the ginger family and is available ground or in pods.

Southern Brunswick Stew

Corn and lima beans provide the tasty fiber venue in this classic comfort-food dish. Serve with a salad and multigrain bread for dipping.

1 whole chicken, quartered (about 3½ lb.)

¼ cup vegetable oil

1 cup white whole-wheat flour

Salt and pepper

½ tsp. ground paprika

1 medium onion, chopped

1 medium celery stalk, diced

1 medium green bell pepper, ribs and seeds removed, and chopped

¼ cup apple juice

1 (15-oz.) can low-sodium chicken broth

1 (15-oz.) can diced tomatoes

1 (10-oz.) pkg. frozen corn

1 (10-oz.) pkg. frozen baby lima beans

1 TB. chopped fresh parsley

Yield: 4 servings		
Prep time: 20 minutes		
Cook time: 1 hour		
Serving size: 2 chicken pieces		
Each serving has:		
8 g fiber		
578 calories		
21 g fat		
59 g carbohydrate		
38 g protein		

1. With a sharp knife or cleaver, cut chicken breasts in ½ and separate thighs from drumsticks. Rinse chicken under cold water and pat dry with paper towels.

2. In a large, nonstick skillet over medium-high heat, heat vegetable oil.

3. In a shallow bowl, whisk together flour, salt, pepper, and paprika. Dredge chicken pieces in flour mixture, and fry chicken in the skillet for about 12 minutes or until browned on both sides. Transfer to a large, heavy pot.

4. Pour off all but 1 tablespoon oil from the skillet, and add onion, celery, and green bell pepper. Reduce heat to medium-low and cook, stirring often, for about 5 minutes or until slightly softened. Pour in apple juice, use a wooden spoon to scrape up all browned bits in skillet, and transfer contents to the pot with chicken.

5. Add broth and tomatoes to the pot, bring to a simmer, reduce heat to low, and cook, covered, for 30 minutes, stirring occasionally. Add corn and lima beans, and simmer, uncovered and stirring often, for about 15 more minutes or until vegetables are tender and stew has thickened.

6. Season with salt and pepper, sprinkle with parsley, and serve immediately.

Grist for the Mill

Lima beans, a member of the legume family, can be found frozen, canned, or dried. They are either baby in size or large (fordhook), and contain a whopping 5 grams fiber per ½ cup.

Stuffed Chicken Breasts with Pecan Crust

Deceptively easy to make, these heavenly creations get their fiber kick from chopped pecans and whole-wheat breadcrumbs, while a creamy garlic and broccoli filling becomes the delicious surprise.

Yield: 4 servings
Prep time: 30 minutes
Cook time: 40 to 45 minutes
Serving size: 1 chicken breast
Each serving has:
6 g fiber
667 calories
34 g fat
49 g carbohydrate
30 g protein

4 TB. unsalted butter

1 small onion, finely chopped

1 garlic clove, minced

1 cup broccoli florets, roughly chopped

Salt and pepper

1 (3-oz.) pkg. cream cheese

4 boneless, skinless chicken breasts

½ cup finely chopped pecans

½ cup whole-wheat bread-crumbs

1 large egg

1. In a medium saucepan over medium-low heat, melt 2 tablespoons butter. Add onion and cook, stirring often, for about 3 minutes or until softened but not browned.

2. Add garlic, broccoli, salt, and pepper, and continue to cook, stirring often, for about 3 more minutes or until broccoli is crisp-tender. Remove from heat, transfer to a small bowl, and stir in cream cheese. Cover and refrigerate for 30 minutes.

3. Preheat the oven to 350°F. Have ready an 8- or 9-inch-square baking dish.

4. Place chicken breasts on a sheet of waxed or parchment paper and flatten with a mallet to double their size. Spread ¼ cream cheese filling in center of each breast, roll up, and secure with toothpicks.

5. In a shallow bowl, combine pecans and breadcrumbs, and season with salt and pepper.

6. In another shallow bowl, beat egg with a fork.

7. Dip each chicken breast in beaten egg, coat with pecan mixture, and place seam side down in the baking dish. Melt remaining 2 tablespoons butter and drizzle over.

8. Bake for 30 to 35 minutes or until crust is golden and chicken is cooked through. Remove toothpicks and serve.

Smooth Move

Save stale whole-wheat and grain breads to make your own breadcrumbs. Pulse bread pieces a few times in a food processor and store in an airtight container in the fridge for up to 2 weeks.

Curry Chicken Kebabs

Aromatic skewers of tender and flavorful chicken and vegetables fit the fiber bill for grill night. A bed of orange-scented rice completes this Indian-inspired meal.

1 TB. curry powder

2 TB. firmly packed brown sugar

Juice of 1 lemon

6 boneless, skinless chicken thighs

1 cup brown basmati rice

1 cup orange juice

1 cup water

1 TB. unsalted butter

½ cup chicken broth

1 tsp. Worcestershire sauce

3 TB. mango chutney

1 large green bell pepper, ribs and seeds removed, and cut into chunks

1 large red onion, peeled and cut into chunks

Salt and pepper

Yield: 4 servings
Prep time: 30 minutes
Cook time: 30 minutes
Serving size: 1 skewer
Each serving has:
5 g fiber
378 calories
9 g fat
45 g carbohydrate
39 g protein

1. In a shallow bowl, stir together curry powder, brown sugar, and lemon juice until smooth.

2. Cut chicken thighs into bite-size pieces and marinate in curry mixture for 20 minutes.

3. Meanwhile, in a medium saucepan over high heat, combine rice, orange juice, water, and butter. Bring to a boil, stir, cover, reduce heat to low, and cook for 25 to 30 minutes or until rice is tender.

4. In a small saucepan over medium heat, combine broth, Worcestershire sauce, and mango chutney. Cook for about 3 minutes or until slightly thickened. Set aside and keep warm.

5. Heat an outdoor or indoor grill to medium-high and coat lightly with oil. Thread metal skewers with chicken, bell pepper, and onion, and season with salt and pepper. Grill kebabs on all sides for about 12 minutes or until browned and chicken juices run clear.

6. To serve, transfer cooked rice to a heated platter, place kebabs on top, and spoon sauce over.

Grist for the Mill

Basmati means "fragrant one" in India, where this aromatic and delicate rice originates. Available in white or brown, basmati rice is a staple of curries and Middle Eastern cuisines.

Chicken and Black Bean Burritos

Fiber-rich black beans pair with chicken in this quick and flavorful Mexican-style dish featuring hot jalapeños, sweet bell pepper, and fragrant cilantro. Serve with guacamole for extra fiber points.

Yield: 4 servings
Prep time: 20 minutes
Cook time: 10 minutes
Serving size: 2 burritos
Each serving has:
11 g fiber
598 calories
18 g fat
85 g carbohydrate
40 g protein

2 TB. vegetable oil

4 boneless, skinless chicken breasts, cut into ½-in. strips

Salt and pepper

1 medium onion, sliced

1 red bell pepper, ribs and seeds removed, and sliced

1 jalapeño pepper, seeded and chopped

1 (15-oz.) can black beans, drained and rinsed

1 tsp. chili powder

1 tsp. ground cumin

1 TB. chopped fresh cilantro

8 (10-in.) whole-wheat tortillas

1 cup shredded cheddar cheese

1. In a large skillet over high heat, heat vegetable oil. Add chicken, season with salt and pepper, and cook, stirring often, for about 5 minutes or until chicken is no longer pink. Using a slotted spoon, transfer chicken to a bowl and set aside.

2. Add onion, red bell pepper, and jalapeño pepper to the skillet. Reduce heat to medium-high, and cook for about 5 minutes or until somewhat softened.

3. Add black beans and return chicken to the skillet. Sprinkle in chili powder and cumin, and cook, stirring often, for 3 more minutes or until heated through. Season with additional salt and pepper if necessary, stir in chopped cilantro, and remove from heat.

4. Fill tortillas with chicken mixture, sprinkle cheese on top, fold up bottom, and roll to close. Place seam side down on a heated platter, and serve immediately.

Smooth Move

Make a batch of these ahead, and wrap them tightly in plastic. When ready to eat, unwrap and heat in the microwave for 1 minute.

Ginger Chicken and Cashew Stir-Fry

As easy as it is healthy, this stir-fry gets its tang from fresh ginger and is particularly suited to the nutty flavor of brown rice.

¼ cup soy sauce

1 TB. cornstarch

1 tsp. sugar

1 lb. chicken tenderloins, trimmed and thinly sliced

2 TB. vegetable or peanut oil

Salt and pepper

2 TB. minced fresh ginger

2 garlic cloves, minced

½ lb. asparagus, cut into 2-in. pieces

8 green onions, cut into 2-in. pieces

1 (3.5-oz.) can water chestnuts, drained

½ cup cashews

⅔ cup low-sodium chicken broth

Toasted sesame oil

Cooked brown rice

Yield: 4 servings
Prep time: 20 minutes
Cook time: 8 minutes
Serving size: about 1 cup
Each serving has:
5 g fiber
354 calories
15 g fat
41 g carbohydrate
28 g protein

1. In a medium bowl, whisk together soy sauce, cornstarch, and sugar. Add chicken, stir to coat, and set aside.

2. In a wok or large skillet over high heat, heat vegetable oil. Add chicken mixture, season with salt and pepper, and stir-fry for about 2 minutes or until no longer pink. Remove from the pan and set aside.

3. Add ginger and garlic (and a little more oil, if necessary, to prevent sticking) to the skillet, and cook, stirring constantly, for 30 seconds without browning. Add asparagus, green onions, water chestnuts, and cashews, and stir-fry for 1 minute.

4. Stir in broth, cover, reduce heat to medium-low, and cook for about 2 minutes or until asparagus is crisp-tender. Return chicken to the pan, and stir-fry to reheat for about 1 more minute. Season with salt and pepper, drizzle a little sesame oil over, and serve with rice.

 Grist for the Mill

Despite its fibrous makeup, gingerroot offers little dietary fiber. Its other attributes are many, however, including anti-inflammatory properties, bacterial protection, and nausea remedy.

Chow-Down Chicken Burgers

A super-flavorful departure from typical burgers, smoke and spice turn this casual dinner fare into a fiesta.

Yield: 4 servings
Prep time: 20 minutes
Cook time: 20 minutes
Serving size: 1 burger
Each serving has:
4 g fiber
450 calories
28 g fat
20 g carbohydrate
27 g protein

1 TB. vegetable oil

½ medium onion, finely chopped

½ medium red bell pepper, ribs and seeds removed, and finely chopped

1 small celery stalk, finely diced

1 small carrot, peeled and finely diced

½ cup roughly chopped mushrooms

Salt and pepper

1 garlic clove, minced

1 lb. ground chicken or turkey

1 large egg white

¼ cup whole-wheat bread-crumbs

1 TB. flax meal

1½ tsp. Old Bay Seasoning

4 whole-grain burger buns

4 TB. mayonnaise

1 TB. sweet pickle relish

4 pieces thinly sliced red onion

4 slices ripe beefsteak tomato

Lettuce leaves

Smooth Move

Prepare burger patties ahead for cooking as part of a barbecue spread. Place on a small baking sheet lined with parchment and top with foil. Keep refrigerated for up to 4 hours.

1. In a medium skillet over medium heat, heat vegetable oil. Add onion, red bell pepper, celery, carrot, and mushrooms, and season with salt and pepper. Cook, stirring often, for about 5 minutes or until vegetables are soft but not browned. Add garlic and cook 1 more minute. Set aside to cool.

2. Preheat an outdoor grill to medium-high, and brush lightly with oil.

3. In a large bowl, combine cooked vegetables, ground chicken, egg white, breadcrumbs, flax meal, Old Bay, salt, and pepper. Mix well with a fork or your hands, and shape into 4 burgers.

4. Grill burgers for about 6 minutes per side or until they're cooked through and nicely browned. Toast buns on the grill, if desired.

5. While burgers are grilling, in a small bowl, combine mayonnaise and sweet pickle relish.

6. To serve, place burger on bun, top with ¼ mayo mixture, onion, tomato, and lettuce.

Cornish Hens with Cornbread-Apple Stuffing

Delicious and tender little game hens are perfect for quickly stuffing. Here, sweet apple, butternut squash, and crunchy walnuts help create the ideal flavor and fiber complement.

2 Cornish game hens

1 TB. unsalted butter

¼ cup finely chopped onion

¼ cup finely chopped celery

1 red delicious apple, cored and cut into ½-in. dice

1 cup peeled and ½-in. diced butternut squash

¼ cup walnut pieces

¼ tsp. dried thyme

2 tsp. finely chopped fresh parsley

Salt and pepper

1 large corn muffin, crumbled

¼ cup low-sodium chicken broth

2 tsp. vegetable oil

½ cup apple juice

Yield: 2 servings
Prep time: 20 minutes
Cook time: 80 minutes
Serving size: 1 hen
Each serving has:
4 g fiber
483 calories
19 g fat
38 g carbohydrate
24 g protein

1. Preheat the oven to 400°F.

2. Remove fat and giblets from game hens. Rinse hens under cold water, and pat dry with paper towels. Set aside.

3. In a skillet over medium heat, melt butter. Add onion and celery, and cook, stirring often, for about 3 minutes or until softened.

4. Add apple, butternut squash, walnut pieces, thyme, parsley, salt, and pepper, and continue to cook, stirring often, for 5 to 7 minutes or until apple and squash are fork-tender. Transfer to a medium bowl.

5. Add crumbled muffin and broth to vegetable mixture, and stir gently to combine. Fill cavities of hens with stuffing, and place on a rack in a roasting pan. Coat skin with oil, season with salt and pepper, and pour apple juice in the bottom of the pan.

6. Roast hens, basting every 15 minutes with pan juices, for about 70 minutes or until skin is crisp and golden and juices run clear when thigh is pierced with a fork.

7. Transfer hens to a platter, let rest for 10 minutes, and serve with pan juices.

 Smooth Move

At holiday time, stuffing can just as easily be made from whole-wheat and whole-grain breads. Cube the bread and allow to air dry before using in your favorite recipe.

Turkey Cutlets with Cranberry Pan Sauce

Out of the pan instead of the can, the tasty cranberry sauce that deliciously coats these tender, savory cutlets will delight all your diners. Serve with a sweet-potato side dish for an any-day Thanksgiving!

Yield: 4 servings
Prep time: 20 minutes
Cook time: 15 minutes
Serving size: 1 cutlet
Each serving has:
3 g fiber
367 calories
12 g fat
35 g carbohydrate
17 g protein

½ cup white whole-wheat flour

¼ tsp. ground sage

Salt and pepper

4 (¼-in.-thick) turkey cutlets (about 4 oz. each)

2 TB. olive oil

2 TB. shelled pumpkin seeds (pepitas)

¼ cup dried cranberries

½ cup low-sodium chicken broth

¼ cup cranberry juice

1 large orange, seeds removed and cut into ¼-in. slices

1 tsp. unsalted butter

1. In a shallow dish, combine flour, sage, salt, and pepper. Dredge turkey cutlets in flour mixture, shaking off any excess, and place on a piece of waxed paper.

2. In a large, nonstick skillet over medium-high heat, heat olive oil. Add cutlets and cook for 2 minutes per side or until lightly brown and not quite cooked all the way through. Transfer cutlets to a plate.

3. Reduce heat to medium. Add pumpkin seeds and cranberries to the skillet, and cook, stirring occasionally, for 1 minute. Pour in broth and cranberry juice, and bring to a simmer.

4. Return cutlets to the pan, place orange slices on top, and continue to cook, covered, for about 3 minutes or until turkey is no longer pink.

5. Transfer cutlets with orange slices to a heated platter. Continue simmering liquid in the skillet for a few more minutes until somewhat thickened. Remove from heat, swirl in butter, and spoon sauce over cutlets. Serve immediately.

Smooth Move

Dried cranberries now come with various enhancements such as cherry, orange, and cinnamon. Try cooking with them in recipes that suit their additional layer of flavor.

Molto Buono Turkey Loaf

Molto buono is Italian for "very good" and it's so appropriate for this meatloaf, which is a great place for hidden fiber. Here, delicious and bold Italian flavors disguise how healthful this really is.

1 lb. lean ground turkey (not breast only)

1 large egg

1 (8-oz.) can tomato sauce

1 small onion, finely chopped

2 garlic cloves, minced

2 TB. finely chopped sun-dried tomatoes

1 tsp. dried oregano

1 tsp. dried basil

1 tsp. dried parsley

1 TB. grated Parmesan cheese

½ cup whole-wheat bread-crumbs

2 TB. toasted wheat germ

1 TB. ground flaxseeds

Salt and pepper

Yield: 4 servings
Prep time: 15 minutes
Cook time: 70 minutes
Serving size: 2 slices
Each serving has:
3 g fiber
210 calories
6 g fat
9 g carbohydrate
15 g protein

1. Preheat the oven to 350°F. Lightly grease a 9×5×3-inch glass loaf dish.

2. In a large bowl, combine turkey, egg, ½ of tomato sauce, onion, garlic, sun-dried tomatoes, oregano, basil, parsley, Parmesan cheese, breadcrumbs, wheat germ, ground flaxseeds, salt, and pepper. Mix well with a fork or your hands.

3. Transfer mixture to the prepared loaf dish, and press down to remove any air pockets. Top with remaining tomato sauce, cover with foil, and bake for about 70 minutes or until an instant-read thermometer inserted in the middle reaches 165°F.

4. Remove from the oven and allow to rest for 10 minutes before slicing.

Grist for the Mill

Ground turkey is available in two varieties, lean and breast only. Lean ground turkey includes some dark meat and is less dry when cooked than ground turkey breast only.

Chapter **14**

Fish and Seafood

In This Chapter

- Fish in a flash
- Fiber comes aboard
- A treasure chest of recipes

If you're fishing for fiber, you've come to the right place. Whether it be succulent shrimp or tender, sweet salmon, these healthy proteins lend themselves beautifully to the addition of fiber-rich ingredients. Beans, rice, and a multitude of veggies are more than happy to accompany fish and seafood in their quest for high fiber.

You might even say, some of these delicious combinations are surely a match made in aquatic heaven!

Cooking Downstream

One of the great things about preparing fish dishes is the relatively short cooking time they require. Shrimp takes a couple minutes at most, while roasted or baked fillets need minimal oven time.

For this reason, it's ideal to have precooked or quick-cooking fiber-containing ingredients such as canned legumes or fresh spinach on hand to use in your recipes. Within no time at all, you can have a delicious and often elegant dinner on the table to everyone's delight and surprise.

Exploring the Delicious Depths

So which ingredients offer the best fiber punch when fish and seafood are on the menu? Beans and peas, frozen or canned, step in nicely in dishes like shellfish paella and halibut stew. Nourishing greens such as chard and spinach, fresh or frozen, can quickly add flavor and fiber to dishes like tilapia Florentine or sautéed shrimp. Corn and crab cakes are an ideal match, while sliced potatoes can create a crispy, fried crust for scrod.

The possibilities are surely as wide as the ocean, so jump in as we test the waters of high-fiber fish cooking!

Jumbo Shrimp with Chard and Cannellini Beans

This easy skillet dish with plenty of garlic tang and a dash of hot pepper is a classic Italian combo. Serve with whole-grain bread or pasta for extra fiber.

2 TB. olive oil

12 uncooked jumbo shrimp, peeled and deveined

Salt and pepper

½ lb. Swiss chard, ribs removed and leaves coarsely chopped

4 garlic cloves, minced

Dash red pepper flakes

½ cup low-sodium chicken broth

1 (15-oz.) can cannellini beans, drained and rinsed

Yield: 2 servings
Prep time: 20 minutes
Cook time: 10 minutes
Serving size: 6 shrimp
Each serving has:
15 g fiber
375 calories
15 g fat
35 g carbohydrate
25 g protein

1. In a large, nonstick skillet over medium-high heat, heat olive oil. Add shrimp, season with salt and pepper, and cook, stirring constantly, for about 2 minutes or until shrimp is pink. Using a slotted spoon, transfer shrimp to a clean bowl and set aside.

2. Add chopped chard to the skillet, and cook, stirring occasionally, for 1 or 2 minutes or until slightly wilted. Add garlic and red pepper flakes, and cook 1 more minute.

3. Reduce heat to low. Pour in broth, cover, and cook for 2 or 3 minutes or until chard is tender.

4. Increase heat to medium. Uncover skillet, add beans and reserved shrimp, and cook, stirring often, for about 3 minutes or until beans and shrimp are heated through. Season with salt and pepper, and serve immediately.

 Grist for the Mill

Swiss chard cultivation originated in Sicily centuries ago and has been a popular ingredient in Mediterranean cooking ever since. It was designated Swiss to distinguish it from French varieties.

Pan-Seared Scallops with Orange Glaze

Large, soft, and sweet scallops pair beautifully with the flavor of orange and ginger in this easy-to-prepare main dish.

Yield: 2 servings
Prep time: 10 minutes
Cook time: 10 minutes
Serving size: 4 ounces scallops (about 5)
Each serving has:
6 g fiber
520 calories
8 g fat
51 g carbohydrate
20 g protein

1 TB. olive oil

8 oz. sea scallops (about 10), rinsed and patted dry

Salt and pepper

1 TB. peeled, minced fresh ginger

6 green onions, cut into 2-in. pieces

½ cup sliced water chestnuts

½ cup orange juice

2 TB. orange marmalade

2 tsp. unsalted butter, softened

2 cups cooked brown rice

1. In a large, nonstick skillet over medium-high heat, heat olive oil. Season scallops with salt and pepper, add to the hot skillet, and quickly sear until lightly browned, about 2 minutes per side. Remove with tongs, and set on a warm plate.

2. Add ginger and green onions to the skillet, and cook, stirring, for about 3 minutes or until slightly softened. Add water chestnuts, and stir 1 more minute.

3. Stir in orange juice and marmalade, and bring to a simmer. Return scallops to the skillet, and stir well to coat. Cook 1 more minute, and swirl in butter. Serve immediately over brown rice.

 Smooth Move _____

Always opt for preserves and marmalades over jellies. The fruit pulp and rind add extra fiber.

Oven-Baked Shellfish Paella

Here's a delicious and simply prepared *paella* featuring succulent shrimp, clams, and mussels that benefits from fiber-rich brown rice laced with aromatic saffron.

1 TB. olive oil

1 medium onion, chopped

½ medium green bell pepper, ribs and seeds removed, and diced

Salt and pepper

3 garlic cloves, minced

1½ cups long-grain brown rice

2¾ cups low-sodium chicken or vegetable broth

1 (15-oz.) can diced tomatoes, drained

1 bay leaf

½ tsp. crushed saffron threads

1 lb. uncooked large shrimp, peeled and deveined

1 doz. clams, scrubbed

1½ doz. mussels, scrubbed and *debearded*

⅔ cup frozen green peas, thawed

2 tsp. finely chopped fresh parsley leaves

Lemon wedges

Yield: *4 servings*		
Prep time: 35 minutes		
Cook time: 60 minutes		
Serving size: about 1½ cups		
Each serving has:		
5 g fiber		
380 calories		
15 g fat		
35 g carbohydrate		
25 g protein		

1. Preheat the oven to 350°F.

2. In a Dutch oven over medium-high heat, heat olive oil. Add onion and green bell pepper, season with salt and pepper, and cook, stirring often, for about 3 minutes or until somewhat softened. Add garlic and cook 1 more minute.

3. Add rice and stir to coat with onion mixture. Add broth, tomatoes, bay leaf, and saffron threads, and bring to a boil, stirring occasionally. Remove from heat, cover, and transfer to the oven. Cook for about 35 minutes or until most liquid is absorbed.

4. Remove from the oven, stir, and place shrimp, clams, mussels, and green peas on top. Cover and return to the oven, and cook for about 20 minutes or until rice is tender, shrimp is opaque, and clam and mussel shells have opened.

5. Let stand, covered, for 5 minutes. Discard any unopened clams or mussels. Sprinkle with parsley, and serve immediately with lemon wedges.

Variation: Classic paella includes spicy chorizo sausage as well as chicken. To add these to your paella, chop a small, dried chorizo sausage and sauté it with the onion and bell pepper. Or brown chicken thighs and drumsticks in a skillet and add them to the pot of rice after the first 20 minutes.

 Fiber Optics

Paella is a Valencian rice dish from Spain, usually made in a large, shallow skillet (*paella*). It includes a variety of fish and shellfish, as well as chicken and vegetables. To **debeard** shrimp means to remove sand and outside beard.

Crispy Corn and Crab Cakes

Corny but true, these tasty crab cakes with a hint of cilantro get a boost of fiber from the addition of corn kernels and a rich creamed corn sauce.

Yield: 4 servings
Prep time: 40 minutes
Cook time: 10 minutes
Serving size: 2 crab cakes
Each serving has:
8 g fiber
755 calories
21 g fat
59 g carbohydrate
36 g protein

1 (15-oz.) can corn kernels, drained

4 green onions, finely chopped

½ medium red bell pepper, ribs and seeds removed, and finely chopped

1 small celery stalk, finely chopped

1 lb. jumbo lump crabmeat, picked over for shells and cartilage

1 tsp. Old Bay Seasoning

1 TB. finely chopped fresh cilantro leaves

½ cup mayonnaise

2 large egg whites

Salt and pepper

3 cups fresh whole-wheat or multigrain breadcrumbs

1 (15-oz.) can cream-style corn

¼ cup heavy cream

2 TB. unsalted butter

Dash cayenne

Vegetable oil

Grist for the Mill

Test oil with a thermometer before frying (it should reach 360°F) or plop a bread cube in the skillet. If it sizzles and browns immediately, the oil is ready.

1. Place ½ of corn kernels in a medium saucepan and set aside.

2. Put remaining corn kernels in a large bowl, and add green onions, red bell pepper, celery, crabmeat, Old Bay, and cilantro. Toss gently to combine.

3. Add mayonnaise, egg whites, salt, pepper, and 1 cup breadcrumbs to crab mixture, and stir just to combine. Form 8 (2-inch) patties, and place on a sheet of waxed paper. Dip each patty into remaining 2 cups breadcrumbs, and press gently to coat. Refrigerate on a baking sheet for at least 20 minutes.

4. Meanwhile, add cream-style corn, heavy cream, butter, and cayenne to the pot with corn kernels, and cook over medium heat, stirring often, for about 3 minutes or until mixture is hot and thick. Season with salt and pepper, set aside, and keep warm.

5. In a large, heavy skillet over medium-high heat, heat enough vegetable oil to come about ¼ inch up the side. Add crab cakes, and fry for 6 to 8 minutes or until golden brown on both sides. Drain crab cakes on paper towels, and serve immediately topped with the corn sauce.

Chilean Sea Bass with Teriyaki Vegetables

Tender, sweet sea bass and crisp-tender vegetables highlight this easy, Asian-style dinner that's both healthy and satisfying.

1 cup low-sodium soy sauce

2 TB. rice vinegar

1½ TB. firmly packed brown sugar

1 TB. peeled and finely chopped fresh ginger

1 large garlic clove, minced

4 (4-oz.) sea bass fillets

2 TB. vegetable or peanut oil

1 cup small broccoli florets

1 large celery stalk, trimmed and thinly sliced on the diagonal

1 medium carrot, peeled and thinly sliced on the diagonal

4 oz. shiitake mushrooms, stemmed and caps thinly sliced

1 cup canned baby corn, drained

8 green onions, cut into 2-in. pieces

1 cup snow peas

Yield: 4 servings
Prep time: 30 minutes
Cook time: 15 minutes
Serving size: 1 fillet with about 1 cup vegetables
Each serving has:
5 g fiber
225 calories
8 g fat
25 g carbohydrate
12 g protein

1. In a shallow bowl, combine soy sauce, rice vinegar, brown sugar, ginger, and garlic. Place sea bass, flesh side down, in soy mixture and marinate in the refrigerator for 30 minutes.

2. Preheat the oven to 400°F.

3. In a large, nonstick skillet over medium-high heat, heat 1 tablespoon vegetable oil. Remove sea bass from marinade, reserving marinade, and add sea bass to the skillet, skin side down. Brown, using a spatula to occasionally press down to keep skin from curling. Transfer to a baking dish, and roast in the oven for about 10 minutes or until opaque in the center.

4. Meanwhile, add remaining 1 tablespoon vegetable oil to the skillet, and heat to nearly smoking. Add broccoli, celery, carrot, mushrooms, and baby corn, and stir-fry for 3 minutes. Add green onions and snow peas, and stir-fry another 3 minutes.

5. Add reserved marinade, stir well, reduce heat to medium-low, and cook for about 3 more minutes or until vegetables are crisp-tender and marinade has thickened into a glaze.

6. To serve, transfer sea bass to a platter and spoon vegetables on top and around.

Variation: Try this same method with scrod, snapper, mahi mahi, or salmon.

 Smooth Move _____

To save on prep time, look for packages of precut stir-fry vegetables in your produce section.

Ten-Minute Tilapia Florentine

Anything with spinach can be designated *Florentine*, but here, there's even more Italian flavor and flair with the addition of pine nuts and sun-dried tomatoes.

2 TB. olive oil

1 tsp. unsalted butter

2 (6-oz.) tilapia fillets

Salt and pepper

¼ cup pine nuts

½ cup chopped marinated sun-dried tomatoes

1 (4-oz.) pkg. baby spinach

2 TB. grated Parmesan cheese

Yield: 2 servings
Prep time: 5 minutes
Cook time: 10 minutes
Serving size: 1 fillet
Each serving has:
5 g fiber
400 calories
25 g fat
15 g carbohydrate
26 g protein

1. In a large, nonstick skillet over medium-high heat, heat 1 tablespoon olive oil with butter.

2. Season tilapia fillets with salt and pepper, and add to the skillet. Sauté, turning over once, for about 5 minutes or until golden and cooked through. Transfer to 2 heated serving plates.

3. Heat remaining 1 tablespoon olive oil in the skillet, add pine nuts and sun-dried tomatoes, and cook, stirring often, for 2 minutes. Add spinach and continue to cook, tossing to coat, until wilted, about 3 minutes.

4. Top each fillet with spinach mixture, and sprinkle Parmesan over top. Serve immediately.

 Grist for the Mill

Before canning, Italians dried tomatoes on their tile roofs for the winter when fresh tomatoes weren't available. Today, Italians rarely make or use sun-dried tomatoes, while we cooks in the United States are devoted fans.

Thyme-Honored Salmon with Peas

Fiber-rich, sweet fresh peas star in this oven-roasted salmon dish with the tang of mustard and the fragrance of thyme.

Yield: *4 servings*
Prep time: 25 minutes
Cook time: 45 minutes
Serving size: 1 fillet
Each serving has:
5 g fiber
375 calories
15 g fat
35 g carbohydrate
25 g protein

¼ **cup honey mustard**

2 **TB. vegetable oil**

3 **medium red-skinned potatoes, skin on and cut into ½-in. dice**

Salt and pepper

1½ **cups fresh shelled peas**

4 **(4-oz.) salmon fillets, skin and bones removed**

1 **TB. chopped fresh thyme or 1 tsp. dried thyme leaves**

Lemon wedges

1. Preheat the oven to 400°F. Lightly grease a rimmed baking sheet.

2. In a large bowl, whisk together honey mustard and vegetable oil. Add potatoes, salt, and pepper, and toss well to coat. Transfer mixture to the prepared baking sheet, and roast in the oven, stirring occasionally, for about 15 minutes or until potatoes begin to soften.

3. Add peas to the baking sheet with potatoes, and continue roasting, stirring occasionally, for about 15 more minutes or until vegetables are tender.

4. Remove from the oven, and use a spatula to scoop peas and potatoes to the center of the pan. Place salmon on top, season with salt and pepper, and sprinkle with thyme. Return to the oven, and roast for 12 to 15 minutes or until salmon is cooked through and is beginning to brown.

5. Transfer salmon and vegetables to a platter, and serve immediately with lemon wedges.

Variation: Eliminate the potatoes and fresh peas. Coat the salmon fillets with the mustard mixture and roast as above, adding 1½ cups thawed frozen peas during the last 5 minutes. Break the cooked fillets into bite-size pieces and serve over cooked bowtie pasta, (1 cup per person) garnished with dill sprigs.

Grist for the Mill

Green peas, also called garden peas or English peas, have one of the highest concentrations of fiber in the vegetable world per weight. In the eighteenth century, they were considered highly fashionable in European culinary circles, and Thomas Jefferson was known to grow more than 30 varieties.

Skillet Scrod with Potato Crust

Paper-thin slices of potato form the crispy crust of this flavorful fish entrée that's topped off with sautéed fennel.

2 TB. unsalted butter

1 medium fennel bulb, trimmed, cored, and thinly sliced

1 medium leek, white part only, thinly sliced

½ tsp. dried oregano

Salt and pepper

1 egg, lightly beaten

2 (6-oz.) scrod or grouper fillets

2 medium red-skinned potatoes

2 TB. olive oil

Yield: 2 servings
Prep time: 20 minutes
Cook time: 20 minutes
Serving size: 1 fillet
Each serving has:
3 g fiber
425 calories
24 g fat
15 g carbohydrate
32 g protein

1. In a skillet over medium heat, melt butter. Add fennel, leek, oregano, salt, and pepper. Cook, stirring often, for about 8 minutes or until vegetables are softened. Set aside and keep warm.

2. Season fish with salt and pepper, and lightly brush with egg on one side.

3. Slice unpeeled potatoes paper thin (about ¹/₈-inch thick), and layer ¹/₂ of slices over egg-coated side of fish.

4. In a large skillet over medium-high heat, heat olive oil. Carefully place fillets into the skillet, potato side down, and fry for about 4 or 5 minutes or until edges of potatoes begin to brown.

5. Meanwhile, brush other side of fillets with egg and layer with remaining potatoes. Carefully flip fish over and continue cooking for about 4 more minutes or until potatoes are browned and fish is opaque.

6. Drain fish on a paper towel, and season with salt and pepper. Serve each fillet topped with fennel mixture.

 Smooth Move

You can use a mandoline, a French vegetable slicer, to make the paper-thin slices of potato for this recipe. Inexpensive plastic versions called Japanese mandolines are available at cooking supply stores and online.

Nutty Seared Ahi Tuna

Nuts and seeds provide the fiber in this easy tuna dish featuring a hot wasabi dressing all on a bed of tangy watercress.

Yield: 2 servings
Prep time: 12 minutes
Cook time: 6 minutes
Serving size: 1 fillet
Each serving has:
7 g fiber
485 calories
30 g fat
17 g carbohydrate
35 g protein

2 tsp. wasabi powder

1 TB. hot water

2 TB. soy sauce

2 TB. orange juice

½ cup chopped peanuts

3 TB. sesame seeds

2 TB. toasted wheat germ

2 (6-oz.) ahi or sushi-grade tuna fillets

1 TB. peanut or vegetable oil

2 cups watercress

1. In a small bowl, whisk together wasabi powder and hot water until smooth. Whisk in soy sauce and orange juice, and set aside.

2. On a large piece of waxed paper, combine peanuts, sesame seeds, and wheat germ. Lightly coat tuna fillets with some peanut oil, and press them into peanut mixture on both sides to coat.

3. Brush remaining oil in a nonstick skillet. Over high heat, cook tuna for 2 or 3 minutes per side or until crust is browned but fish is still pink inside. Transfer to a cutting board.

4. To serve, scatter watercress over 2 plates, slice tuna and place on top, and drizzle wasabi mixture over all.

 Grist for the Mill

Unlike hot peppers that burn the tongue, wasabi, or Japanese horseradish, affects the nasal passages and can clear your sinuses in no time! It's also believed to have anti-cancer benefits.

Halibut and Saffron Bean Stew

Thick and hearty, with a hint of aromatic saffron, this stew is surprisingly quick to make and delightful to eat. Serve with multigrain bread for dipping.

3 TB. olive oil

1 medium onion, chopped

1 large celery stalk, chopped

1 large carrot, peeled and diced

4 garlic cloves, chopped

1 (15-oz.) can diced tomatoes with juice

1 (8-oz.) bottle clam juice

1 cup water

Pinch saffron threads

1 (15-oz.) can navy beans, drained

1 (15-oz.) can Roman or borlotti beans, drained

1½ lb. halibut fillets, cut into chunks

Salt and pepper

1 TB. chopped fresh parsley

Yield: 4 servings
Prep time: 20 minutes
Cook time: 20 minutes
Serving size: about 2 cups
Each serving has:
17 g fiber
450 calories
13 g fat
55 g carbohydrate
28 g protein

1. In a large, heavy-bottomed pot over medium heat, heat olive oil. Add onion, celery, and carrot, and cook, stirring occasionally, for about 6 minutes or until softened. Add garlic and cook 1 more minute.

2. Stir in tomatoes, clam juice, water, and saffron. Increase heat to high and bring to a boil. Reduce heat to medium-low, and simmer, stirring occasionally, for 5 minutes.

3. Add navy beans, Roman beans, and halibut, and simmer, covered, for about 5 minutes or until halibut is opaque and stew is piping hot. Season with salt and pepper, and serve sprinkled with parsley.

 Grist for the Mill

Anchors aweigh! Navy beans got their name in the late nineteenth century because they were a staple of U.S. ship cuisine. They are also the state vegetable of Massachusetts.

Chapter 15

Here's the Beef, Veal, and Pork

In This Chapter

- ◆ Comforting beef dishes
- ◆ Grilling and skilleting
- ◆ Fibering up some classics

When meat's on the menu, what's a fiber-conscious cook to do? There's no denying that even those who are monitoring their healthy proteins and fats may at times want to sink their teeth into a good side of beef.

Being a bit extravagant doesn't mean the whole meal has gone up in fiberless flames. On the contrary, meats such as beef, veal, and pork are excellent vehicles for adding healthful vegetables and adornments, and in this chapter, you get a real good taste of what I mean!

Sneaking in Some Fiber

Beef stew or pot roast would be nothing without the intensely flavored carrots, potatoes, and other root vegetables that cook up with them. And adding a few extra fiber-rich ingredients such as peas, parsnips, or beans can really beef up the fiber content in a delicious way. Whole grains can even make an appearance in the form of dumplings to soak up that rich, tasty gravy from the stewing pot, and contribute their own form of fiber to your meal. But that's just the beginning.

Accompanying sauces such as a peanut satay may be the fiber provider instead, as well as that buttery corn ragout that tops your veal chop. Creative combinations like these are bound to make you wonder if you've really added fiber at all when it's not staring you bluntly in the face like a pile of lima beans.

And if you're fooled as the cook, just think of the reception you'll get from family and friends! "I thought you were cooking high fiber. This is delicious!" You'll, of course, be smiling to yourself, as they dig into your moist meatloaf laced with flaxseed meal or that succulent pork tenderloin topped with cider-braised onions and apple. *This is just too easy*, you'll be thinking. Instead of wondering where the beef is, they'll be utterly baffled trying to figure where the fiber is. Don't you love it?

Winter Beef Stew with Whole-Grain Dumplings

Guaranteed to warm you from head to toe, this comforting and delicious stew, featuring the intense flavors of garlic and root vegetables, offers excellent amounts of fiber.

2 TB. vegetable oil

1½ lb. stewing beef, cubed and trimmed of excess fat

Salt and pepper

Flour

1 medium onion, chopped

1 large celery stalk, chopped

2 garlic cloves, minced

1 TB. tomato paste

1 TB. grape or currant jelly

2 cups low-sodium beef broth

2 cups water

1 bay leaf

2 large carrots, peeled and cut into 1-in. chunks

2 medium turnips, peeled and quartered

2 medium red-skinned potatoes, cubed

2 cups white whole-wheat flour

1 TB. toasted wheat germ

1 TB. baking powder

1 tsp. salt

1 TB. chopped fresh parsley

2 large eggs

¾ cup buttermilk

Yield: 4 servings
Prep time: 20 minutes
Cook time: 2 hours, 10 minutes
Serving size: about 2 cups
Each serving has:
11 g fiber
725 calories
34 g fat
65 g carbohydrate
38 g protein

1. In a large, heavy-bottomed pot over medium-high heat, heat vegetable oil. Season beef with salt and pepper, dredge in flour, shake off excess, and fry beef in oil for 5 to 7 minutes or until browned on all sides. Remove beef from the pot, and set aside.

2. Add onion and celery to the pot, and cook over medium heat, stirring often, for about 4 minutes or until softened. Add garlic and cook 1 more minute.

3. Stir in tomato paste and jelly, and continue to cook, stirring constantly, for 2 minutes. Add broth, water, and bay leaf, increase heat to high, and bring to a boil. Return beef to pot, reduce heat to medium-low, and simmer, covered, for about 1½ hours or until nearly fork-tender.

4. Add carrots and cook at a simmer for 15 minutes. Add turnips and potatoes, and cook, stirring occasionally, for 20 to 30 minutes or until beef and vegetables are completely tender. Add water, if necessary, to prevent sticking and maintain gravy consistency.

5. Meanwhile, in a medium bowl, make dumplings by whisking together 2 cups white whole-wheat flour, wheat germ, baking powder, salt, and parsley.

6. In another bowl, beat together eggs and buttermilk. Add egg mixture to flour mixture, and stir quickly with a fork to combine. Do not overmix.

7. Drop heaping tablespoons of dumpling mixture into simmering stew. Reduce heat to low, cover, and cook for about 10 minutes or until dumplings are firm and puffy. Serve immediately from the pot.

 Smooth Move _____

Dumplings made from whole-grain flours are a great way to add fiber to any broth-based soup or stew. They're also a nice alternative to serving bread with your meal.

Easy Horseradish Pot Roast

Tangy horseradish adds pizzazz to this old-fashioned dish that's fibered up with plenty of flavor-packed vegetables and beans.

1 (3- to 4-lb.) chuck roast on the bone

Salt and pepper

⅓ cup prepared horseradish

3 TB. vegetable oil

1 large onion, chopped

1 TB. all-purpose flour

¼ cup apple juice

2 cups low-sodium beef broth

2 cups water

1 sprig fresh thyme

4 medium carrots, peeled and cut into 1-in. pieces

3 medium parsnips, cut into thirds

1½ lb. *fingerling* or baby white or red potatoes

¾ cup frozen fordhook lima beans

½ cup frozen green peas

Yield: 4 servings
Prep time: 15 minutes
Cook time: 2½ hours
Serving size: about 2 cups
Each serving has:
8 g fiber
560 calories
25 g fat
38 g carbohydrate
45 g protein

1. Trim roast of excess fat, and season with salt and pepper. Spread horseradish on both sides.

2. In a large, heavy-bottomed pot over medium-high heat, heat vegetable oil. Add roast and brown well on both sides. Remove roast from the pot, and set aside.

3. Add onion to the pot, and cook, stirring up browned bits on bottom of pot, for 2 minutes. Stir in flour, and cook for 1 minute.

4. Pour in apple juice, and cook until evaporated. Add broth, water, and thyme. Increase heat to high, and bring to a boil. Return roast to the pot, reduce heat to medium-low, cover, and cook at a simmer for about 1½ to 2 hours or until fork-tender. Add water, if necessary, to prevent sticking.

5. Add carrots, parsnips, and potatoes, and cook, covered, for about 20 minutes or until fork-tender. Uncover, add lima beans and peas, and cook, stirring occasionally, for about 8 minutes or until tender and heated through. Serve immediately.

Fiber Optics

Fingerling potatoes are small, finger-shaped potatoes that are low in starch. Varieties include Rose Finn, French, and Russian Banana.

Stir-Fried Mongolian Beef with Broccoli

Flavored with sweet hoisin sauce and fragrant sesame oil, you can make this dish as hot as you like by adjusting the red pepper flakes. Serve with brown short-grain or basmati rice for extra fiber.

Yield: 2 servings
Prep time: 40 minutes
Cook time: 6 minutes
Serving size: about 1½ cups
Each serving has:
5 g fiber
500 calories
27 g fat
30 g carbohydrate
35 g protein

½ cup soy sauce

2 TB. hoisin sauce

1 TB. toasted sesame oil

2 tsp. sugar

1 large garlic clove, minced

1 tsp. red pepper flakes

¾ lb. beef flank steak, thinly sliced

1 TB. peanut or vegetable oil

4 green onions, cut into 2-in. pieces

2 cups small broccoli florets

1. In a medium bowl, whisk together soy sauce, hoisin sauce, toasted sesame oil, sugar, garlic, and red pepper flakes. Add sliced beef, and toss well to coat. Refrigerate for 30 minutes.

2. In a wok or large, nonstick skillet over high heat, heat vegetable oil. Add green onions and broccoli, and stir-fry for 2 minutes. Drain beef, reserving marinade, and add to the wok, continuing to stir-fry over high heat for about 3 minutes more or until beef begins to brown.

3. Add remaining marinade, and continue to cook for about 1 more minute or until beef and vegetables are lightly coated with sauce. Serve immediately.

 Smooth Move _____

Look for precooked fiber-rich Asian noodles such as brown rice udon or soba in your supermarket that can be reheated quickly and take the place of rice.

Beef Skewers with Peanut Satay

Deliciously nutty satay sauce and butter leaf lettuce for wrapping accompany these quickly grilled, tender morsels of beef.

1 small head butter leaf or Boston lettuce	**1 lb. filet mignon or sirloin steak, thinly sliced**
1 cup chunky peanut butter	**20 bamboo skewers**
¼ cup low-sodium soy sauce	**Salt and pepper**
2 TB. firmly packed brown sugar	**¼ tsp. curry powder**
Juice of 1 lemon	**Vegetable oil for grilling**
Dash Tabasco sauce	**1 bunch green onions, chopped**
½ cup hot water	

Yield: 4 servings
Prep time: 30 minutes
Cook time: 4 minutes
Serving size: 5 skewers
Each serving has:
8 g fiber
575 calories
36 g fat
23 g carbohydrate
40 g protein

1. Remove core from lettuce, separate leaves, and wash and dry. Set aside.

2. In a food processor fitted with a steel blade, add peanut butter, soy sauce, brown sugar, lemon juice, and Tabasco sauce, and pulse a few times to combine. While running, pour in enough hot water to thin out into a sauce. Transfer to a dipping bowl, and set aside.

3. Thread beef slices onto skewers. Season with salt and pepper, and sprinkle lightly with curry powder.

4. Heat an indoor or outdoor grill to high and brush lightly with oil. Grill skewered beef for about 2 minutes per side or until edges are brown. Transfer to a heated platter.

5. Serve immediately with satay sauce, chopped green onions for sprinkling, and lettuce leaves for wrapping.

 Smooth Move

Thinly slicing beef, pork, or chicken for skewering or stir-fries is a snap when it's partially frozen.

Skillet Steak and Onion on Toast

Rib-eye fans, here's one for you! Perfectly seared succulent steak topped with sweet, herbed onions and mushrooms finds a home on fiberful toast slathered with garlic.

Yield: 2 servings

Prep time: 8 minutes

Cook time: 18 minutes

Serving size: 1 steak

Each serving has:

5 g fiber

410 calories

15 g fat

40 g carbohydrate

22 g protein

---

1 TB. unsalted butter

1 TB. olive oil

1 large Vidalia or other sweet onion, thinly sliced

8 oz. white button mushrooms, thinly sliced

Salt and pepper

2 TB. chopped fresh thyme or 2 tsp. dried

¼ cup apple juice

2 tsp. vegetable oil

2 (¾-in.-thick) rib-eye steaks

2 (1-in.-thick) slices whole-grain sourdough bread, toasted

1. In a large, nonstick skillet over medium-high heat, heat butter and olive oil. Add onion and mushrooms, season with salt and pepper, and cook, stirring occasionally, for about 8 minutes or until softened and golden. Add thyme and cook for 1 more minute. Stir in apple juice, and set aside, keeping warm.

2. In a large, heavy skillet over medium-high heat, heat vegetable oil.

3. Season both sides of steaks with salt and pepper, and add to the skillet. Cook for about 4 minutes per side for medium-rare or longer for desired doneness.

4. To serve, place 1 slice of toast in the middle of each of 2 plates, top with steak, and spoon onions and mushrooms over.

 Grist for the Mill

Many steak aficionados consider rib-eye steaks the best cut. The extensive marbling provides mucho flavor and tenderness. Kansas City is famous for them.

Veal Chops with Summer Corn Ragout

Tender veal rests on a delicious bed of fresh corn *ragout* flavored with pungent cumin and sweet basil in this easy but elegant presentation.

2 TB. olive oil

2 (10- to 12-oz.) rib veal chops

Salt and pepper

¼ tsp. ground cumin

1 shallot, minced

½ medium red bell pepper, ribs and seeds removed, and diced

1½ cups fresh or frozen corn kernels

½ cup low-sodium chicken broth

Dash paprika

2 tsp. unsalted butter

¼ cup torn fresh basil leaves

Yield: 2 servings	
Prep time: 10 minutes	
Cook time: 22 minutes	
Serving size: 1 veal chop	
Each serving has:	
40 g fiber	
550 calories	
35 g fat	
15 g carbohydrate	
44 g protein	

1. In a large, nonstick skillet over medium-high heat, heat 1 tablespoon oil.

2. Season chops on both sides with salt, pepper, and cumin, and add to the skillet. Cook for about 3 minutes per side or until brown. Transfer to a plate and set aside.

3. Add remaining 1 tablespoon olive oil to the skillet. Add shallot and red bell pepper, and cook, stirring often, for about 3 minutes or until vegetables are soft. Stir in corn, and cook 1 more minute.

4. Add broth and paprika, return chops to the skillet, cover, and cook for about 10 minutes or until veal is no longer pink. Transfer chops to serving dishes.

5. Stir butter and basil into the skillet corn mixture, and cook for 1 minute. Spoon corn ragout over veal chops, and serve immediately.

 Fiber Optics

Ragout (pronounced *ra-GOO*) is a French term for a hearty stew or sauce prepared with or without meat.

Veal Parmesan Deluxe

A popular Italian entrée gets a burst of fiber in this delectable version made with whole-grain breadcrumbs and a kicked-up sauce featuring tasty artichokes and zucchini.

Yield: *4 servings*
Prep time: 30 minutes
Cook time: 40 minutes
Serving size: 1 cutlet
Each serving has:
5 g fiber
730 calories
30 g fat
60 g carbohydrate
39 g protein

1 TB. olive oil

1 medium zucchini, halved lengthwise and sliced

Salt and pepper

1½ cups marinara sauce

1 cup artichoke hearts

4 veal cutlets (1½ lb. total)

2 large eggs, beaten

3 cups whole-grain or whole-wheat breadcrumbs

½ cup grated Parmesan cheese

4 TB. vegetable oil

2 cups shredded mozzarella cheese

1. Preheat the oven to 350°F.

2. In a large skillet over medium heat, heat olive oil. Add zucchini, season with salt and pepper, and cook, stirring often, for about 4 minutes or until vegetables are softened and lightly browned. Add marinara sauce and artichoke hearts, and continue to cook for about 3 minutes or until heated through. Set aside.

3. Place cutlets between 2 sheets of waxed paper, and gently pound to ⅛-inch thickness. Season both sides with salt and pepper.

4. Place beaten eggs in a shallow bowl. In another small bowl, stir together breadcrumbs and Parmesan cheese. Dip veal, 1 cutlet at a time, into egg, allow excess to drip off, and dredge in breadcrumb mixture. Place coated cutlets on a sheet of waxed paper.

5. In a large, nonstick skillet over medium-high heat, heat 2 tablespoons vegetable oil. Add 2 cutlets, and fry for about 3 minutes per side or until golden brown. Transfer to a large baking dish. Add remaining 2 tablespoons vegetable oil to the skillet, and fry remaining cutlets. Transfer to the baking dish with others, trying not to overlap.

6. Spoon marinara sauce with vegetables evenly over cutlets, sprinkle with mozzarella, and bake for 15 to 20 minutes or until sauce is bubbly and cheese has melted. Serve immediately.

 Smooth Move

Leftover canned artichoke hearts make great fiber additions to salads and pizzas. Just ½ cup contains 5 grams fiber.

Pork Chops with Sauerkraut and Potatoes

Serve this terrific dish, featuring the tang of sauerkraut and the irresistible flavor of bacon with chunky applesauce for the ideal savory-and-sweet combo—as well as extra fiber.

4 bacon slices

8 thin-cut loin or rib pork chops

Salt and pepper

4 medium Idaho or russet potatoes, peeled and cut into eighths

2 (15-oz.) cans sauerkraut, drained

Yield: 4 servings	
Prep time: 10 minutes	
Cook time: 55 minutes	
Serving size: 2 pork chops	
Each serving has:	
7 g fiber	
400 calories	
25 g fat	
26 g carbohydrate	
18 g protein	

1. Preheat the oven to 375°F.

2. In a large, nonstick skillet over medium-high heat, fry bacon until crisp. Drain bacon on paper towels and pour off ½ of accumulated grease.

3. Season pork chops with salt and pepper, and add to the skillet. Fry for about 2 minutes per side or until browned. Transfer to a 9×13-inch casserole dish.

4. Add potatoes to the skillet and cook, scraping up browned bits, for 3 minutes. Transfer to the edges of the casserole dish.

5. Add sauerkraut to the skillet and cook, stirring, for 3 minutes or until heated through. Place on top of pork chops in the casserole dish, and arrange cooked bacon strips across the top.

6. Bake for about 40 minutes or until pork chops are no longer pink and potatoes have browned. Serve immediately.

 Grist for the Mill

In addition to its fiber content, sauerkraut is an excellent source of vitamin C, which is retained through its fermentation process. An average serving also offers more probiotics (beneficial bacteria that keeps our digestion on track) than yogurt.

Quick Pork Tenderloin and Apples

Lean and luscious, this quick preparation will become a staple in your dinner repertoire. Serve with a baked sweet potato for the perfect high-fiber meal.

Yield: 4 servings
Prep time: 10 minutes
Cook time: 40 minutes
Serving size: 4 to 6 ounces
Each serving has:
4 g fiber
345 calories
13 g fat
21 g carbohydrate
35 g protein

1 TB. vegetable oil

1 (1½- to 2-lb.) unseasoned pork tenderloin

Salt and pepper

1 large onion, halved and sliced

3 firm apples, such as Gala or Red Delicious, unpeeled, cored, and quartered

2 sprigs fresh sage

½ cup apple cider

1. Preheat the oven to 400°F.

2. In a large skillet over high heat, heat vegetable oil.

3. Season tenderloin with salt and pepper. Add to the skillet and brown on all sides. Transfer to a roasting pan.

4. Reduce heat to medium. Add onion to the skillet, season with salt and pepper, and cook, stirring often, for about 4 minutes or until softened. Add apples and sage, and cook for 2 more minutes.

5. Transfer contents of the skillet to the roasting pan with pork, and bake, occasionally stirring vegetables, for 20 to 25 minutes or until an instant-read thermometer inserted in the center of tenderloin reads 140°F. Remove pork from the pan and place on a cutting board to rest.

6. Add cider to the roasting pan with onions and apples, and return to the oven to cook for 10 more minutes.

7. To serve, thinly slice tenderloin, place on a heated platter, and scatter onions and apple with cider sauce around.

 Grist for the Mill

Depending on whether you plan to cook your apple or eat it out of hand, choosing the correct apple can make a big difference in the outcome. Tender, less-firm apples such as MacIntosh are better for eating raw as they tend to break down under heat.

Spicy Sausage and Peppers

Feel the heat as you tuck into this hearty main course, featuring hot sausage and plenty of garlic. Sweet Italian sausage may be substituted for the faint of heart.

2 TB. olive oil	**4 garlic cloves, chopped**
8 hot Italian sausages	**1 (15-oz.) can tomato sauce**
2 medium onions, sliced	**1 cup water**
2 medium green bell peppers, ribs and seeds removed, and sliced	**1 tsp. dried oregano**
	1 tsp. dried basil
1 medium red or yellow bell pepper, ribs and seeds removed, and sliced	**1 tsp. dried parsley**
	2 medium red-skinned potatoes, skin on and cubed
Salt and pepper	**Whole-grain Italian bread**

Yield: 4 servings
Prep time: 15 minutes
Cook time: 40 minutes
Serving size: 2 sausages
Each serving has:
5 g fiber
380 calories
26 g fat
25 g carbohydrate
12 g protein

1. In a large, heavy-bottomed pot over medium-high heat, heat olive oil. Pierce sausages several times with a fork, and add to the pot. Fry sausages for about 6 minutes or until browned on all sides. Remove sausages and set aside.

2. Add onions, green bell peppers, and red bell peppers to the pot. Season with salt and pepper, and fry, stirring often, for about 5 minutes or until somewhat softened. Add garlic and cook 1 more minute.

3. Increase heat to high. Stir in tomato sauce, water, oregano, basil, and parsley, and bring to a boil. Cut browned sausages in $^1/_2$ and return to the pot.

4. Reduce heat to medium-low. Add potatoes, cover, and cook at a simmer for about 25 minutes or until vegetables are tender.

5. Serve in bowls with sauce spooned over top and bread on the side.

Grist for the Mill

For sausages to be classified as Italian in the United States, they must be 85 percent meat and contain fennel or anise.

Meatloaf Supreme

Everyone has a classic meatloaf recipe. Here's one that not only fits the fiber bill but offers plenty of rich flavor and moistness. Serve with a baked potato and high-fiber vegetable side dish for a complete fiber-rich meal.

Yield: 6 servings
Prep time: 15 minutes
Cook time: 1 hour 5 minutes
Serving size: 1 slice
Each serving has:
4 g fiber
435 calories
29 g fat
13 g carbohydrate
30 g protein

2 lb. meatloaf mix (ground beef, veal, and pork)

2 large eggs, beaten

1 small onion, finely chopped

1 small carrot, peeled and grated

½ green bell pepper, ribs and seeds removed, and finely chopped

1¼ cups whole-wheat breadcrumbs

¼ cup flaxseed meal

2 TB. toasted wheat germ

½ cup ketchup

½ cup hickory-smoked BBQ sauce

2 tsp. prepared mustard

Salt and pepper

1. Preheat the oven to 350°F. Lightly grease a 9×5-inch loaf pan.

2. In a large mixing bowl, combine meatloaf mix, eggs, onion, carrot, green bell pepper, breadcrumbs, flaxseed meal, wheat germ, ketchup, BBQ sauce, mustard, salt, and pepper. Mix well with a fork or your hands. Transfer to the loaf pan, and pat down firmly.

3. Cover pan with aluminum foil, and bake for 45 minutes. Remove foil, drain off some accumulated fat, and bake, uncovered, for 20 more minutes or until top is browned and an instant-read thermometer inserted in the center reads 160°F.

4. Allow to rest for 10 minutes, loosen sides with a knife, and transfer to a heated serving platter.

 Smooth Move

Leftover meatloaf makes the best sandwich in the world! Use a hearty, multigrain bread for a good dose of additional fiber.

Chapter 16

Vegetarian Main Courses

In This Chapter

◆ Super-satisfying vegetarian entrées

◆ Protein-packed beans, legumes, and grains

◆ Unique ingredients and flavors

It might seem a no-brainer to prepare fiberful vegetarian fare. After all, doesn't vegetarian food just boil down to lots of beans, vegetables, and some tofu thrown in for good measure? If that's your view, I guarantee your horizons will be pleasantly broadened in this chapter.

Have you ever tasted a vegetarian chili or stew you really enjoyed? In this chapter, I introduce you to a few that will no doubt become lifelong dinner companions and open your eyes to the wonders of truly delicious vegetarian cooking.

It Don't Amount to a Hill of Beans

There's no doubt, beans and legumes are a great jumping-off point in meat-less cooking, simply because they provide the protein you'd normally consume from animal sources. But they're only a portion of the arsenal at your disposal in preparing a fiber-rich meal that excludes meat.

Did you know that many whole grains also contain protein as well as fiber? When pairing these foods with beans and vegetables, your protein intake is no longer in question. The real question becomes how to make all these naturally fiber-rich ingredients team up to create a winning main course that's both satisfying and delicious.

Fortunately, for meat-eating skeptics, that question is answered in this chapter. From three-bean chili to ratatouille, the intense flavors of herbs and spices kick up the interest of common ingredients. And the addition of unique and exotic flavors such as coconut and sweet chili sauce take your taste buds to places of culinary delight. What a splendid way to reach your fiber goals.

Three-Alarm Three-Bean Chili

Spicy and satisfying, this meatless chili offers loads of fiber and tangy Tex-Mex flavor in every bite.

2 TB. olive oil

1 large onion, diced

1 large green bell pepper, ribs and seeds removed, and diced

Salt and pepper

1 jalapeño pepper, seeded and minced

1 garlic clove, minced

1 TB. chili powder

1 tsp. ground cumin

½ tsp. paprika

¼ tsp. cayenne

1 (28-oz.) can crushed tomatoes

1 (8-oz.) can tomato sauce

Pinch sugar

1 (15-oz.) can red kidney beans, drained and rinsed

1 (15-oz.) can white kidney beans (cannelloni), drained and rinsed

1 (15-oz.) can black beans, drained and rinsed

Sour cream

Chopped fresh cilantro leaves

Yield: 4 servings	
Prep time: 10 minutes	
Cook time: 30 minutes	
Serving size: 1½ cups	
Each serving has:	
16 g fiber	
430 calories	
8 g fat	
68 g carbohydrate	
20 g protein	

1. In a large, heavy-bottomed pot over medium-high heat, heat olive oil. Add onion and green bell pepper, season with salt and pepper, and cook, stirring often, for about 6 minutes or until softened. Stir in jalapeño and garlic, and cook 1 more minute.

2. Add chili powder, cumin, paprika, and cayenne, and cook, stirring constantly, for 1 minute. Add tomatoes, tomato sauce, and sugar, and bring to a boil. Reduce heat to medium-low, and cook at a simmer for 10 minutes.

3. Add red kidney beans, white kidney beans, and black beans. Simmer for 12 to 15 minutes or until thickened and piping hot. Serve immediately with a dollop of sour cream and a sprinkling of chopped cilantro.

 Smooth Move

Make your chili less alarming by reducing or eliminating the cayenne and minced jalapeño pepper.

Cajun Red Beans and Rice

The spicy and seductive flavors of Louisiana beckon in this hearty rendition of the Southern classic featuring flavorful brown rice and creamy red beans.

Yield: 4 servings	
Prep time: 15 minutes	
Cook time: 25 minutes	
Serving size: about 1½ cups	
Each serving has:	
13 g fiber	
375 calories	
8 g fat	
63 g carbohydrate	
12 g protein	

2 TB. olive oil

1 medium onion, chopped

1 medium green bell pepper, ribs and seeds removed, and chopped

1 medium celery stalk, chopped

2 garlic cloves, minced

1 tsp. *Cajun seasoning*

1 cup low-sodium vegetable broth

1 (15-oz.) can stewed tomatoes, roughly chopped

2 (15-oz.) cans red beans or kidney beans, drained and rinsed

Salt and pepper

3 cups cooked long-grain brown rice

1. In a large, nonstick skillet over medium-high heat, heat olive oil. Add onion, green bell pepper, and celery, and cook, stirring often, for about 8 minutes or until softened. Stir in garlic and Cajun seasoning, and cook for 1 more minute.

2. Add broth and tomatoes, bring to a simmer, and cook, stirring occasionally, for 5 minutes. Stir in beans and continue cooking for 10 more minutes or until creamy and piping hot. Season with salt and pepper.

3. Serve immediately, ladled over hot rice.

 Fiber Optics

Cajun seasoning is a blend of salt, pepper, spices, and herbs traditionally used in Louisiana cooking. Find it in the spice aisle of your supermarket.

Hearty Shepherd's Pie

Meaty lentils and peas take the place of ground beef in this delicious casserole topped with creamy, rich mashed potatoes.

1 TB. vegetable oil

1 medium onion, chopped

1 small celery stalk, chopped

2 medium carrots, peeled and diced

Salt and pepper

2 TB. all-purpose flour

½ tsp. dried thyme

2 (15-oz.) cans cooked lentils

¾ cup frozen peas, thawed

1 cup vegetable broth or water

3 Idaho or russet potatoes, peeled and diced

2 TB. unsalted butter, softened

Dash paprika

Yield: 4 servings
Prep time: 15 minutes
Cook time: 1 hour, 20 minutes
Serving size: about 2 cups
Each serving has:
13 g fiber
335 calories
9 g fat
49 g carbohydrate
14 g protein

1. In a large, nonstick skillet over medium-high heat, heat vegetable oil. Add onion, celery, and carrots, and season with salt and pepper. Cook, stirring occasionally, for about 8 minutes or until softened.

2. Stir in flour, and cook for 2 minutes. Add thyme, lentils, peas, and broth, and continue cooking, stirring often, for about 5 minutes or until broth has thickened and vegetables are heated through. Set aside.

3. Preheat the oven to 350°F. Lightly grease a 9×13-inch casserole dish.

4. In a medium saucepan, place potatoes, a good pinch of salt, and cold water to cover. Bring to a boil over high heat, and boil for about 12 minutes or until potatoes are fork-tender. Drain and set aside.

5. Transfer lentil mixture to the casserole dish, and spread evenly. Place potatoes in a medium bowl. Add butter, and mash potatoes to desired consistency. Season with salt and pepper, and spread on top of lentil mixture. Use the tines of a fork to create ridges, and sprinkle paprika over top of casserole.

6. Bake for about 40 minutes or until potatoes begin to brown and lentil mixture is bubbly. Serve immediately.

 Grist for the Mill

Buona Fortuna! In Italy, lentils are always eaten on New Year's Eve for good luck because they represent the coins of future wealth.

Colossal Stuffed Artichokes

Meaty leaves filled with a delicious garlic-and-breadcrumb stuffing will lead you to the final delectable heart of this high-fiber vegetable.

Yield: 2 servings
Prep time: 15 minutes
Cook time: 45 to 60 minutes
Serving size: 1 artichoke
Each serving has:
9 g fiber
440 calories
25 g fat
38 g carbohydrate
16 g protein

2 large globe artichokes

½ lemon

1½ cups whole-wheat bread-crumbs

2 TB. toasted wheat germ

¼ cup grated Parmesan cheese

4 garlic cloves, minced

1 tsp. grated lemon zest

3 TB. extra-virgin olive oil

Salt and pepper

1. Cut off stems of artichokes so they stand upright. Using a sharp knife, cut off the top ¼ of artichokes. With kitchen scissors, trim ½ inch off remaining leaves. Turn upside down and twist on a solid surface to open leaves. Rinse under cold water, rub with lemon, and set aside.

2. In a medium bowl, stir together breadcrumbs, wheat germ, Parmesan cheese, garlic, and lemon rind. Add olive oil slowly, stirring to moisten crumb mixture, and season with salt and pepper.

3. Open artichoke leaves with your fingers, one at a time, and spoon a little stuffing inside each. Place any leftover stuffing in middle of artichokes and press down.

4. Place artichokes snuggly in a medium saucepan and add enough water to come up 1 inch on the sides. Bring to a boil, reduce heat to low, cover, and cook 45 to 60 minutes or until leaves are easily removed when pulled. Check water level occasionally and add a small amount when low.

5. Using tongs, carefully remove artichokes from the pan and place on paper towels to drain. Serve immediately.

Smooth Move

The inner inedible spiny part of the artichoke just above the heart, called the choke, can be removed more easily when cooked than when raw. To remove before cooking, use a grapefruit knife to scrape it away from the heart.

Whole-Wheat Thin-Crust Pizza

You'll be in pizza heaven after you dive into this mouthwatering rendition of America's favorite slice featuring sliced mushrooms and tender spinach.

1 (12-in.) whole-wheat thin-crust pizza or 1 Whole-Wheat Pizza Dough (recipe in Chapter 21)

½ cup marinara sauce

1 cup shredded mozzarella cheese

½ cup cooked frozen spinach, drained well

½ cup sliced fresh mush-rooms

Yield: 2 servings
Prep time: 10 minutes
Cook time: 10 minutes
Serving size: ½ of pizza
Each serving has:
8 g fiber
610 calories
20 g fat
67 g carbohydrate
40 g protein

1. Preheat the oven to 450°F. Position the oven rack in the middle of the oven.

2. Place prebaked pizza crust on a work surface, and evenly spread marinara sauce on top. Sprinkle with mozzarella, and evenly distribute spinach and mushrooms.

3. Bake on the oven rack for 8 to 10 minutes or until pizza is crisp and cheese has melted. (For homemade dough, add 5 to 8 minutes to baking time.) Using metal spatulas, transfer pizza to a cutting board. Slice and serve.

 Smooth Move

For an easy and equally fiberful alternative topping, purchase grilled vegetables from your supermarket deli section. Look for eggplant, peppers, onions, or zucchini.

Peanut-Crusted-Tofu Stir-Fry

Crunchy, fiber-rich peanuts highlight this vegetarian delight of healthful tofu and vegetables in a tangy chili sauce.

Yield: 4 servings
Prep time: 15 minutes
Cook time: 12 minutes
Serving size: about 1½ cups
Each serving has:
3 g fiber
445 calories
16 g fat
45 g carbohydrate
31 g protein

1 (15-oz.) block extra-firm *tofu*, drained and patted dry

½ cup whole-wheat breadcrumbs

¼ cup chopped peanuts

2 TB. toasted wheat germ

Salt and pepper

2 TB. peanut or vegetable oil

2 large eggs, beaten

1 bunch green onions, trimmed and cut into 2-in. pieces

1 medium red bell pepper, ribs and seeds removed, and thinly sliced

1 cup thinly sliced napa cabbage

¾ cup prepared sweet chili sauce

3 cups cooked brown short-grain or basmati rice

1. Cut tofu into 16 (1-inch) cubes, and pat dry with paper towels. Set aside.

2. In a shallow bowl, combine breadcrumbs, peanuts, wheat germ, salt, and pepper.

3. In a large, nonstick skillet over medium-high heat, heat peanut oil. Dip tofu cubes into egg, shake off excess, and dredge in peanut mixture. Add tofu to the skillet, and fry, turning occasionally to brown evenly, for about 5 minutes or until golden. Transfer to a paper towel to drain.

4. Increase heat to high. Add green onions, red bell pepper, and cabbage to the skillet, and stir-fry for about 4 minutes or until vegetables are slightly softened. Stir in chili sauce, and cook for 2 more minutes or until bubbly. Return tofu to the skillet, toss gently to coat, and serve immediately over rice.

Fiber Optics

Tofu, or bean curd, is made from coagulated soy milk that's pressed into cubes. A good source of protein for vegetarians, tofu also contains a good amount of fiber.

Coconut-Curried Vegetarian Stew

Wonderfully aromatic and flavorful, this mildly seasoned Thai-inspired dish is terrific for fiber-seeking vegetarians.

2 tsp. yellow mustard seeds

2 TB. vegetable oil

1 medium onion, chopped

½ medium red bell pepper, ribs and seeds removed, and diced

Salt and pepper

1 TB. finely chopped fresh ginger

1 garlic clove, minced

1 TB. curry powder

2 cups vegetable broth or water

⅓ cup dried red lentils, picked over and rinsed

2 medium carrots, peeled and cut into ½-in. pieces

1 (13-oz.) can unsweetened coconut milk

2 large red potatoes, peeled and cubed

1 cup cauliflower florets

1 cup canned chickpeas, drained and rinsed

½ cup frozen peas, thawed

Yield: 4 servings
Prep time: 15 minutes
Cook time: 30 minutes
Serving size: about 1½ cups
Each serving has:
12 g fiber
480 calories
25 g fat
50 g carbohydrate
13 g protein

1. Heat a large, heavy-bottomed pot over high heat. Add mustard seeds and cook, shaking the pan occasionally, for about 3 minutes or until mustard seeds pop.

2. Reduce heat to medium. Add vegetable oil, onion, red bell pepper, salt, and pepper, and cook for about 5 minutes or until vegetables are slightly softened.

3. Add ginger and garlic, and cook, stirring, for 1 more minute. Add curry powder, broth, lentils, and carrots. Bring to a boil, reduce heat to medium-low, and cook at a simmer for 5 minutes.

4. Add coconut milk, potatoes, and cauliflower, and continue to simmer for about 12 minutes or until vegetables are fork-tender.

5. Stir in chickpeas and peas, and cook for about 5 minutes or until thickened and heated through. Season with salt and pepper, and serve immediately.

 Smooth Move

Chalk up even more fiber by serving this stew with whole-wheat pitas or naan bread for dipping.

Ratatouille Casserole

The herbes de Provence waft through the kitchen as this delectable, colorful casserole bakes and bubbles.

Yield: 4 servings
Prep time: 20 minutes
Cook time: 45 minutes
Serving size: about 1¹⁄₂ cups
Each serving has:
3 g fiber
185 calories
8 g fat
22 g carbohydrate
4 g protein

2 TB. extra-virgin olive oil

2 medium zucchini, cut into ¹⁄₂-in. rounds

1 medium yellow squash, cut into ¹⁄₂-in. rounds

1 large green bell pepper, ribs and seeds removed, and cut into 1-in. pieces

2 small red onions, cut into ¹⁄₄-in. rounds

2 small eggplant, skin on and cut into ¹⁄₂-in. rounds

4 plum tomatoes, cut into ¹⁄₂-in. rounds

Salt and pepper

2 tsp. *herbes de Provence*

¹⁄₂ cup vegetable broth

1 cup whole-wheat or whole-grain breadcrumbs

1. Preheat the oven to 350°F. Lightly coat a shallow oval or rectangular 1¹⁄₂-quart baking dish with 1 teaspoon olive oil.

2. Layer zucchini, squash, green bell pepper, onions, eggplant, and tomatoes in the baking dish in rows, domino fashion, staggering them to distribute different vegetables throughout. Season with salt and pepper, and sprinkle herbes de Provence over top.

3. Pour vegetable broth around the edges of the baking dish, and drizzle remaining olive oil over top. Lightly press breadcrumbs over top of casserole to cover vegetables.

4. Bake for about 45 minutes or until vegetables are fork-tender, most of liquid has evaporated, and crumb topping is golden. Allow to rest for 10 minutes before serving.

Fiber Optics

Herbes de Provence is a blend of dried herbs that hail from the Provence area of France. The mixture typically contains rosemary, marjoram, basil, bay leaf, thyme, and lavender. Find it in your supermarket spice aisle.

Pasta Dishes

In This Chapter

◆ Whole-wheat and whole-grain pastas

◆ Fibered-up semolina pasta

◆ Pasta classics … with a twist

If you've taken a stroll down the pasta aisle of your supermarket lately, you know pasta producers have hopped on the health bandwagon and are offering everything from omega-3–enriched ziti to whole-wheat spaghetti. What was once an easy choice has become a studious affair entailing much label reading and comparison shopping. Is this rotelle better for me than that one? Should I switch entirely to whole-grain macaroni for fiber? Doesn't it taste a bit funny? … And what about that low-carb brand? (Sorry, that's another book.)

Don't despair, my pasta-loving friends. I'm here to separate the wheat from the chaff, so to speak, and advise you on the merits of the multitude of various grain pastas that grace grocery store shelves.

The Personality of Pasta

If you've ever been disappointed in the outcome of a dish made with whole-wheat penne, you've come to the right place. The key to taking advantage of healthful grain pastas is completely incumbent upon the other ingredients you're preparing them with. Here's the deal:

Nutty, dense, whole-grain spaghetti is bold in flavor. It must keep company with other bold flavors; otherwise, it will overpower your recipe. A simple, light marinara sauce cannot compete with the intensity of flavor whole-grain and whole-wheat pastas possess. Sun-dried tomatoes, broccoli rabe, and sausage are a few of the fellows that can do the job. They put whole-grain spaghetti in its place and make it a team player.

Traditional semolina pasta is a natural at getting along with everybody. For our purposes, however, we want it to get along with some fiber-rich ingredients because plain pasta lacks the fiber content of pastas made with whole grains. Beans, chunky tomatoes, and even root vegetables are all good choices for fibering up basic pasta and adding interest and flavor.

So what the pasta pot boils down to is the old wise advice of choosing the right guy, or in this case—macaroni—for the job. After that, the rest is a cake walk. (Oh wait, that's another chapter.)

Big-Bowl Pasta and Fagioli

The Italian definition of comfort in a bowl, this quick version of a classic dish made with little tube pasta and beans in tomato sauce is hearty, flavorful, and undeniably satisfying.

8 oz. ditalini pasta	1 garlic clove, minced
1 TB. olive oil	½ cup low-sodium chicken broth
1 small onion, minced	
1 small celery stalk, finely chopped	1 (8-oz.) can tomato sauce
	1 (15-oz.) can pork and beans, undrained
1 small carrot, peeled and cut into small dice	
	Extra-virgin olive oil
Salt and pepper	

Yield: *4 servings*
Prep time: 15 minutes
Cook time: 10 to 12 minutes
Serving size: about 1 cup
Each serving has:
12 g fiber
375 calories
4 g fat
60 g carbohydrate
13 g protein

1. Cook pasta according to package directions and set aside.

2. In a large pot over medium-high heat, heat olive oil. Add onion, celery, carrot, salt, and pepper, and cook, stirring often, for about 5 minutes or until softened. Add garlic and cook 1 more minute.

3. Stir in broth and tomato sauce, and bring to a low boil, stirring often. Reduce heat to medium. Add beans and pasta, and cook for about 3 minutes or until heated through and bubbly. Stir often to prevent sticking.

4. Season with salt and pepper, and serve in large bowls with a drizzle of extra-virgin olive oil.

Grist for the Mill

I'm no fool! In 1927, Van and Schenk immortalized this popular peasant dish in song—"Don't be a fool, eat pasta fazool."

Penne with Sun-Dried-Tomato Pesto

Both sweet and sharp tasting, sun-dried-tomato pesto is the perfect partner for whole-wheat penne pasta.

Yield: 4 servings
Prep time: 12 minutes
Cook time: 9 minutes
Serving size: about 1 cup
Each serving has:
10 g fiber
280 calories
12 g fat
30 g carbohydrate
11 g protein

1 cup oil-packed sun-dried tomatoes, drained

⅓ cup torn fresh basil leaves

2 TB. slivered almonds

2 garlic cloves

½ cup extra-virgin olive oil

½ cup grated Parmesan cheese, plus more for sprinkling

¾ lb. whole-wheat penne pasta

¼ cup light cream

Salt and pepper

1. Bring a large pot of water to a boil over high heat.

2. In a food processor fitted with a steel blade, combine sun-dried tomatoes, basil, almonds, and garlic, and pulse until chopped. While the processor is running, slowly add olive oil until a paste forms. Transfer to a bowl, and stir in Parmesan cheese.

3. Cook pasta according to package directions, reserve ½ cup of cooking liquid, and drain. Add pesto to the pot, and stir together with reserved liquid. Return pasta to the pot, add cream, and toss well to coat.

4. Season with salt and pepper, and serve with a sprinkle of Parmesan cheese.

 Smooth Move _____

Make batches of sun-dried-tomato pesto and keep it refrigerated for up to 2 weeks. Use as a topping for grilled chicken or fish.

Spinach Spaghetti Puttanesca

Named after the ladies of the night, this dish is spicy, bold, and deliciously alluring, with the assertive flavor of garlic and the sassy taste of capers and olives.

2 TB. olive oil

4 garlic cloves, sliced

½ (1-oz.) can anchovy fillets, chopped

1 (15-oz.) can crushed tomatoes

½ cup pitted kalamata olives, roughly chopped

2 TB. small capers, drained

¼ tsp. red pepper flakes

Pinch sugar

¾ lb. spinach spaghetti or linguine

Salt

2 TB. roughly chopped fresh Italian parsley leaves

Yield: 4 servings
Prep time: 12 minutes
Cook time: 18 minutes
Serving size: about 1 cup
Each serving has:
11 g fiber
417 calories
10 g fat
60 g carbohydrate
15 g protein

1. Bring a large pot of salted water to a boil over high heat.

2. In a large, nonstick skillet over medium-high heat, heat olive oil. Add garlic and anchovies, and cook, stirring often, for 2 minutes. Reduce heat to medium-low. Add crushed tomatoes, olives, capers, red pepper flakes, and sugar, and simmer, stirring occasionally, for about 15 minutes or until thickened.

3. Cook spaghetti according to the package directions, drain, and return to the hot pot. Add cooked tomato sauce, and toss well to coat. Season with salt, if necessary, and serve immediately, sprinkled with parsley.

Smooth Move

A multigrain Italian bread dipped in extra-virgin olive oil is the perfect beginning for pasta and increases your overall dinner fiber intake.

Harvest Whole-Wheat Lasagna

The intense, sweet flavor of roasted butternut squash pairs well with creamy ricotta and nutty whole-wheat lasagna in this easy pasta favorite.

Yield: 4 servings
Prep time: 15 minutes
Cook time: 45 minutes
Serving size: 1 slice
Each serving has:
6 g fiber
490 calories
25 g fat
38 g carbohydrate
3 g protein

9 pieces (8 oz.) whole-wheat lasagna

2 cups butternut squash, cut into ½-in. dice

2 TB. olive oil

1 tsp. dried oregano

Salt and pepper

1 (15-oz.) pkg. whole or part-skim ricotta cheese

1 egg, lightly beaten

2 TB. grated Parmesan cheese

Dash ground nutmeg

1 (28-oz.) jar marinara or spaghetti sauce

1½ cups shredded mozzarella cheese

1. Cook lasagna according to package directions, drain, and rinse under cold water. Set aside.

2. Preheat the oven to 375°F.

3. In a medium bowl, combine squash, olive oil, oregano, salt, and pepper, and toss well. Transfer to a large, rimmed baking sheet, spread out evenly, and roast in the oven, stirring occasionally, for about 15 minutes or until tender and lightly golden.

4. In a medium bowl, stir together ricotta cheese, egg, Parmesan, nutmeg, salt, and pepper.

5. Spread ¼ marinara sauce on the bottom of a 9×13-inch casserole dish, and place 3 lasagna noodles in a single layer over sauce. Spread ½ of ricotta mixture over lasagna, and distribute ½ of roasted butternut squash on top. Spread ⅓ remaining sauce over squash, and sprinkle with ⅓ of mozzarella cheese. Top with 3 lasagna noodles and repeat.

6. Cover top noodles with remaining sauce and mozzarella, and bake for about 30 minutes or until bubbly around the edges and cheese has melted. Let rest 10 minutes before slicing and serving.

Variation: Add 1½ cups cooked crumbled Italian sausage to the layers and substitute 1 (28-ounce) jar Alfredo sauce for the marinara sauce to make a rich, meat-based lasagna.

 Smooth Move

Try using a chunky garden-vegetable variety of spaghetti sauce for even more fiber, flavor, and texture.

Whole-Grain Linguine with Turkey Sausage

The bold flavors of sausage and broccoli rabe are the perfect complement to hearty, whole-grain linguine and tangy Romano cheese.

3 uncooked turkey sausages, casings removed

2 TB. olive oil

2 garlic cloves, sliced

1 bunch *broccoli rabe*, cleaned and trimmed of hard stems

Salt and pepper

⅔ cup low-sodium chicken broth

8 oz. whole-grain linguine or spaghetti

1 TB. unsalted butter

⅓ cup grated Romano cheese plus more for sprinkling

Yield: 2 servings
Prep time: 15 minutes
Cook time: 20 minutes
Serving size: about 2 cups
Each serving has:
8 g fiber
800 calories
30 g fat
80 g carbohydrate
40 g protein

1. Bring a large pot of salted water to a boil over high heat.

2. In a large, nonstick skillet over medium-high heat, cook sausage with oil, using a fork to break up sausage, for about 6 minutes or until lightly browned. Add garlic and cook 1 more minute.

3. Add broccoli rabe, season with salt and pepper, and cook, stirring often, for 2 minutes. Add broth, bring to a boil, cover, and reduce heat to low. Cook for about 8 minutes or until broccoli rabe is fork-tender yet firm.

4. Meanwhile, cook linguine according to package directions. Drain and add to the skillet with sausage and broccoli rabe. Add butter and Romano cheese, and toss well to combine. Serve immediately with additional Romano for sprinkling.

Fiber Optics

Broccoli rabe, or *rapini*, is a commonly used vegetable in Mediterranean cooking. It belongs to the turnip family, although it resembles small heads of broccoli. Its flavor is somewhat bitter and bold.

Best-Ever Baked Ziti

Delicious morsels of fried eggplant and creamy dollops of goat cheese enhance this healthful dish made with whole-wheat pasta.

Yield: 4 servings
Prep time: 10 minutes
Cook time: 35 minutes
Serving size: about 2 cups
Each serving has:
8 g fiber
725 calories
28 g fat
80 g carbohydrate
30 g protein

¾ lb. whole-wheat or whole-grain ziti or penne

3 TB. olive oil

1 medium eggplant, peeled and cut into 1-in. dice

Salt and pepper

2 TB. chopped fresh basil leaves

1 (28-oz.) jar marinara or spaghetti sauce

1 (3-oz.) log goat cheese, cut into small chunks

½ cup grated Parmesan cheese

1 cup shredded mozzarella cheese

1. Cook ziti according to the package directions. Set aside.

2. Preheat the oven to 350°F.

3. In a large, nonstick skillet over medium-high heat, heat olive oil. Add eggplant, season with salt and pepper, and fry, stirring often, for about 6 minutes or until tender and browned. Add a little oil if necessary to prevent sticking. Stir in basil, and transfer to a 9×13-inch casserole dish.

4. Add marinara sauce, goat cheese, and cooked ziti to the casserole dish, stirring well to combine. Sprinkle with Parmesan cheese, and top with mozzarella cheese.

5. Bake for 25 to 30 minutes or until bubbly and cheese has melted. Serve immediately.

Grist for the Mill

Baked ziti is the most popular dish served at Italian-American weddings. *Ziti* is also the Italian word for "bridegrooms."

Tortellini with Walnuts and Gorgonzola

Stuffed pasta enrobed in a creamy, rich sauce gets a fiber boost from delicious toasted walnuts, sweet shallots, and flavorful garlic.

1 (8-oz.) pkg. mushroom tortellini

½ cup walnut pieces

1 TB. olive oil

1 shallot, minced

1 garlic clove, minced

⅓ cup heavy cream

¼ cup crumbled gorgonzola cheese

Salt and pepper

1 TB. chopped fresh chives

Yield: 2 servings
Prep time: 10 minutes
Cook time: 15 minutes
Serving size: about 1½ cups
Each serving has:
5 g fiber
850 calories
21 g fat
80 g carbohydrate
28 g protein

1. Prepare mushroom tortellini according to package directions. Set aside.

2. In a large, nonstick skillet over high heat, toast walnuts, shaking the pan often, for about 3 minutes or until fragrant and lightly browned. Transfer to a small bowl, and set aside.

3. Reduce heat to medium-high, and add olive oil to the skillet. Add shallot and cook, stirring occasionally, for about 3 minutes or until softened. Add garlic and cook 1 more minute.

4. Add heavy cream, and bring to a simmer. Add gorgonzola, salt, and pepper, and continue to cook, stirring occasionally, for 3 minutes.

5. Return walnuts to the skillet, and add cooked tortellini. Stir well to coat, remove from heat, cover, and set aside for 2 minutes. Serve sprinkled with chives.

Grist for the Mill

The shape of tortellini pasta was inspired by the navel of Lucrezia Borgia, a Renaissance femme fatale who employed both a chef and a poisoner to cater to her guests.

Pumpkin Ravioli with Pepitas

Both sweet and savory, with the addition of dried cranberries and crunchy pumpkin seeds, this delectable dish is a snap to make with prepared ravioli.

Yield: 2 servings
Prep time: 20 minutes
Cook time: 12 minutes
Serving size: about 1½ cups
Each serving has:
8 g fiber
400 calories
29 g fat
31 g carbohydrate
7 g protein

1 (8-oz.) pkg. pumpkin or butternut squash ravioli

1 TB. olive oil

1 TB. unsalted butter

½ medium red onion, thinly sliced

Salt and pepper

2 cups trimmed and washed beet tops or red chard

½ cup low-sodium chicken broth

¼ cup light cream

⅓ cup pepitas (toasted pumpkin seeds)

¼ cup dried cranberries

¼ cup crumbled goat cheese

1. Prepare ravioli according to the package directions. Set aside.

2. In a large, nonstick skillet over medium heat, heat olive oil and butter. Add red onion, sprinkle with salt and pepper, and cook, stirring occasionally, for about 4 minutes or until softened.

3. Add beet tops and broth, increase heat to medium-high, and cook for about 4 minutes or until greens are wilted.

4. Add cream, cooked ravioli, pepitas, and cranberries, and gently toss to combine. Cook for 2 minutes, remove from heat, cover, and set aside for 2 minutes. Serve topped with goat cheese.

 Smooth Move _____

Pumpkin ravioli is often seasonally available. When you find it, buy extra and store it in your freezer to enjoy any time of year.

Gnocchi with Garlic-Sautéed Broccoli

Potato gnocchi and crisp-tender broccoli florets take on the zesty flavor of garlic in this tasty and satisfying entrée.

1 lb. frozen potato gnocchi, cooked according to package directions

3 TB. olive oil

6 garlic cloves, minced

Salt and pepper

2 cups broccoli florets, cooked to crisp-tender

⅓ cup grated Romano cheese, plus more for sprinkling

Extra-virgin olive oil

Yield: 4 servings
Prep time: 20 minutes
Cook time: 8 minutes
Serving size: about 1½ cups
Each serving has:
8 g fiber
310 calories
15 g fat
33 g carbohydrate
8 g protein

1. Cook gnocchi according to package directions. Set aside.

2. In a large, nonstick skillet over medium heat, heat olive oil. Add garlic, sprinkle with salt and pepper, and cook, stirring often, for about 2 minutes or until somewhat softened but not browned.

3. Add broccoli, stir well to coat, and cook for 2 minutes more. Add gnocchi and Romano cheese, stir to combine, and continue cooking for 2 minutes or until piping hot.

4. Drizzle in a little extra-virgin olive oil, and season with salt and pepper. Serve immediately, sprinkled with more Romano cheese.

 Smooth Move

Gnocchi can also be made from ricotta cheese, but the potato-based gnocchi offer more fiber.

Part 6

Supplemental Sides

If coming up with interesting, tasty side dishes has never been your forte, life is about to change. Your repertoire is going to expand by leaps and bounds after you explore the following recipes. Move over, boiled carrots and white rice! Part 6 contains some clever combinations that will knock your socks off and lure everyone to the table.

From potato gratin to Hoppin' John, vegetables never tasted so delectable. With a sharp knife and an eye toward fiber, you'll impress them all when you serve these supplemental side dishes full of flavor and excitement. Rice and whole-grain pilafs and risottos are included as well, all prepared with the tastiest ingredients and a mind for easy cooking and serving. And although they say we can't live by bread alone, after you try the upcoming selections, you may wonder, why not?

Chapter 18

Potatoes and Roots

In This Chapter

- Popular potato and yam dishes
- Stellar sides from fiber-rich vegetables
- Learning to love your roots

Root vegetables, or those that grow underground, have some of the highest concentrations of fiber you can find in your produce section. Potatoes, yams, and carrots are a few of the already-familiar fiber-rich gems that await you.

But how about parsnips, rutabagas, or kohlrabi? Many people are confused about how to prepare and eat these veggies. But there's no need to be intimidated by the unusual shapes and appearance. Celery root surely won't win any vegetable beauty contests, but its wondrous flavor and texture will quickly win you over. And the uniquely flavored parsnip is a great source of dietary fiber. You'll soon become fast friends.

In this chapter, you are introduced to some terrific recipes that make use of these healthy tubers and roots, while expanding your potato horizons with some delicious, out-of-the-ordinary combinations. The more tricks you have up your sleeve in preparing these fiber-rich friends, the more likely you are to serve them up more than a couple times a week. Make a point of getting to know at least one strange root vegetable a week and master it's cooking. It will be worth the effort in the long run, and eventually, instead of running away from them at the supermarket, you'll be seeking them out with anticipation.

Superstar Side Dishes

All the side dishes in this chapter go equally well with any number of meat, fish, or poultry preparations, from a simply prepared roasted chicken breast to a grilled steak.

When the focus is on the roots, it's okay to opt for an easy-cooking method for your protein selection, because the fiber content, not to mention nutritional value, will be impressively high. Throw in a green vegetable or salad, and you're well on your way to meeting your fiber goals at dinner.

Easy Idaho Oven Fries

This crispy and flavorful alternative to traditional fries also offers a bit of fiber by roasting with the skins on.

4 medium Idaho or russet potatoes, skin on

Salt and pepper

Red cayenne (optional)

1. Preheat the oven to 400°F.

2. Cut potatoes in $\frac{1}{2}$ lengthwise, and cut each $\frac{1}{2}$ into 4 wedges.

3. Place potatoes on a baking sheet sprayed with cooking oil, and season with salt, pepper, and red cayenne (if using). Bake for about 20 minutes per side or until crisp, brown, and fork-tender. Serve immediately.

 Smooth Move

For even more fiber, try oven-frying sweet potatoes using the same method.

Yield: 4 servings	
Prep time: 10 minutes	
Cook time: 40 minutes	
Serving size: 8 fries	
Each serving has:	
3 g fiber	
90 calories	
1 g fat	
20 g carbohydrate	
1 g protein	

Smashed Red-Skinned Potatoes

Leaving the skin on adds a bit of fiber in this chunky version of mashed potatoes.

Yield: 4 servings
Prep time: 15 minutes
Cook time: 30 minutes
Serving size: about 1 cup
Each serving has:
4 g fiber
275 calories
10 g fat
36 g carbohydrate
4 g protein

2 lb. red-skinned potatoes (about 4 or 5 medium), cut into 1-in. cubes

1 tsp. salt

2 TB. unsalted butter, softened

⅔ cup sour cream

1 TB. chopped fresh chives

Freshly ground black pepper

1. Place cubed potatoes in a large pot, and add salt and enough cold water to cover. Bring to a boil over heat, reduce heat to medium-low, and simmer for 12 to 15 minutes or until fork-tender. Pour into a colander and allow to drain for about 15 minutes or until potato edges begin to look dry.

2. In a large bowl, combine potatoes, butter, sour cream, chives, and pepper. Mash with a potato masher, leaving some lumps. Season with salt, and serve immediately.

Variation: Add 3 whole, peeled cloves of garlic to the potato water to cook, and mash along with the potatoes.

 Grist for the Mill _____

More than 99 percent of all potatoes cultivated worldwide are descendants of the species that originated in Chile.

Russet and Sweet Potato Gratin

This delectable version of scalloped potatoes flavored with savory broth and rich cream makes use of the fiber-rich yam, or sweet potato.

1 cup light cream

½ cup low-sodium chicken broth

1 garlic clove, minced

Dash nutmeg

1 tsp. salt

Freshly ground black pepper

3 large Idaho or russet potatoes, peeled and sliced ¼-in. thick

3 medium yams or sweet potatoes, peeled and sliced ¼-in. thick

Yield: 6 servings
Prep time: 20 minutes
Cook time: 40 to 50 minutes
Serving size: about 1 cup
Each serving has:
4 g fiber
200 calories
7 g fat
30 g carbohydrate
4 g protein

1. Preheat the oven to 350°F. Butter a 9×13-inch glass baking dish.

2. In a large bowl, whisk together cream, broth, garlic, nutmeg, salt, and pepper. Add Idaho potatoes and yams, and toss well to coat.

3. Transfer to the prepared baking dish, and arrange potato slices evenly. Cover with foil, and bake for 30 minutes.

4. Remove the foil, and continue to bake for 10 to 20 more minutes or until potatoes are fork-tender. Remove from the oven, and allow to rest for 10 minutes before serving.

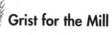 **Grist for the Mill**

Are those yams, ma'am? Yams, although commonly called sweet potatoes, are a different type of root vegetable and are not actually grown or marketed in the United States. Neither is a sweet potato truly a type of potato. It's okay—we love 'em anyway.

Honey-Glazed Baby Carrots

Here's a sweet, roasted dish that goes well with everything from chicken to meatloaf. The addition of dried currants and sunflower seeds helps hike up the fiber.

Yield: 4 servings
Prep time: 5 minutes
Cook time: 25 to 30 minutes
Serving size: about ¹/₂ cup
Each serving has:
4 g fiber
175 calories
7 g fat
24 g carbohydrate
3 g protein

1 (16-oz.) bag peeled baby carrots

1 TB. vegetable oil

Salt and pepper

¹/₃ cup *dried currants*

¹/₄ cup sunflower seeds

1 TB. honey

1. Preheat the oven to 375°F.

2. Place carrots in a medium roasting pan, add vegetable oil, salt, and pepper, and toss to coat.

3. Roast in the oven for about 15 minutes or until nearly fork-tender. Stir in currants and sunflower seeds, and roast for about 10 to 15 more minutes or until carrots are cooked through.

4. Remove from the oven, stir in honey to coat, and serve immediately.

Fiber Optics

Dried currants, like raisins, are made from dehydrated grapes, specifically the Zante Currant grape. They are black, small, and seedless, and they contain a good concentration of fiber.

Whipped Root Vegetable Casserole

The best of all roots unite in this delicious side dish casserole that's topped off with a sweet and crunchy nut finish.

½ **large rutabaga, peeled and cubed**

1 **medium celery root, peeled and cubed**

3 **medium sweet potatoes, peeled and cubed**

2 **large carrots, peeled and diced**

2 TB. **unsalted butter**

¼ **cup heavy cream**

Salt and pepper

½ **cup chopped pecans**

½ **cup chopped walnuts**

1 TB. **sugar**

½ tsp. **ground cinnamon**

Yield: 6 servings
Prep time: 30 minutes
Cook time: 60 minutes
Serving size: about 1 cup
Each serving has:
5 g fiber
300 calories
20 g fat
25 g carbohydrate
4 g protein

1. Place rutabaga, celery root, sweet potatoes, and carrots in a large saucepan, and add enough water to cover. Bring to a boil over high heat, reduce heat to medium-low, and simmer for about 20 minutes or until vegetables are fork-tender. Drain and transfer to a large bowl.

2. Preheat the oven to 350°F. Butter a 9×13-inch glass or ceramic casserole dish.

3. Add butter, heavy cream, salt, and pepper to root vegetables, and, using a mixer, beat until smooth. Transfer to the prepared casserole dish, and spread out evenly using a rubber spatula.

4. In a small bowl, combine pecans, walnuts, sugar, and cinnamon, and sprinkle over top of root mixture. Bake for about 40 minutes or until hot throughout and top begins to brown. Serve immediately.

 Grist for the Mill

Will it ever turn up? Every year the town of Cumberland, Wisconsin, holds a Rutabaga Festival in honor of the homely yellow turnip, although nary a rutabaga can be found. It seems you can take the rutabaga out of the festival, but not the festival out of the rutabaga.

Parsnip and Pear Compote

Not only do the sweet and unique flavors of pears and parsnips pair up well taste-wise, but together they account for two of the highest fiber-rich vegetables and fruits around.

Yield: 4 servings
Prep time: 15 minutes
Cook time: 30 minutes
Serving size: ²/₃ cup
Each serving has:
5 g fiber
110 calories
5 g fat
14 g carbohydrate
2 g protein

4 medium parsnips, peeled and diced

2 TB. unsalted butter

2 firm Bosc pears, cored and diced

2 TB. light cream

Salt

Pinch ground allspice

1. Place parsnips in a medium saucepan, cover with cold water, and bring to a boil over high heat. Reduce heat to medium-low, and simmer for about 20 minutes or until fork-tender. Drain and set aside.

2. Meanwhile, in a medium skillet over medium-low heat, melt butter. Add pears and cook, stirring often, for 5 minutes or until softened but still a bit firm.

3. Add cooked parsnips to the skillet, and stir in cream, salt, and allspice. Continue cooking, mashing some parsnips with the back of a fork, for about 5 minutes. Stir well to combine, and serve immediately.

 Grist for the Mill

The parsnip contains more vitamins and minerals than its cousin, the carrot, as well as twice as much fiber.

Roasted Beets and Sweets

Two powerhouses of fiber team up in this herb-scented dish that's particularly delicious with roasted chicken.

1 bunch beets (about 1½ lb. or 4 medium beets) trimmed, peeled, and cut into ½-in. dice

2 medium yams or sweet potatoes, peeled and cut into 1-in. dice

3 TB. olive oil

1 sprig fresh rosemary

1 small bunch fresh thyme

1 bay leaf

Salt and pepper

Yield: 4 servings
Prep time: 20 minutes
Cook time: 45 minutes
Serving size: about 1 cup
Each serving has:
4 g fiber
170 calories
10 g fat
19 g carbohydrate
2 g protein

1. Preheat the oven to 425°F.

2. Place beets and sweet potatoes in a medium roasting pan, and drizzle with olive oil. Toss in rosemary, thyme, and bay leaf, and season with salt and pepper.

3. Roast in the oven, stirring occasionally, for about 45 minutes or until vegetables are tender and potatoes are browned. Discard herbs and bay leaf, and serve immediately.

 Smooth Move

Fresh beets can also be roasted whole with their skins on. After they're cooked but while they're still warm, rub the skins off with a paper towel. Keep the beets refrigerated, and add them diced or sliced to salads or vegetable medleys.

Chapter 19

Beans and Greens and Things

In This Chapter

- An assortment of bountiful beans
- Greens with great taste
- Fiber-rich vegetables for all

Everyone knows that beans of all descriptions contain a good amount of fiber and are healthy to eat. You also know that eating greens is as important as wearing clean underwear—at least that's what Mom used to think. So why don't we do it (eat our greens, that is)? And how come serving up a generous helping of beans is something we usually leave to the vegetarians?

I'd guess it's because our first introduction was marred by overcooking, underseasoning, and a general lack of creativity in presentation. On the other hand, if you are of a younger generation that's been raised on fast food, you may not even know what a vegetable is (and no, ketchup doesn't count).

A Quintessential Gold Mine

Welcome to the world of the healthiest food around. Nutritionally speaking, you can't do much better than beans, greens, and other colored things that fall into the vegetable category. Bite for bite, they are worth their weight in gold to our bodies and, as far as fiber is concerned (except for whole grains, which we get to in a future chapter), this is where the action is.

From black beans to green peas, and collards to cauliflower, fiber seekers can't do much better than the delicious selections in this chapter.

Do Me a Flavor

One of the tricks to cooking up appetizing vegetables is in the preparation. Boiling, in addition to leaching out nutrients, can also remove flavor. Roasting and sautéing, however, can intensify flavor as well as retain vitamins and minerals. Cooking with herbs, spices, and condiments can create palatable interest, while serving with sauces and glazes adds another dimension to the dish.

Learning to create exciting combinations of beans, greens, and other vegetables helps you in your efforts to provide more fiber for your family at mealtime, making you happier and healthier as well. So let's stir up a mess o' greens and beans and things, and start cookin'.

Easy BBQ Baked Beans

Deliciously doctored traditional pork and beans results in a thick and rich baked bean dish like no other, perfect for barbecues and picnics.

4 slices bacon, diced

1 medium onion, diced

2 (16-oz.) cans pork and beans

¼ cup ketchup

¼ cup firmly packed brown sugar

2 tsp. Worcestershire sauce

1 tsp. prepared mustard

Yield: 4 servings
Prep time: 15 minutes
Cook time: 50 minutes
Serving size: about 1 cup
Each serving has:
6 g fiber
325 calories
16 g fat
36 g carbohydrate
9 g protein

1. Preheat the oven to 350°F.

2. In a skillet over medium-high heat, fry bacon and onion for about 5 minutes or until bacon is crisp.

3. Drain off excess fat, and transfer bacon and onion to a 2-quart casserole dish. Stir in beans, ketchup, brown sugar, Worcestershire sauce, and mustard, combining well.

4. Bake, stirring occasionally, for about 45 minutes or until thickened and bubbly. Allow to cool for 10 minutes before serving.

Variation: For a vegetarian version, omit the bacon and fry the onion in 1 tablespoon vegetable oil. Replace the pork and beans with vegetarian beans, omit Worcestershire sauce, and add ¼ teaspoon liquid smoke.

Grist for the Mill

Original Boston baked beans got their name because New England Puritans were famous for baking beans, particularly on Saturday for the next day's meal, because cooking on the Sabbath was prohibited. Must be why they seem to taste even better the next day!

More Peas, Please Medley

All varieties of peas are high in fiber, and here, a few of them come together in a delicious and buttery side dish.

Yield: 4 servings
Prep time: 10 minutes
Cook time: 8 minutes
Serving size: about 1 cup
Each serving has:
5 g fiber
155 calories
9 g fat
13 g carbohydrate
6 g protein

3 TB. unsalted butter

1 shallot, peeled and minced

1 (10-oz.) pkg. frozen peas, thawed

1 cup sugar snap peas, ends and tough strings removed

1 cup snow peas, ends and tough strings removed

¼ cup low-sodium chicken broth

Salt and pepper

1. In a large, nonstick skillet over medium heat, melt 2 tablespoons butter. Add shallot, and cook, stirring often, for about 2 minutes.

2. Increase heat to medium-high. Add thawed peas and sugar snap peas to the skillet, stir to coat, and cook, stirring occasionally, for 3 minutes. Add snow peas, stir to combine, and cook 2 more minutes.

3. Pour broth in the skillet, cover, reduce heat to medium-low, and cook for about 2 minutes or until all peas are crisp-tender.

4. Remove from heat, swirl in remaining 1 tablespoon butter, season with salt and pepper, and serve immediately.

 Smooth Move

Add leftover pea medley to stews and soups at the end of the cooking time for extra fiber.

Quick Smokehouse Hoppin' John

Black-eyed peas and collards combine in this classic mouth-watering Southern dish that's loaded with fiber and smoky flavor.

2 TB. vegetable oil

1 medium onion, chopped

2 garlic cloves, chopped

1 (16-oz.) pkg. prewashed and cut *collard* greens

1 ham hock or smoked turkey wing

½ cup low-sodium chicken broth

1 (15-oz.) can black-eyed peas, drained

Salt and pepper

Cooked brown or white rice

Yield: 4 servings
Prep time: 15 minutes
Cook time: 30 minutes
Serving size: 1¹/₂ cups
Each serving has:
9 g fiber
235 calories
10 g fat
25 g carbohydrate
11 g protein

1. In a large, heavy pot over medium-high heat, heat vegetable oil. Add onion, and cook, stirring often, for about 3 minutes or until softened. Stir in garlic, and cook 1 more minute.

2. Add collards, ham hock, and broth, and stir well. Cook, covered, over low heat for about 20 minutes or until greens are tender.

3. Stir in peas, season with salt and pepper, and cook, uncovered, for 5 minutes. Remove ham hock, and serve immediately with rice.

Fiber Optics

Collards are members of the cabbage family and are prized for their dark-green edible leaves. They contain high levels of vitamin C and soluble fiber and may also offer anti-cancer protective properties.

Butter Beans and Kale with Sage

Here's another super-tasty bean-and-green combo that also contains fiber-rich, sweet butternut squash and tangy olives. Practically a meal in itself!

Yield: *4 servings*
Prep time: 20 minutes
Cook time: 35 minutes
Serving size: 1½ cups
Each serving has:
10 g fiber
300 calories
9 g fat
45 g carbohydrate
9 g protein

2 TB. olive oil

1 medium onion, diced

2 garlic cloves, minced

1 small butternut squash, peeled, seeded, and cut into 1-in. cubes (about 2 cups)

1 medium red bell pepper, ribs and seeds removed, and diced

1 medium bunch kale, stems removed, washed, and cut into strips

1 cup low-sodium chicken broth

1 TB. finely chopped fresh sage leaves

2 (15-oz.) cans butter beans, drained and rinsed

½ cup pitted kalamata olives, roughly chopped

Salt and pepper

Smooth Move

To save preparation time, look for packages of peeled and cubed butternut squash as well as prewashed and cut kale.

1. In a large, heavy pot over medium heat, heat olive oil. Add onion and garlic, and cook, stirring often, for 2 minutes.

2. Add butternut squash, red bell pepper, and kale, and stir well to combine. Cook for 2 more minutes. Add broth and sage, and bring to a simmer over medium-high heat. Cover, reduce heat to low, and cook, stirring occasionally, for about 20 minutes or until vegetables are tender.

3. Stir in beans and olives, and cook until heated through. Season with salt and pepper, and serve immediately.

Do-It-Yourself Refried Beans

After tasting the delicious difference when you make them yourself, you'll never buy canned refried beans again!

1 TB. vegetable oil

1 small onion, minced

1 jalapeño pepper, seeded and minced, or more to taste

2 (15-oz.) cans pinto beans, drained and rinsed

1 tsp. fresh lime juice

¼ cup water

½ tsp. ground cumin

Salt and pepper

Shredded cheddar cheese

Yield: 4 servings
Prep time: 10 minutes
Cook time: 15 minutes
Serving size: about 1 cup
Each serving has:
6 g fiber
130 calories
4 g fat
17 g carbohydrate
6 g protein

1. In a medium nonstick skillet over medium-high heat, heat vegetable oil. Add onion and jalapeño, and cook, stirring often, for about 4 minutes or until softened. Reduce heat to prevent browning.

2. Add pinto beans, lime juice, water, and cumin, and stir well to combine. Cook over medium heat for about 3 minutes or until beans are heated through.

3. Remove from heat and, using a potato masher or back of a fork, coarsely mash bean mixture until smooth yet still a bit lumpy. Return to heat, season with salt and pepper, and cook, stirring constantly, for 2 minutes or until piping hot. Serve immediately with a sprinkling of shredded cheese.

Smooth Move _____

You can also serve these beans as a hot dip with raw veggies and tortilla chips, or as a fiber-rich filling for a burrito or taco.

Roasted Green and Yellow String Beans

Here's a deliciously unusual way to prepare string beans flavored with fragrant olive oil and pungent garlic, that's guaranteed to have them requesting seconds.

Yield: *4 servings*
Prep time: 15 minutes
Cook time: 45 minutes
Serving size: about 1 cup
Each serving has:
8 g fiber
250 calories
19 g fat
15 g carbohydrate
5 g protein

1 lb. fresh green beans, stalk ends trimmed and left whole

½ lb. yellow (wax) beans, stalk ends trimmed and left whole

8 garlic cloves, peeled and smashed

3 TB. olive oil

Salt and pepper

⅓ cup pine nuts

1. Preheat the oven to 400°F.

2. Place green and yellow beans in a large roasting pan. Add garlic and olive oil, season with salt and pepper, and stir well to coat.

3. Roast in the oven, stirring occasionally, for about 40 minutes or until beans are shriveled and tender. Stir in pine nuts, and continue to roast for 5 more minutes. Serve immediately.

Grist for the Mill

Snap to it! Green and yellow string beans are also known as snap beans because at their peak of freshness, they make a snap sound when broken in half. Feel free to use this test at the supermarket—just don't tell them who sent you.

Sugar-Glazed Acorn Squash

Brown sugar adds a delightfully sweet touch to these easy-to-make acorn squash pieces that are finished with candied walnuts.

2 medium *acorn squash*, cut into quarters and seeded

Salt and pepper

4 tsp. unsalted butter

8 tsp. dark brown sugar

¼ cup candied (glazed) walnuts

Yield: 4 servings
Prep time: 10 minutes
Cook time: 50 minutes
Serving size: 2 pieces
Each serving has:
3 g fiber
200 calories
8 g fat
28 g carbohydrate
3 g protein

1. Preheat the oven to 375°F. Line a rimmed baking sheet with foil and spray lightly with oil.

2. Sprinkle squash pieces with salt and pepper and place cut side down on the prepared baking sheet. Bake, turning over once, for 30 minutes.

3. Turn squash pieces cut sides up, place ½ teaspoon of butter in each cavity, and sprinkle 1 teaspoon brown sugar on top of butter. Return to the oven and continue baking, occasionally brushing flesh of squash with a pastry brush to coat with butter and sugar mixture, for about 20 minutes more or until squash is nicely glazed and fork-tender.

4. Transfer to a platter to serve, and sprinkle with walnuts.

Fiber Optics

Acorn squash belong to the winter squash family, which includes butternut, buttercup, and turban, all good sources of dietary fiber as well as potassium.

Buttery Brussels Sprouts with Chestnuts

Although brussels sprouts are a good source of fiber on their own, when paired with their favorite partner, fiber-rich chestnuts, they will surpass your fiber as well as flavor expectations.

Yield: 4 servings
Prep time: 20 minutes
Cook time: 10 minutes
Serving size: ¾ cup
Each serving has:
5 g fiber
175 calories
6 g fat
24 g carbohydrate
4 g protein

1 lb. brussels sprouts, trimmed and halved through core

2 TB. unsalted butter

1 cup jarred or canned steamed chestnuts, crumbled

Salt and pepper

1 tsp. lemon juice

1. Bring a medium saucepan of salted water to a boil over heat. Add brussels sprouts, and simmer for about 6 minutes or until fork-tender but not mushy. Drain and set aside.

2. In a skillet over medium heat, melt butter. Add brussels sprouts and chestnuts, and season with salt and pepper. Stir well to coat, and cook, covered, for 2 minutes or until piping hot.

3. Stir in lemon juice, and serve immediately.

 Grist for the Mill

Brussels sprouts got their name from the Belgian city because they were originally cultivated there sometime in the early thirteenth century. They resemble mini cabbages and are sometimes sold on the stem during the winter holidays.

Broccoli and Cauliflower Bake with Crumb Topping

Two of our favorite cruciferous vegetables combine for a dressed-up presentation that includes a touch of tangy sour cream and a deliciously crisp finish.

½ **cup sour cream**

¼ **cup (½ stick) plus 1 TB. unsalted butter**

½ **tsp. prepared mustard**

Salt and pepper

2 cups broccoli florets, cooked to crisp-tender

2 cups cauliflower florets, cooked to crisp-tender

1 TB. olive oil

⅔ **cup whole-wheat bread-crumbs**

Yield: 4 servings
Prep time: 15 minutes
Cook time: 30 minutes
Serving size: about 1 cup
Each serving has:
7 g fiber
400 calories
20 g fat
40 g carbohydrate
10 g protein

1. Preheat the oven to 350°F. Lightly grease a 1-quart baking dish.

2. In a small saucepan over medium heat, combine sour cream, ¼ cup butter, mustard, salt, and pepper. Cook over medium heat, stirring often, for about 5 minutes or until smooth.

3. Place cooked broccoli and cauliflower in the prepared baking dish, and pour hot sour cream mixture over evenly.

4. In another small saucepan over heat, melt olive oil and remaining 1 tablespoon butter. Remove from heat, stir in breadcrumbs, season with salt and pepper, and sprinkle topping over florets.

5. Bake for about 25 minutes or until topping is golden and sauce is bubbly. Remove from the oven and allow to rest for 5 minutes before serving.

 Smooth Move

Look for bags of broccoli and cauliflower florets packaged together in your supermarket to save preparation time. You can cook florets to crisp-tender in the microwave with a little water in 5 minutes.

Chapter 20

Whole-Grain Pilafs and Risottos

In This Chapter

- ◆ Cooking a variety of grains
- ◆ Pilafs with pizzazz
- ◆ Easy risotto making

Gone are the days when our grain choices were limited to Minute Rice and Uncle Ben. Even brown rice has been given a run for its money. From brown basmati to kasha, we now have a wide range of international grains available, many of which were diet staples for foragers and farmers centuries ago. Not only is their fiber content high, but their nutrient value can be downright impressive.

Ounce for ounce, these mega-powerhouses of healthy fiber are a great way to introduce Rice-A-Roni fans to the benefits of making pilafs and risottos with whole grains. Chewy and flavorful, they also absorb the flavors imparted from other ingredients and come together to create sensational side dishes that go with just about any entrée you choose.

Having a few of these in your high-fiber repertoire will be tremendously helpful to you when trying to chalk up some fiber gram points.

I Left My Rice in San Francisco

In the following pages, we first explore some unusual grains and unique combinations like a brown and wild rice pilaf studded with sweet apricots and almonds. Pilafs lend themselves superbly to the addition of fruit and nuts, two fiber-friendly allies we've seen on more than one occasion. Then we venture into the exotic with a curry-scented couscous and a Moroccan-spiced quinoa, both perfect accompaniments for chicken or lamb on the grill. Finally, we take on the delicate creation of risotto and find that, not only is it easy to make, but it can sometimes contain grains other than white arborio rice—a pleasant surprise for all you fiber-seeking risotto lovers.

All in all, this is a chapter you'll want to refer to on many occasions when you need a healthy alternative to that San Francisco treat. Ding! Ding!

Brown and Wild Rice Pilaf

Nutty and fragrant, brown and wild rice come together in this terrific side dish that's particularly tasty with roasted or grilled chicken.

1 cup brown long-grain rice

½ cup *wild rice*

1½ cups low-sodium chicken broth

1½ cups water

⅓ cup chopped dried apricots

¼ cup sliced almonds

1 TB. unsalted butter

1 TB. chopped fresh parsley leaves

Salt and pepper

Yield: 4 servings
Prep time: 5 minutes
Cook time: 45 minutes
Serving size: about 1 cup
Each serving has:
5 g fiber
315 calories
9 g fat
48 g carbohydrate
9 g protein

1. In a medium saucepan over high heat, combine brown and wild rice. Stir in broth and water, and bring to a boil.

2. Stir in apricots, reduce heat to low, cover, and cook for 40 to 45 minutes or until liquid is absorbed and rice is tender.

3. Stir in almonds, butter, parsley, salt, and pepper. Let stand 5 minutes, and serve.

Fiber Optics

Wild rice is technically not a type of rice but rather a seed in the wild grass family. It grows in shallow, muddy waters and is high in fiber, vitamins E and B, and protein.

Kasha Mia Pilaf

Aromatic roasted buckwheat stars in this fiber-rich pilaf with sweet onions and carrots and a hint of dill.

Yield: 4 servings
Prep time: 10 minutes
Cook time: 25 minutes
Serving size: ³/₄ cup
Each serving has:
3 g fiber
175 calories
11 g fat
13 g carbohydrate
3 g protein

1 TB. vegetable oil

1 TB. unsalted butter

1 medium sweet onion, such as Maui or Vidalia, halved and thinly sliced

1½ cups peeled and shredded carrots

Salt and pepper

1 cup whole-grain kasha

1½ cups water

⅓ cup walnut pieces

1 TB. chopped fresh dill

1. In a large, nonstick skillet over medium heat, heat vegetable oil and butter. Add onion and cook, stirring occasionally, for about 8 minutes or until onion is soft and lightly browned.

2. Stir in carrots, season with salt and pepper, and cook, stirring often, for 2 more minutes.

3. Add kasha to the skillet, and stir well to combine. Pour in water, bring to a boil, cover, and reduce heat to low. Cook for 12 to 15 minutes or until liquid is absorbed and kasha is tender.

4. Stir in walnuts and dill, season with salt and pepper, and serve immediately.

 Smooth Move _____

Look for bags of preshredded carrots in the salad section of your supermarket's produce aisle. Use in salads, pilafs, and soups for a quick fiber addition.

Moroccan Quinoa

A powerhouse of nutrition, quinoa takes on the flavors of the Middle East in this delicious dish, perfect alongside grilled meats and vegetables.

1 TB. olive oil

1 TB. unsalted butter

1 medium red onion, chopped

1 medium celery stalk, diced

Salt and pepper

1 garlic clove, minced

¼ tsp. ground cumin

¼ tsp. coriander

¼ tsp. turmeric

¼ tsp. ginger

1 cup *quinoa*, rinsed and drained

2 cups water

1 tsp. fresh lemon juice

1 TB. chopped fresh cilantro

1 TB. chopped fresh mint

1 medium tomato, seeded and diced

Yield: *4 servings*
Prep time: 15 minutes
Cook time: 25 minutes
Serving size: ⅔ cup
Each serving has:
4 g fiber
235 calories
9 g fat
32 g carbohydrate
7 g protein

1. In a heavy, medium saucepan over medium heat, heat olive oil and butter. Add red onion and celery, season with salt and pepper, and cook, stirring occasionally, for about 6 minutes or until softened. Add garlic, and cook 1 more minute.

2. Stir in cumin, coriander, turmeric, and ginger, and cook for 2 minutes. Stir in quinoa, and cook for 1 minute.

3. Add water, bring to a boil, reduce heat to low, and cook, covered, for about 15 minutes or until liquid is absorbed and quinoa is tender.

4. Stir in lemon juice, cilantro, mint, and tomato. Season with salt and pepper, and serve immediately.

Fiber Optics

Quinoa is a South American grain with a delicate texture and flavor. It is high in protein and fiber, and can be found in the rice aisle of most supermarkets.

Lentil Curry Couscous

Tender couscous pairs with fiber-rich lentils in this flavorful, exotic dish with hints of curry and cinnamon.

Yield: 4 servings
Prep time: 10 minutes
Cook time: 40 minutes
Serving size: about 1 cup
Each serving has:
11 g fiber
310 calories
6 g fat
49 g carbohydrate
7 g protein

3 cups low-sodium chicken or vegetable broth

1 tsp. curry powder

½ tsp. ground turmeric

½ cup red lentils, picked over and rinsed

1 cup *couscous*

⅓ cup currants or raisins

⅓ cup frozen peas, thawed

1 cinnamon stick

¼ cup sliced almonds

4 green onions, thinly sliced

Salt and pepper

1. In a medium saucepan over high heat, bring broth to a boil. Stir in curry powder, turmeric, and lentils. Reduce heat to low, cover, and cook for 25 to 30 minutes or until lentils are tender.

2. Add couscous, currants, and peas, and stir well to combine. Place cinnamon stick on top, cover, and remove from heat. Let stand for 10 minutes.

3. Fluff couscous mixture with a fork, and gently stir in almonds and green onions. Season with salt and pepper, and serve immediately.

Fiber Optics

Couscous, a staple of Middle Eastern cuisine, is made from semolina and resembles small granules. In Western markets, couscous is usually presteamed for quick cooking.

Rustic Risotto with Cabbage and Chickpeas

Hearty and full of flavor, risotto goes country-style with fiber-rich cabbage and beans, enhanced with the tang of lemon zest.

6 large savoy cabbage leaves, hard centers removed

2 TB. unsalted butter

2 tsp. olive oil

3 shallots, finely chopped

Salt and pepper

1½ cups arborio rice

1 qt. low-sodium chicken broth, kept hot on the back burner

½ cup canned chickpeas, drained and rinsed

⅓ cup canned cannellini beans, drained and rinsed

1 tsp. grated lemon zest

½ cup grated Parmesan cheese

Yield: 4 servings		
Prep time: 12 minutes		
Cook time: 30 minutes		
Serving size: about 1 cup		
Each serving has:		
4 g fiber		
265 calories		
10 g fat		
30 g carbohydrate		
11 g protein		

1. Bring a medium pot of salted water to a boil over high heat. Submerge cabbage leaves in boiling water, and cook for 5 minutes. Drain, rinse under cold water, pat dry, and roughly chop. Set aside.

2. In a large saucepan over medium heat, heat butter and olive oil. Add shallots and chopped cabbage, season with salt and pepper, and cook, stirring, for about 3 minutes or until softened. Do not brown.

3. Add rice and cook, stirring constantly, for 1 minute.

4. Using a ½-cup ladle, begin adding hot broth to rice, stirring constantly each time, until liquid has been absorbed. Be sure to keep rice at a low simmer while stirring. When about ½ cup broth remains, stir in chickpeas and cannellini beans.

5. Add remaining broth, and cook, stirring, until rice is tender and creamy but still firm to the bite. Rice should require about 25 minutes of cooking from beginning to end.

6. Remove from heat, and stir in lemon zest and Parmesan cheese. Season with salt and pepper, and serve immediately.

 Grist for the Mill

The characteristic smell of cooking cabbage is due to the release of sugars in the leaves. The older the cabbage, the more intense the aroma.

Mushroom-Barley Risotto

Nutty barley takes the place of rice in this earthy mushroom and herb–flavored risotto.

Yield: 4 servings
Prep time: 20 minutes
Cook time: 55 minutes
Serving size: about 1 cup
Each serving has:
9 g fiber
375 calories
12 g fat
36 g carbohydrate
13 g protein

1 TB. olive oil

1 TB. unsalted butter

1 small onion, finely chopped

10 oz. *crimini* or white button mushrooms, sliced

1 large portobello mushroom, stem and gills removed and cap chopped

Salt and pepper

1 large garlic clove, minced

2 TB. chopped fresh parsley

2 tsp. chopped fresh thyme

1 tsp. chopped fresh sage

1 cup pearl barley

5 cups low-sodium chicken or vegetable broth

¼ cup heavy cream

½ cup grated Parmesan cheese

1. In a heavy, large saucepan over medium heat, heat olive oil and butter. Add onion and cook, stirring often, for about 3 minutes or until onion is soft. Add sliced crimini mushrooms and chopped portobello, season with salt and pepper, and cook, stirring occasionally, for about 10 minutes or until lightly golden.

2. Stir in garlic, parsley, thyme, and sage, and cook for 2 minutes. Add barley, stir well to coat, and cook 1 more minute.

3. Add 4 cups broth and bring to a boil. Reduce heat to medium-low, cover, and cook for about 30 minutes or until liquid is nearly absorbed.

4. Stir cream into remaining broth and add to the saucepan with barley. Continue to cook, uncovered, stirring often, for about 10 minutes or until barley is tender and mixture is creamy.

5. Remove from heat, stir in Parmesan cheese, season with salt and pepper, and serve immediately.

Variation: Make a mixed-grain risotto by substituting ²/₃ of barley with ¹/₃ cup wheat berries and ¹/₃ cup brown rice.

Fiber Optics

Crimini mushrooms are immature portobello mushrooms. They are often sold as "baby bellas."

Brown Rice and Butternut Risotto

Creamy and sweet butternut squash takes center stage in this healthy rendition made with aromatic brown rice.

1 TB. olive oil	**¼ cup chopped hazelnuts**
1 small onion, finely chopped	**1 TB. chopped fresh basil**
1 garlic clove, minced	**1 tsp. dried oregano**
1 cup brown arborio or short-grain rice	**1 TB. unsalted butter**
¼ cup apple cider	**½ cup grated Parmesan cheese**
6 cups low-sodium chicken broth, kept hot on the back burner	**Salt and pepper**
	¼ cup crumbled feta cheese
1 small butternut squash, peeled, seeded, and cut into ½-in. dice	

Yield: 4 servings

Prep time: 15 minutes

Cook time: 45 minutes

Serving size: about 1 cup

Each serving has:

4 g fiber

465 calories

19 g fat

45 g carbohydrate

13 g protein

---

1. In a heavy, medium saucepan over medium heat, heat olive oil. Add onion and cook, stirring often, for about 3 minutes or until softened. Add garlic and cook 1 more minute.

2. Add rice and cook, stirring constantly, for 1 minute. Add apple cider, and cook, stirring, for about 2 minutes or until liquid is absorbed.

3. Using a ½-cup ladle, begin adding hot broth to rice, stirring constantly each time, until liquid has been absorbed. Be sure to keep rice at a low simmer while stirring. When ½ of broth remains, add butternut squash, hazelnuts, basil, and oregano, and continue cooking, adding broth and stirring constantly, until rice and squash is tender and mixture is creamy. Rice should take about 45 minutes from beginning to end.

4. Remove from heat, stir in Parmesan cheese, and season with salt and pepper. Serve immediately topped with feta.

Variation: Try this with *2 cups blanched asparagus pieces* instead of the butternut squash. Eliminate hazelnuts and sprinkle sliced almonds on top before serving. Top with shaved Asiago instead of feta.

 Smooth Move

To bring back the creamy consistency of leftover risotto, add a little water to the mixture and stir constantly while heating over medium-low heat.

Chapter 21

The Harvest Bread Box

In This Chapter

- ◆ Baking with whole-grain flour
- ◆ Quick breads and biscuits
- ◆ Yeast rolls and loaves

Commercial bread manufacturers have learned that fiber sells bread. Whether it be whole wheat, bran, seeded, sprouted, or even "double fiber," they know consumers are looking for the buzz words that will convince them they're improving their fiber intake in the sliced bread aisle. And rightly so. Eating bread made with whole grains is one of the best ways to up your fiber intake.

Well, almost. If the first ingredient listed on the package is enriched white flour, it doesn't matter what else the label says. If it's fiber you're after, you need to see words like *whole grain* and *whole wheat* right up at the top of the ingredient list. Otherwise, you might as well buy that mushy white sandwich bread the kids like—your fiber benefit will be nearly the same: zip.

Getting a Rise Out of Whole Grains

Breads, rolls, and biscuits that feature whole grains and their flours are the best bet for fiber-seeking consumers. And one of the best ways to ensure that you're getting what you want is to make it yourself.

Yes, bread baking can be a long process at times, particularly when yeast is involved, but who can resist the aroma of fresh baked bread as it wafts through the house?

The Quick and the Bread

Having said that, there are many types of breads, leavened by other ingredients such as baking powder and eggs, that are a snap to prepare and smell just as good. You'll find both types in this chapter, for when you're feeling ambitious or when time is of the essence.

You'll also find recipes for some basics that will serve you well and help to increase your fiber tally. Easy, homemade whole-grain croutons are one staple you'll enjoy, while whole-wheat pizza dough will no doubt become a featured star of your repertoire. Quick breads like those made from stone-ground cornmeal or grated zucchini and walnuts will also become favorites as part of a meal or simply on their own.

So preheat the oven and get baking! When you taste that first slice, you and everyone else will be so glad you did.

Whole-Grain Croutons

Increase your fiber by making these crunchy and delicious home-made croutons flavored with garlic and Parmesan for salads and soups.

3 cups cubed whole-grain bread	**1 TB. grated Parmesan cheese**
Olive oil cooking spray	**1 tsp. dried parsley**
¼ tsp. garlic salt	

Yield: 6 servings
Prep time: 10 minutes
Cook time: 10 minutes
Serving size: ½ cup
Each serving has:
3 g fiber
105 calories
2 g fat
17 g carbohydrate
2 g protein

1. Preheat the oven to 350°F. Lightly spray a large, rimmed baking sheet with olive oil.

2. Spread bread cubes evenly on the prepared baking sheet, and coat them lightly with olive oil cooking spray.

3. Bake, occasionally shaking the pan, for about 10 minutes or until toasted and golden. Sprinkle with garlic salt, Parmesan cheese, and parsley, and toss well to coat.

4. Transfer to paper towels to cool, and store in an airtight container for up to 4 days.

 Smooth Move _____

Crush leftover croutons and use them as a crumb topping for casseroles or for breading oven-baked or fried cutlets or fish.

Whole-Wheat Pizza Dough

Perfectly crisp on the outside and soft and chewy on the inside, this healthful and versatile pizza dough will serve you well.

Yield: 1 (12-inch) pizza
Prep time: 25 minutes
Cook time: 18 minutes
Serving size: ½ of pizza
Each serving has:
7 g fiber
830 calories
9 g fat
145 g carbohydrate
11 g protein

½ tsp. sugar

¾ cup warm water (about 110°F)

1½ tsp. active dry yeast

1½ tsp. olive oil

¼ tsp. salt

1 cup whole-wheat flour

¾ cup all-purpose flour

1. In a medium bowl, dissolve sugar in warm water. Sprinkle yeast over top, and let stand for about 10 minutes or until foamy.

2. Stir in olive oil and salt, and add whole-wheat flour and ½ cup all-purpose flour. Stir well to combine, and turn out onto a floured work surface.

3. Using remaining ¼ cup all-purpose flour, knead dough for about 10 minutes or until all flour is absorbed and it's formed a round smooth ball. Place in a lightly oiled bowl, cover with a towel, and allow to rise in a warm place for 1 hour.

4. Tip dough onto a lightly floured surface, form into a tight ball, cover with the towel, and let stand for 20 minutes.

5. Preheat the oven to 375°F.

6. Roll out dough with a floured rolling pin to 12 inches in diameter. Slightly curl edges inward, transfer to a baking sheet lined with parchment paper, prick dough surface all over with a fork, and bake for 10 minutes to set.

7. Proceed with Whole-Wheat Thin-Crust Pizza (recipe in Chapter 16) or add your favorite toppings, and bake at 450°F for 12 to 18 minutes.

 Smooth Move

Not sure if your yeast is still good? Test a small amount in a water and sugar solution—a method called "proofing." If it foams, it's still viable.

Quick Cornbread

Stone-ground cornmeal provides a deliciously intense corn flavor, while whole-wheat pastry flour adds nuttiness and fiber.

1 cup stone-ground cornmeal

½ cup whole-wheat *pastry flour*

½ cup all-purpose flour

2 TB. sugar

1 TB. baking powder

1 tsp. salt

1 cup milk

2 TB. unsalted butter, melted and cooled

2 large eggs, beaten

Yield: 9 servings
Prep time: 10 minutes
Cook time: 25 minutes
Serving size: 1 (3-inch) square
Each serving has:
2 g fiber
150 calories
5 g fat
20 g carbohydrate
4 g protein

1. Preheat the oven to 400°F. Lightly grease a 9-inch-square baking pan.

2. In a medium bowl, whisk together cornmeal, whole-wheat pastry flour, all-purpose flour, sugar, baking powder, and salt.

3. In a small bowl, whisk together milk, melted butter, and eggs. Add milk mixture to flour mixture, and stir with a fork until just combined.

4. Pour batter into the prepared baking pan, spread evenly, and bake for 20 to 25 minutes or until edges are golden and a toothpick inserted in the center comes out clean.

5. Cut into squares and serve warm, or cover and keep for up to 3 days.

Variation: For extra fiber, reduce milk to ³/₄ cup and add 1 (8-ounce) can cream-style corn.

 Fiber Optics

Pastry flour, available in white or whole wheat, is a low-gluten flour often used in baking. A ¼ cup measure of whole-wheat pastry flour contains 2 grams fiber.

Super-Seeded Rolls

Far from heavy, these super-light wheat rolls with the tasty addition of crunchy seeds are a delight to serve at any meal.

Yield: 2 dozen rolls
Prep time: 30 minutes
Cook time: 15 minutes
Serving size: 2 rolls
Each serving has:
3 g fiber
130 calories
5 g fat
18 g carbohydrate
4 g protein

2 (4-oz.) pkg. active dry yeast (4½ tsp.)

1¾ cups warm water (about 110°F)

⅓ cup sugar

1 tsp. salt

¼ cup (½ stick) unsalted butter, melted and cooled

1 large egg, beaten

2½ cups whole-wheat flour

2 TB. toasted wheat germ

2¼ cups all-purpose flour

2 tsp. poppy seeds

2 tsp. celery seeds

1 tsp. caraway seeds

1 tsp. sesame seeds

1 large egg white, slightly beaten

1. In a large bowl, add yeast to warm water and let stand for about 10 minutes or until foamy. Add sugar, salt, melted butter, and beaten egg, and stir well to combine.

2. In another large bowl, whisk together whole-wheat flour, wheat germ, and all-purpose flour. Stir into yeast mixture ½ cup at a time until dough begins to pull away from the bowl.

3. Turn out dough onto a floured work surface, and knead for about 10 minutes or until smooth and elastic. Place in a lightly oiled bowl, cover with a towel, and allow to rise in a warm place for 1 hour.

4. Punch dough in the bowl to deflate, cover again, and allow to rise in a warm place for another 30 minutes. Meanwhile, lightly grease 2 (12-cup) muffin pans and set aside.

5. Turn out dough on a lightly floured surface, punch down, and divide into 24 equal pieces. Form each piece into a small round, and place in prepared muffin pans.

6. In a small bowl, combine poppy seeds, celery seeds, caraway seeds, and sesame seeds. Brush each roll with egg white, and sprinkle seeds evenly on top. Set aside, uncovered, to rise for 30 minutes.

7. Preheat the oven to 400°F. Bake rolls for 12 to 15 minutes or until golden brown. Remove from the oven and transfer rolls to wire racks to cool, or serve warm. Store in an airtight plastic bag for up to 3 days.

 Smooth Move

Breads like these that require a lot of rising time are always well worth the effort. Fill in the waiting time by prepping ingredients for your dinner entrée.

Better-for-You Biscuits

Who doesn't love the delicious tenderness of warm buttermilk biscuits straight from the oven? Here, white whole-wheat flour secretly adds the fiber you're after.

1½ cups white whole-wheat flour

½ cup all-purpose flour

1 TB. sugar

1 TB. baking powder

½ tsp. baking soda

½ tsp. salt

6 TB. (¾ stick) unsalted butter, diced and softened

1 cup buttermilk

Yield: 10 biscuits
Prep time: 10 minutes
Cook time: 18 minutes
Serving size: 2 biscuits
Each serving has:
3 g fiber
235 calories
11 g fat
34 g carbohydrate
5 g protein

1. Preheat the oven to 375°F.

2. In a large mixing bowl, whisk together white whole-wheat flour, all-purpose flour, sugar, baking powder, baking soda, and salt. Using a pastry blender, cut butter into flour mixture until mixture resembles small peas (or use a food processor, pulsing several times).

3. Add buttermilk and stir quickly to combine without overmixing. Let dough rest for 5 minutes.

4. Turn out dough onto a lightly floured surface, and roll out to ³/₄ inch thickness. Using a 2-inch biscuit cutter or the open end of a drinking glass dipped in flour, cut out biscuits and transfer to a nonstick or parchment paper–covered baking sheet.

5. Bake for 15 to 18 minutes or until bottoms are lightly golden and a toothpick inserted in the center comes out clean. Serve warm or store in an airtight container for 2 days.

Variation: You can make this by replacing the sugar with 2 tablespoons honey and add 2 tablespoons honey-toasted wheat germ to the flour mixture.

Smooth Move

Don't feel like running out for buttermilk but craving some delicious warm biscuits? In a pinch, you can substitute 1 cup milk mixed with 1 tablespoon vinegar. Let it stand for 10 minutes before using.

Zucchini-Walnut Bread

This moist and almost cakelike quickbread, scented with spice and dotted with tasty walnut morsels, is particularly delicious toasted and buttered as a side at dinnertime.

Yield: 1 loaf
Prep time: 15 minutes
Cook time: 60 minutes
Serving size: ⅙ of loaf
Each serving has:
5 g fiber
410 calories
28 g fat
29 g carbohydrate
9 g protein

2 large eggs

⅔ cup sugar

½ cup vegetable oil

1 cup shredded zucchini, including skin (about 1 medium)

½ tsp. vanilla extract

1 cup white whole-wheat flour

½ cup all-purpose flour

2 TB. flax meal

½ tsp. salt

½ tsp. baking soda

¼ tsp. baking powder

½ tsp. ground cinnamon

⅛ tsp. ground nutmeg

1 cup walnut pieces

1. Preheat the oven to 350°F. Grease a 9×5-inch loaf pan.

2. In a medium bowl, beat together eggs, sugar, and vegetable oil. Add zucchini and vanilla extract, and beat 1 more minute.

3. In another medium bowl, whisk together white whole-wheat flour, all-purpose flour, flax meal, salt, baking soda, baking powder, cinnamon, and nutmeg.

4. Add flour mixture to wet mixture in 2 batches, beating well each time to combine. Stir in walnuts.

5. Pour batter into the prepared loaf pan, and bake for 50 to 60 minutes or until golden and a toothpick inserted in the center comes out clean. Cool in the pan for 10 minutes, loosen the edges with a knife, and transfer to a wire rack to cool completely. Slice with a serrated knife.

Smooth Move _____

Zucchini is one of the easiest vegetables to grow, and home gardeners are usually stuck with an overabundance at harvest time. For winter zucchini bread making, shred as you would for the recipe and store 1-cup amounts in airtight bags in your freezer. Thaw on a plate before using.

Whole-Grain Pumpkin Seed Loaf

Fiber-rich, chewy, and slightly sweet, this bread, including hearty oats and crunchy pepitas, is terrific for sandwiches and toast.

1 cup milk

½ cup old-fashioned rolled oats

¼ cup warm water (about 110°F)

1 (4-oz.) pkg. active dry yeast (2¼ tsp.)

¼ cup honey

2 TB. unsalted butter, melted and cooled

1½ cups white whole-wheat flour

1 cup *bread flour*

½ TB. salt

1 egg white, slightly beaten

2 TB. pepitas (toasted pumpkin seeds)

Yield: 1 loaf
Prep time: 30 minutes
Cook time: 40 minutes
Serving size: 2 slices (¹⁄₆ of loaf)
Each serving has:
4 g fiber
265 calories
8 g fat
38 g carbohydrate
9 g protein

1. In a small saucepan over medium heat, heat milk. Do not boil. Stir in oats, and set aside.

2. In a large bowl, combine warm water, yeast, and 1 teaspoon honey. Let stand for about 10 minutes or until foamy. Stir in oat mixture, remaining honey, and butter.

3. In a medium bowl, whisk together white whole-wheat flour, ½ cup bread flour, and salt. Add to yeast mixture, and stir until a soft dough forms, adding more bread flour if necessary.

4. Turn out dough onto a lightly floured surface, and knead for about 10 minutes or until smooth and elastic, using remaining flour. Transfer to a lightly oiled bowl, cover with a towel, and allow to rise in a warm place for 1 hour.

5. Grease a 9×5-inch loaf pan.

6. Punch down dough, turn out onto a lightly floured surface, and knead again for 2 minutes. Shape into a log and place in the prepared loaf pan. Cover with a towel, and allow to rise in a warm place for another hour.

7. Preheat the oven to 375°F.

8. Brush top of loaf with egg white, and sprinkle pepitas over top. Bake for 30 to 40 minutes or until golden and hollow-sounding when tapped. Tent with foil to prevent overbrowning.

9. Run a knife around the edges of loaf, remove from the pan, and transfer to a wire rack to cool. Slice with a serrated knife. Store wrapped in plastic for up to 4 days.

 Fiber Optics

Bread flour is a high-gluten flour that contains malted barley to help the yeast rise in bread recipes, particularly those that contain heavy flours or grains.

Rosemary Potato Focaccia

This moist Italian bread, garlicky and fragrant with rosemary, benefits from the addition of mashed potatoes by contributing both fiber and moistness.

1 (4-oz.) pkg. active dry yeast (2¼ tsp.)

1 cup warm water (about 110°F)

2½ cups white whole-wheat flour

2 cups all-purpose flour

2 cups cooked mashed Idaho or russet potatoes

1 TB. salt

3 garlic cloves, smashed

2 tsp. crumbled dry rosemary

⅓ cup extra-virgin olive oil

1 lb. baby red potatoes, very thinly sliced

Yield: 1 loaf		
Prep time: 15 minutes		
Cook time: 45 minutes		
Serving size: ⅙ of loaf		
Each serving has:		
4 g fiber		
275 calories		
8 g fat		
42 g carbohydrate		
8 g protein		

1. In a small bowl, combine yeast and warm water, and let stand for about 10 minutes or until foamy.

2. In a large bowl, whisk together white whole-wheat flour and 1½ cups all-purpose flour. Add potatoes and salt, and stir until mixture resembles coarse meal. Add yeast mixture, and combine well.

3. Turn out dough onto a lightly floured surface, and knead, using remaining flour as necessary, for about 8 minutes or until smooth and elastic. Transfer to a lightly oiled bowl, cover with a towel, and allow to rise in a warm place for 1 hour.

4. Meanwhile, in a small bowl, combine garlic, rosemary, and olive oil. Set aside.

5. Oil a rimmed baking sheet.

6. Turn out dough onto the prepared baking sheet, and press down to flatten into a ½-inch-thick oval. Cover with a towel, and allow to rise in a warm place for 30 minutes.

7. Preheat the oven to 400°F.

8. Layer potato slices over top of focaccia, and brush with oil mixture, discarding garlic. Sprinkle lightly with salt, and bake in the lower third of the oven for 40 to 50 minutes or until golden. Cool in the pan on a wire rack and serve warm, or cool and store wrapped in plastic for up to 2 days.

Variation: Eliminate the potato topping and add 4 sliced plum tomatoes and $1/2$ cup sliced olives halfway through the baking time, brushing with the oil mixture.

 Grist for the Mill _____

Focaccia comes from the Latin word *focus,* meaning "center." It refers to the place in the home, usually the fireplace, where bread is always baked.

Part 7

Desserts and Sweet Treats

No cookbook is complete without something that satisfies the sweet tooth and brings your meal to a perfect (and sometimes decadent) conclusion. Cooking high fiber is no exception, and in fact, just may introduce you to some of the best desserts you've ever created. From cobblers to pies, cakes to cookies, and parfaits to sorbets, who knows? You may want to shake things up at dinner and serve dessert first.

Every healthy diet has room for treats, so don't deprive yourself! Besides, with an eye toward fiber, these selections aren't really a bad thing—they just taste like they are. So let's get to it, my fiber friends—dessert awaits.

Chapter 22

Fruit Cobblers, Puddings, and Pies

In This Chapter

- ◆ Fiberful fruit desserts
- ◆ Tips for incorporating grains and nuts
- ◆ New twists on old favorites

From peaches to blueberries, and bananas to apples, fruit-based desserts can be a healthful treat for a fiber seeker with a sweet tooth. Fresh is usually the best bet, but don't hesitate to make use of frozen or even canned fruits when needed. In general, the fiber content is the same, and when certain types of fruit are out of season, the flavor will even surpass their fresh counterparts.

Go Nuts for Fruit

In this chapter, you get recipes for everything from cobblers to tarts to banana cream pie, all with a view toward increasing your fiber intake with little twists and enhancements.

Whole grains and breads make an appearance in rice and bread puddings, while an easy whole-wheat piecrust, suitable for any recipe you may already have in your file, provides extra fiber as well. A pecan crust, utilizing healthy nut fiber and fat, will become a favorite in no time.

In fact, nuts add flavor and crunch to many of the recipes here, always great partners for fruit.

The Proof Is in the Pudding

Compared to store-bought fruit pies and other desserts, as tempting as they may sometimes be, the high-fiber treats in this chapter are far more nutritious. And although you'll find butter and other ingredients that do contain fat, you'll find no trace of trans fats here, which is definitely a plus.

Rest assured that your family will be better served as they relish each homemade bite.

Cherry-Peach Cobbler

Sweet, succulent cherries combine with juicy peaches in this heavenly dessert—that's good for you, too!

1 lb. fresh peaches peeled, pitted, and cut into ½-in.-thick slices, or 1 lb. frozen, thawed and drained

1 (15-oz.) can dark pitted cherries in heavy syrup, drained and syrup reserved

½ cup water

½ cup sugar

1½ TB. cornstarch

1 tsp. almond extract

4 TB. unsalted butter, diced

1½ cups all-purpose flour

1 TB. honey-toasted wheat germ

1½ tsp. baking powder

1 tsp. baking soda

½ tsp. salt

⅔ cup buttermilk

Yield: 4 servings
Prep time: 30 minutes
Cook time: 40 minutes
Serving size: about 1 cup
Each serving has:
4 g fiber
400 calories
12 g fat
59 g carbohydrate
5 g protein

1. Preheat the oven to 400°F. Lightly butter a 9-inch-square baking dish.

2. Place peaches and cherries in the prepared baking dish and gently toss.

3. In a medium saucepan over medium-high heat, combine reserved cherry syrup, water, sugar, and cornstarch. Cook for about 2 minutes or until sugar is dissolved. Stir in almond extract, pour over peaches and cherries, and dot with 1 tablespoon diced butter.

4. For topping: in a medium bowl, whisk together flour, wheat germ, baking powder, baking soda, and salt. Work in remaining 3 tablespoons diced butter with a pastry blender until mixture resembles a coarse meal. Add buttermilk, and stir just to combine.

5. Turn out dough onto a floured surface, and pat into roughly the size of the baking dish. Transfer with metal spatulas to the baking dish, and place on top of fruit. Make slight indentations with your fingertips so dough appears "cobbled."

6. Bake for 30 to 40 minutes or until top is golden and fruit is bubbly. Cool slightly before serving.

Smooth Move

Keep a jar of fiber-rich toasted wheat germ (honey or regular) on hand in the fridge for adding small amounts to your baking.

Whole-Wheat Blackberry Cobbler

Fiberful blackberries take center stage in this delectably sweet and satisfying dessert. Top with vanilla ice cream for a bit of extravagance.

Yield: 6 servings
Prep time: 20 minutes
Cook time: 35 minutes
Serving size: about ¾ cup
Each serving has:
8 g fiber
400 calories
12 g fat
60 g carbohydrate
7 g protein

⅔ cup blackberry jam or preserves

½ cup water

1 tsp. lemon juice

1 (16-oz.) bag frozen blackberries, thawed, or 4 cups fresh

1 TB. unsalted butter, diced

1 cup whole-wheat flour

1 cup all-purpose flour

2 TB. sugar

1 TB. baking powder

½ tsp. salt

¼ cup vegetable oil

¾ cup milk

1. Preheat the oven to 350°F. Lightly butter a 9-inch-square baking dish.

2. In a medium saucepan over medium heat, combine blackberry jam, water, and lemon juice. Cook, stirring often, for about 5 minutes or until bubbly. Stir in blackberries, pour into baking dish, and dot with butter.

3. For topping: in a medium bowl, whisk together whole-wheat flour, all-purpose flour, sugar, baking powder, and salt.

4. In a measuring cup, combine vegetable oil and milk, and add all at once to flour mixture. Stir just to combine.

5. Drop dough by heaping spoonfuls over blackberries, and bake for 25 to 35 minutes or until topping is golden and fruit is bubbly. Cool slightly before serving.

Variation: Replace blackberries with raspberries and use raspberry jam, or try a combination of berries.

 Grist for the Mill

Frozen blackberries are sometimes really Marion berries, a close cousin developed and grown in Oregon. They are equally sweet and fiber rich.

Chocolate-Raspberry Bread Pudding

The richness of dark chocolate and the tart zing of raspberries join forces in this surprisingly fiberful yet decadent dessert.

4 cups cubed, crustless, soft honey-wheat sandwich bread

1 cup heavy cream

1 cup half-and-half

5 TB. unsweetened cocoa powder

1 cup semisweet miniature chocolate chips

3 large eggs

½ cup sugar

1½ cups fresh raspberries

Whipped cream

Yield: 6 servings
Prep time: 20 minutes
Cook time: 35 minutes
Serving size: about ³/₄ cup
Each serving has:
8 g fiber
510 calories
30 g fat
60 g carbohydrate
11 g protein

1. Preheat the oven to 325°F. Lightly butter a 2-quart baking dish.

2. Place bread in a large mixing bowl.

3. In a medium saucepan over low heat, whisk together heavy cream, half-and-half, and cocoa powder until warm and bubbling around edges. Add ¹/₂ cup chocolate chips, remove from heat, and stir until melted.

4. In a medium bowl, whisk together eggs and sugar until pale yellow. Slowly whisk in warm chocolate mixture, and pour over bread cubes. Toss gently and set aside to absorb for 20 minutes.

5. Gently stir in remaining ¹/₂ cup chocolate chips and 1 cup raspberries. Transfer to the baking dish, distribute evenly, and bake for about 30 minutes or until custard is set and a toothpick inserted in the center comes out clean.

6. Serve warm with remaining raspberries and whipped cream.

 Smooth Move

Reheat leftover bread pudding in the microwave for 30 seconds to replicate that "just baked" consistency.

Fresh Berry Summer Pudding

This unbaked, low-fat, English-style pudding gets its fiber from white whole-grain bread and its delicious sweetness (and more fiber!) from fresh summer berries.

Yield: 4 servings
Prep time: 30 minutes
Cook time: 5 minutes
Serving size: about 1½ cups
Each serving has:
6 g fiber
320 calories
5 g fat
64 g carbohydrate
5 g protein

1 lb. fresh strawberries, washed, hulled, and roughly chopped

½ cup sugar

1 lb. fresh blueberries, stems removed and rinsed

9 slices white whole-grain bread, crusts removed

Whipped cream

1. Lightly butter a 2-quart round glass bowl.

2. In a medium bowl, combine strawberries with 2 tablespoons sugar. Break down berries slightly with a potato masher or fork, and set aside.

3. In a medium saucepan over medium heat, combine remaining sugar and blueberries, and cook, stirring often, for about 5 minutes or until berries begin to break and sauce is formed. Strain and reserve liquid. Add blueberries to strawberries, and stir to combine.

4. Line the prepared bowl with 6 bread slices, overlapping to cover. Press firmly to seal. Pour berries into bowl, and top with remaining bread slices to cover. Pour reserved blueberry liquid over top, cover with plastic wrap, and place a medium-size plate on top. Press down firmly, and top with a 1- or 2-pound weight, such as a large can. Refrigerate overnight.

5. To unmold, remove weight, plate, and plastic. Cover with a large, rimmed platter and flip over. Lift up glass bowl and spoon excess juices on top of bread to saturate. Serve immediately with whipped cream.

 Grist for the Mill

Crushing fresh fruit with sugar and allowing it to create its own juices is called *maceration*. Sometimes brandy or another type of alcohol is added as well.

Brown Rice Pudding with Raisins and Cinnamon

Creamy and rich rice pudding is made fiberful with nutty brown rice and sweet golden raisins.

2 cups whole milk	**3 cups cooked brown basmati or long-grain rice**
⅓ cup sugar	**2 large eggs, separated**
¾ cup golden raisins	**1 TB. unsalted butter**
1 (3-in.) cinnamon stick	**Ground cinnamon**
1 tsp. vanilla extract	

Yield: 6 servings
Prep time: 10 minutes
Cook time: 20 minutes
Serving size: ⅔ cup
Each serving has:
3 g fiber
310 calories
7 g fat
54 g carbohydrate
8 g protein

1. In a medium saucepan over medium heat, combine 1½ cups milk, sugar, raisins, and cinnamon stick. Bring to a simmer, stirring often, and cook for about 3 minutes or until sugar is dissolved.

2. Stir in vanilla extract and rice, decrease heat to medium-low heat, and cook, stirring often, for about 15 minutes or until thickened and creamy. Reduce heat as necessary to prevent sticking.

3. In a small bowl, whisk together egg yolks with remaining ½ cup milk.

4. In another small bowl, beat egg whites to stiff peaks.

5. Remove cinnamon stick from rice. Slowly stir in egg yolk mixture, and continue to cook over low heat, stirring constantly, for 2 minutes. Remove from heat, stir in butter until melted, and gently fold in egg whites.

6. Transfer to individual pudding cups or a medium serving bowl. Sprinkle with cinnamon, and serve warm or chilled.

 Grist for the Mill

Cinnamon has been shown to help regulate glucose levels as well as remedy toothaches and bad breath.

Crumb-Topped Mince Tarts

Fruitful and nutty mincemeat gets a fiber makeover in these cute little tarts that echo the flavors and spices of the winter holidays.

Yield: 18 tarts
Prep time: 40 minutes
Cook time: 20 minutes
Serving size: 2 tarts
Each serving has:
3 g fiber
245 calories
12 g fat
24 g carbohydrate
8 g protein

1 recipe Easy Whole-Wheat Piecrust (recipe later in this chapter)

1 cup prepared *mincemeat*

½ cup diced, unpeeled apple

¼ cup raisins

¼ cup chopped pecans

Dash ground ginger

¼ cup (½ stick) unsalted butter, diced

¼ firmly packed light brown sugar

½ cup white whole-wheat flour

¼ tsp. ground cinnamon

Confectioners' sugar

1. Preheat the oven to 375°F. Lightly coat 2 mini muffin tins with baking spray.

2. On a lightly floured surface, roll out Easy Whole-Wheat Piecrust to ¹/₈-inch thickness. Use a 2-inch round cutter to make 18 circles. Gather dough and reroll as necessary. Place circles in the muffin tins, pressing into the bottom and up the sides of each muffin cup. Transfer tins to the refrigerator, and chill for 10 minutes.

3. Meanwhile, in a medium bowl, stir together mincemeat, apple, raisins, pecans, and ginger.

4. In another medium bowl, using a fork, combine butter, brown sugar, white whole-wheat flour, and cinnamon until crumbs form.

5. Fill each muffin tin with mincemeat mixture, and top each with a heaping spoonful of crumb mixture, pressing down gently. Bake for about 20 minutes or until tops are lightly golden and filling is bubbly. Cool 15 minutes in tins before carefully removing and transferring to a wire rack. Serve warm or at room temperature, dusted with confectioners' sugar.

Fiber Optics

Mincemeat is a mixture of dried fruit and spices, sometimes also containing liquor. Originally, it always contained beef suet, hence its name, but the beef suet has since been replaced with a solid vegetable oil.

Easy Whole-Wheat Piecrust

Crisp yet flaky, this slightly sweet, wholesome pie crust will fill in nicely for fiber-seeking bakers.

½ **cup whole-wheat flour**

½ **cup all-purpose flour**

¼ **tsp. salt**

1 **TB. sugar**

5 **TB. cold unsalted butter**

3 or 4 **TB. ice-cold water**

Yield: 1 (9-inch) crust
Prep time: 12 minutes
Serving size: ¹/₆ of crust
Each serving has:
2 g fiber
165 calories
10 g fat
17 g carbohydrate
3 g protein

1. In a medium bowl, whisk together whole-wheat flour, all-purpose flour, salt, and sugar.

2. Cut butter into flour mixture with a pastry blender, or use a food processor, pulsing on and off until mixture resembles coarse meal.

3. Add water, 1 tablespoon at a time, stirring or processing until dough comes together.

4. Form dough into a disc, wrap in plastic, and refrigerate for at least 2 hours before rolling out on a floured surface.

 Smooth Move

Make double or triple the recipe and keep extra crust portions frozen for later use. Defrost overnight in the refrigerator.

Nutty Pecan Crust

Sweet and delicious pecans are the base for this easy crust that's prebaked and ready for any creamy, rich filling.

Yield: 1 (9-inch)
deep-dish crust
Prep time: 5 minutes
Cook time: 12 minutes
Serving size: ¹⁄₆ of crust
Each serving has:
2 g fiber
255 calories
21 g fat
15 g carbohydrate
2 g protein

2½ cups ground pecans

⅓ cup sugar

¼ tsp. ground cinnamon

4 TB. unsalted butter, melted

1. In a medium bowl, whisk together ground pecans, sugar, and cinnamon. Stir in melted butter to moisten.

2. Press evenly into a 9-inch deep-dish pie pan, up the sides and on the bottom. Chill for 40 minutes.

3. Preheat the oven to 350°F.

4. Bake crust for 10 to 12 minutes or until lightly browned. Do not overbake. Cool completely before filling.

Grist for the Mill

The word *pecan* comes from the Native American Algonquin language and means "requiring a stone to crack." Must have been a pretty tough nut!

Bananarama Cream Pie

A silky smooth and superlicious treat featuring sweet, ripe bananas and a cool, creamy custard, this pie is guaranteed to please.

1 cup granulated sugar

3 large eggs, beaten

3 TB. cornstarch

2 cups milk

Pinch salt

1 tsp. vanilla extract

1 cup heavy whipping cream

3 TB. confectioners' sugar

3 large ripe bananas, sliced

1 recipe Nutty Pecan Crust, baked (recipe earlier in this chapter)

Yield: 1 (9-inch) deep-dish pie
Prep time: 20 minutes
Cook time: 6 minutes
Serving size: ¹/₆ of pie
Each serving has:
4 g fiber
560 calories
31 g fat
65 g carbohydrate
9 g protein

1. In a medium bowl, whisk together sugar and eggs until slightly pale yellow. Add cornstarch, milk, and salt. Whisk to combine.

2. Transfer to a medium saucepan over medium-high heat, and cook, stirring constantly, for about 6 minutes or until thickened. Remove from heat and stir in vanilla extract. Transfer to a clean bowl, cover surface with plastic wrap, allow to cool slightly, and transfer to the refrigerator and chill for 1 hour.

3. In a medium bowl, and using a mixer on high, beat whipping cream, adding confectioners' sugar a little at a time, until soft peaks form. Gently fold ¹/₂ of whipped cream into pudding mixture. Refrigerate remaining whipped cream.

4. Place ¹/₂ of sliced bananas on bottom of piecrust, spoon ¹/₂ of pudding mixture over, and repeat with remaining bananas and pudding. Cover top decoratively with remaining whipped cream, and chill pie for at least 3 hours before serving.

 Grist for the Mill

Cornstarch is always added to a cold liquid for quick dissolving without lumps. It must be cooked, however, before it reaches its full thickening power.

Variation: This one's for you chocoholics: melt together 4 ounces semisweet chocolate chips with ¹/₄ cup heavy cream and 1 tablespoon unsalted butter. Pour all but 1 tablespoon into the bottom of baked nut crust and chill before continuing with recipe. Drizzle remaining chocolate mixture over top of pie before serving.

Almond-Streusel Pumpkin Pie

A sweet and crunchy streusel tops this velvety-smooth, sweetly spiced fiber-rich pumpkin favorite.

Yield: 1 (9-inch) pie
Prep time: 30 minutes
Cook time: 60 minutes
Serving size: 1/6 of pie
Each serving has:
5 g fiber
470 calories
20 g fat
65 g carbohydrate
9 g protein

**1 frozen (9-in.) piecrust or
1 recipe Easy Whole-Wheat
Piecrust**

1 (15-oz.) can pure pumpkin

**1 cup firmly packed light
brown sugar**

1 tsp. ground cinnamon

¼ tsp. ground ginger

⅛ tsp. ground nutmeg

Pinch ground cloves

¼ tsp. salt

3 large eggs

**1¼ cups heavy whipping
cream**

**⅓ cup white whole-wheat
flour**

**2 TB. cold, unsalted butter,
diced**

**½ cup sliced almonds,
roughly crumbled**

Confectioners' sugar

 Smooth Move

Any streusel topping recipe can be made fiber friendly by substituting whole-wheat flour for all-purpose flour and adding chopped nuts. Try it on cakes, pies, and baked fruit desserts.

1. If using Easy Whole-Wheat Piecrust, roll out crust, transfer to a 9-inch pie dish, and chill for 20 minutes.

2. Preheat the oven to 375°F.

3. Line chilled piecrust with parchment paper and weigh down with dry beans or pie weights. Bake for about 15 minutes or until set and just beginning to show color. Remove paper and weights and set aside. Reduce the oven temperature to 350°F.

4. In a medium bowl, beat together pumpkin, ¾ cup brown sugar, ½ teaspoon cinnamon, ginger, nutmeg, cloves, and salt. Add eggs 1 at a time and beat in. Add cream and beat well to combine. Pour into prepared piecrust.

5. In a small bowl, whisk together flour, remaining ¼ cup brown sugar, and remaining ½ teaspoon cinnamon. Cut in butter with a fork or pastry blender, and stir in almonds. Sprinkle streusel on top of pumpkin filling, and bake for about 1 hour or until browned and set.

6. Cool completely and dust with confectioners' sugar before slicing and serving.

Apple-Walnut Pie

America's favorite pie gets fiber conscious with a hearty double whole-wheat crust and sweet, crunchy, glazed walnuts.

2 recipes Easy Whole-Wheat Piecrust (recipe earlier in this chapter)

8 Granny Smith apples, peeled, cored, and cut into ¼-in. slices

⅔ cup sugar

1 tsp. lemon juice

1 tsp. ground cinnamon

1 TB. all-purpose flour

1 cup sugar-glazed walnuts

Yield: 1 (9-inch) deep-dish pie
Prep time: 30 minutes
Cook time: 60 minutes
Serving size: ⅙ of pie
Each serving has:
7 g fiber
510 calories
28 g fat
55 g carbohydrate
10 g protein

1. Preheat the oven to 375°F.

2. Roll out 1 disc of piecrust dough on a floured surface to 10 inches round, and carefully transfer to a pie pan. Crimp edges and patch dough where necessary. Refrigerate for 15 minutes.

3. Meanwhile, roll out other disc of piecrust dough for top and set aside.

4. In a large bowl, combine apples, sugar, lemon juice, cinnamon, and flour, tossing gently to coat apples. Stir in glazed walnuts.

5. Transfer apple mixture to chilled piecrust and arrange apples evenly. Place top dough on apple mixture, and pinch together both crusts at edges to seal. Cut 3 small slits in center of pie, and bake for 50 to 60 minutes or until crust is golden and apples are fork-tender. Cover edges of crust loosely with foil if necessary to prevent overbrowning.

6. Cool on a wire rack at least 1 hour before slicing and serving.

Grist for the Mill

Walnuts are one of the few plant-based sources of omega-3 fatty acid, an essential nutrient most commonly found in fish.

Chapter 23

Cakes, Cookies, and Bars

In This Chapter

◆ Indulgent, delicious cakes

◆ Cookie jar favorites

◆ Fiber-rich fruit and grain bars

When you think about your favorite cakes and cookies, do you assume they can't possibly fit into your fiber plan? Have you written off moist cakes with creamy frosting, fudgy brownies, and rich, sweet cookies?

There's no need to moan and groan any longer. In this chapter, you find that many of your favorite goodies are still on the menu, and tasting better than ever!

Picking Flours

By substituting traditional white flour with fiberful flours like whole wheat and white whole wheat, you're headed in the right direction for a sweet yet healthful indulgence. In addition, utilizing the fiber content of fruits, nuts, oats, and even cocoa powder helps bring you even closer to your goal.

From carrot cake cupcakes to old-fashioned fig bars, you'll be baking up a storm of delicious, rich treats that are a far cry from bland and dry high-fiber sweets you may have tried in the past. Who knew they could taste so great?

Cuckoo for Cocoa Powder

The key to delectable high-fiber baking is taking advantage of the qualities of your ingredients. Bananas and applesauce, although fiberful, also impart moisture. Dried fruit and nuts, also good sources of fiber, contribute chewiness and crunch. The final result happily reflects all these desirable qualities, which are important for successful baking.

So you see, it's not such a difficult prospect after all. Besides, any healthy recipe that calls for cocoa powder in abundance has got to be a good thing, right?

Carrot Cake Cupcakes

Sweet carrots, coconut, and pineapple add fiber, moistness, and flavor to these tasty cakes topped with a creamy frosting.

1 cup granulated sugar

½ cup vegetable oil

2 large eggs

½ cup white whole-wheat flour

½ cup all-purpose flour

1 tsp. baking soda

¾ tsp. ground cinnamon

½ tsp. salt

¼ tsp. ground nutmeg

2 (8-oz.) cans crushed pineapple, drained

1 cup peeled and grated carrots

¾ cup sweetened flaked coconut

1 (8-oz.) pkg. light cream cheese

4 TB. unsalted butter, softened

1 tsp. lemon juice

2½ cups confectioners' sugar

¼ cup chopped walnuts

Yield: 1 dozen cupcakes
Prep time: 30 minutes
Cook time: 20 minutes
Serving size: 1 cupcake
Each serving has:
2 g fiber
325 calories
15 g fat
40 g carbohydrate
6 g protein

1. Preheat the oven to 350°F. Line a 12-cup muffin pan with cupcake liners.

2. In a large bowl, beat together sugar and vegetable oil. Add eggs and beat well to combine.

3. In a medium bowl, whisk together white whole-wheat flour, all-purpose flour, baking soda, cinnamon, salt, and nutmeg. Beat flour mixture into egg mixture until just combined.

4. Stir in pineapple, carrots, and coconut, and spoon batter into muffin cups. Bake for about 20 minutes or until golden and a toothpick inserted in the center comes out clean. Remove cupcakes from the pan and cool completely on a wire rack.

5. *For frosting:* in a medium bowl, beat together cream cheese and butter until smooth. Add lemon juice, and beat 1 minute more. Add confectioners' sugar, ½ cup at a time, beating well after each addition.

6. Spread frosting on cupcakes, and sprinkle tops with walnuts. Keep refrigerated.

 Grist for the Mill

Coconut water, the liquid found inside a fresh coconut, contains a surprisingly high level of fiber. It's consumed as a refreshing drink in the tropics and is good for replenishing potassium, an important electrolyte, after rigorous exercise.

Banana-Chocolate-Chip Cake

This delicious snacking cake, moist and flavorful from ripe bananas and deliciously dotted with chocolate chips and nuts, will satisfy everyone's desire for something sweet.

Yield: 9 servings
Prep time: 15 minutes
Cook time: 40 minutes
Serving size: 1 (3-inch-square) piece
Each serving has:
3 g fiber
380 calories
20 g fat
45 g carbohydrate
5 g protein

½ cup vegetable oil

¾ cup sugar

2 large eggs, slightly beaten

1½ tsp. vanilla extract

1½ cups mashed ripe bananas (about 2 large)

1 cup all-purpose flour

½ cup whole-wheat flour

1 tsp. baking powder

½ tsp. baking soda

½ tsp. ground cinnamon

½ tsp. salt

¾ cup mini semisweet chocolate chips

½ cup chopped pecans

1. Preheat the oven to 350°F. Grease a 9-inch-square cake pan.

2. In a large bowl, beat together vegetable oil and sugar. Add eggs and vanilla extract, beating well to combine. Stir in bananas.

3. In a medium bowl, whisk together all-purpose flour, whole-wheat flour, baking powder, baking soda, cinnamon, and salt. Add flour mixture to banana mixture in 2 batches, stirring each time just to combine.

4. Stir in chocolate chips and pecans, pour into prepared baking pan, and spread evenly. Bake for 35 to 40 minutes or until light golden and a toothpick inserted in the center comes out clean. Cool on a wire rack before slicing and serving.

 Smooth Move _____

To increase fiber and nutrition in your baking recipes, you can substitute up to ⅓ of the white flour called for with whole-wheat flour without a noticeable change in taste and texture.

Spanish Bar Cake

This moist, delicious spice cake, once limited to supermarket bakeries, gets the home cook's fiber seal of approval for terrific texture and taste.

1 cup white whole-wheat flour

1 cup all-purpose flour

1½ cups granulated sugar

1½ tsp. baking soda

1 TB. unsweetened cocoa powder

¾ tsp salt

1 tsp. ground cinnamon

1 tsp. nutmeg

1 tsp. allspice

½ cup vegetable oil

2 cups applesauce

2 large eggs

1½ cups *baking raisins*

5 TB. unsalted butter, softened

1 tsp. vanilla extract

3 TB. milk

3 cups confectioners' sugar or to taste

Yield: 1 (2-layer) bar cake		
Prep time: 20 minutes		
Cook time: 35 minutes		
Serving size: ⅛ of cake		
Each serving has:		
4 g fiber		
580 calories		
20 g fat		
85 g carbohydrate		
6 g protein		

1. Preheat the oven to 350°F. Grease a 9×13-inch cake pan.

2. In a large bowl, whisk together white whole-wheat flour, all-purpose flour, sugar, baking soda, cocoa powder, salt, cinnamon, nutmeg, and allspice.

3. In another large bowl, beat together vegetable oil, applesauce, and eggs.

4. Add flour mixture to oil mixture in batches, beating well after each addition. Stir in raisins, and pour into prepared baking pan, spreading out evenly. Bake for 30 to 35 minutes or until a toothpick inserted in the center comes out clean. Cool completely in pan on a wire rack.

5. *For frosting:* in a medium bowl, beat together butter, vanilla extract, and milk until smooth. Add confectioners' sugar, 1 cup at a time, beating well after each addition. Add more sugar, if necessary, to reach a spreadable consistency.

6. Loosen edges of cake with a sharp knife and cut into 2 length-wise pieces. Remove 1 piece using 2 metal spatulas, and transfer to a platter. Spread $1/2$ of frosting over cake (not on sides), and place other $1/2$ of cake on top. Spread remaining frosting on top (again not on sides), and decorate by running the tines of a fork lengthwise down frosting.

7. Chill for 1 hour before slicing. Keep any leftover cake refrigerated.

Fiber Optics

Baking raisins have been preplumped for recipes, so they have a moister texture. To plump raisins yourself, let regular raisins stand in boiling water for 10 minutes, drain, and pat dry.

Nutz for Peanuts Drop Cookies

If you love peanuts, you'll adore these chunky and chewy treats, especially when they're warm and gooey from the oven.

½ cup chunky peanut butter

½ cup (1 stick) unsalted butter, softened

½ cup granulated sugar

½ cup firmly packed light brown sugar

1 large egg

1 cup all-purpose flour

¼ cup whole-wheat flour

¾ tsp. baking soda

½ tsp. baking powder

1 cup lightly salted peanuts

½ cup milk chocolate chunks or chips

Yield: about 3 dozen
Prep time: 15 minutes
Cook time: 10 minutes
Serving size: 3 cookies
Each serving has:
4 g fiber
350 calories
21 g fat
32 g carbohydrate
8 g protein

1. Preheat the oven to 375°F.

2. In a large bowl, beat together peanut butter, butter, sugar, and brown sugar until light and fluffy. Add egg and beat well to combine.

3. In a medium bowl, whisk together all-purpose flour, whole-wheat flour, baking soda, and baking powder. Add flour mixture to peanut butter mixture in 2 batches, beating well after each addition. Stir in peanuts and chocolate chunks.

4. Drop batter in heaping tablespoonfuls onto a nonstick cookie sheet, spacing them 2 inches apart. Flatten slightly with the back of a fork. Bake for 8 to 11 minutes or until set and lightly golden around edges. Let rest for 2 minutes, and transfer to a wire rack to cool. Repeat with remaining dough. Store cooled cookies in an airtight container for up to 5 days.

 Grist for the Mill

Peanuts are a good source of resveratrol, the same phytochemical found in red wine that can reduce the risk of cancer and heart disease.

Whole-Wheat-Orange Shortbread

Nutty, tender, and not too sweet, with a delicious hint of fresh orange, these cookies are terrific with your next cup of tea.

Yield: 2 dozen	

Prep time: 10 minutes

Cook time: 20 minutes

Serving size: 3 cookies

Each serving has:

3 g fiber

225 calories

15 g fat

19 g carbohydrate

3 g protein

2 cups whole-wheat flour

½ cup *raw sugar*

1 tsp. salt

2 tsp. finely grated orange zest

1 cup (2 sticks) unsalted butter, diced

1. Preheat the oven to 350°F. Line a large baking sheet with parchment paper.

2. In a food processor, combine whole-wheat flour, raw sugar, salt, and orange zest, and pulse several times. Add diced butter, and pulse on and off until dough comes together but is still crumbly.

3. Turn out dough onto a clean work surface, and shape into 2 (6-inch-long) logs. Slice logs into ¹/₂-inch-thick circles and transfer to baking sheet. Use a fork to poke several holes in each cookie, and bake for 15 to 20 minutes or until golden brown. Transfer to a wire rack to cool completely, and store in an airtight container for up to 1 week.

Fiber Optics

Raw sugar, also called turbinado sugar, is crystallized from the initial pressing of sugar cane, retaining some of the natural molasses flavor.

Deep Chocolate Brownies

Brownies with fiber? You bet! Fudgy, moist, and deeply chocolaty, you'll get rave reviews with these extra-special delights.

1 cup (2 sticks) unsalted butter	1 tsp. vanilla extract
2 cups firmly packed dark brown sugar	1½ cups whole-wheat flour
¾ cup unsweetened cocoa powder	1 tsp. baking powder
	1 tsp. salt
4 large eggs, slightly beaten	1 cup bittersweet chocolate chips
	½ cup chopped walnuts

> *Yield: 12 large brownies*
>
> **Prep time:** 20 minutes
> **Cook time:** 30 minutes
> **Serving size:** 1 (3-inch-square) brownie
>
> **Each serving has:**
> 5 g fiber
> 450 calories
> 27 g fat
> 46 g carbohydrate
> 6 g protein

1. Preheat the oven to 350°F. Lightly grease a 9×13-inch baking pan.

2. In the top of a double boiler over medium heat, melt butter and brown sugar, stirring often, until sugar is dissolved. Whisk in cocoa powder, remove from heat, transfer to a large bowl, and set aside to cool for 10 minutes.

3. Add eggs and vanilla extract to warm chocolate mixture, and whisk to combine.

4. In a small bowl, whisk together whole-wheat flour, baking powder, and salt. Add to chocolate mixture, and stir with a wooden spoon until smooth. Add chocolate chips and walnuts, stir to combine, and pour into the prepared baking pan, spreading evenly.

5. Bake for about 30 minutes or until a toothpick inserted in the center comes out with wet crumbs and top appears set. Cool completely on a wire rack before cutting into squares. Keep in an airtight container for up to 4 days.

 Smooth Move

If you don't have a double boiler, you can rig one by placing a stainless-steel bowl over a saucepan of simmering water.

Rolled Oat and Raisin Bars

Hearty, chewy, and oh so delicious, you may be tempted to grab a few of these oatmeal bars at breakfast time!

Yield: 24 bars
Prep time: 25 minutes
Cook time: 40 minutes
Serving size: 2 bars
Each serving has:
9 g fiber
465 calories
15 g fat
70 g carbohydrate
12 g protein

4 cups old-fashioned rolled oats

1 cup white whole-wheat flour

1 cup all-purpose flour

½ cup firmly packed light brown sugar

1 cup chopped walnuts

1 tsp. baking soda

1 tsp. salt

½ tsp. ground cinnamon

1½ cups (3 sticks) unsalted butter, melted

2 tsp. vanilla extract

1 cup raisins

1 cup golden raisins

½ cup water

Dash nutmeg

1. Preheat the oven to 350°F. Grease a 9×13-inch baking dish.

2. In a large bowl, stir together rolled oats, whole-wheat flour, all-purpose flour, brown sugar, walnuts, baking soda, salt, and cinnamon. Add melted butter and vanilla extract, and stir well to combine. Set aside.

3. In a medium saucepan, combine raisins, golden raisins, water, and nutmeg. Bring to a boil, reduce heat to low, and cook, stirring occasionally, for 3 minutes.

4. Transfer to a food processor and pulse a few times to chop, but not purée. Strain to remove any excess liquid.

5. Put ¹/₂ of oat mixture in the prepared baking dish, and press down evenly with your fingers. Spread raisins over top, and place remaining oat mixture on top of raisins, pressing down to cover and form an even surface.

6. Bake for 35 to 45 minutes or until browned on top. Cool on a wire rack completely before cutting into bars. Store in an airtight container for up to 4 days.

 Grist for the Mill

Sowing your oats? In addition to fiber, oats are a good source of thiamine (B_1), which can be depleted if you consume lots of alcohol.

Whole-Grain Fig Bars

When compared to commercial versions, these figgy treats made with whole-wheat flour win in the fiber and flavor departments, hands down.

⅓ cup unsalted butter, softened

1 cup firmly packed light brown sugar

2 large eggs

1 tsp. vanilla extract

1¼ cups whole-wheat flour

1¼ cups all-purpose flour

¼ tsp. baking soda

2 tsp. baking powder

¼ tsp. salt

1 (8-oz.) pkg. dried figs, stems removed, roughly chopped

½ cup water

¼ cup orange juice

3 TB. granulated sugar

Yield: 24 bars
Prep time: 30 minutes
Cook time: 15 minutes
Serving size: 2 bars
Each serving has:
3 g fiber
215 calories
6 g fat
37 g carbohydrate
3 g protein

1. In a large bowl, beat together butter and brown sugar until fluffy. Add eggs and vanilla extract, and beat until well combined.

2. In a medium bowl, whisk together whole-wheat flour, all-purpose flour, baking soda, baking powder, and salt. Add in 2 batches to egg mixture, beating well after each addition.

3. Transfer dough to a floured surface, form into a disc, wrap in plastic, and refrigerate for 2 hours.

4. Meanwhile, for filling: in a medium saucepan over medium-high heat, combine figs, water, orange juice, and sugar. Bring to a boil, reduce heat to medium-low, and simmer, stirring often, until thickened, about 7 minutes. Set aside to cool for 15 minutes.

5. Transfer to a blender or food processor, and purée until smooth. Transfer to a small bowl, and chill completely in the refrigerator.

6. Preheat the oven to 375°F. Line a large, rimmed baking sheet with parchment paper.

7. Roll out dough on a lightly floured surface into a 12-inch square. Using a pizza cutter dipped in flour, cut dough into 6 equal rectangles.

8. Spoon $\frac{1}{6}$ of filling lengthwise down the center of each rectangle, and fold edges in to meet, pinching them together. Transfer bars seam side down to baking sheet, 2 inches apart. Using the pizza cutter, cut each rectangle into 4 bars without separating them.

9. Bake for 13 to 16 minutes or until golden and puffed. Cool on the pan for 10 minutes, separate bars, and transfer to a wire rack to cool completely. Store in an airtight container for up to 1 week.

Grist for the Mill

Figs contain the highest quantity of fiber of any dried or fresh fruit, boasting nearly 3 grams per individual fruit.

Easy Honey Granola Bars

Use your favorite granola to make these crunchy, satisfying treats flavored with golden honey and your choice of nuts and fruit.

1 cup granola

1 cup quick-cooking oats

½ cup cashew pieces

½ cup dried cranberries

½ cup all-purpose flour

1 large egg, beaten

⅓ cup honey

⅓ cup vegetable oil

¼ cup firmly packed light brown sugar

Yield: 12 bars	
Prep time: 15 minutes	
Cook time: 30 minutes	
Serving size: 1 bar	
Each serving has:	
3 g fiber	
230 calories	
10 g fat	
30 g carbohydrate	
5 g protein	

1. Preheat the oven to 325°F. Grease a 9-inch-square baking pan, and line the bottom with parchment paper, cut to fit.

2. In a medium bowl, combine granola, oats, cashews, cranberries, and flour.

3. In a small bowl, whisk together egg, honey, vegetable oil, and brown sugar. Pour into granola mixture, and stir well to combine.

4. Transfer mixture to the prepared baking pan, pressing down and smoothing over top. Bake for 25 to 30 minutes or until lightly browned on edges.

5. Cool completely on a wire rack, flip out onto a cutting board, remove paper, and cut into 12 bars. Keep in an airtight container or individually wrapped in plastic for up to 1 week.

Variation: Instead of cashews and dried cranberries, feel free to substitute your favorite nuts and dried fruit.

 Smooth Move

Quick-cooking oats are great to add to cookie recipes (even chocolate chip!) for extra fiber and texture. Just a few tablespoons make the difference.

Parfaits, Sundaes, and Sorbets

In This Chapter

◆ Warm fruit parfaits

◆ Sundaes with attitude

◆ Cool, rich sorbets

Ice-cream parlor fans will scream with delight after tasting the creamy, rich desserts in this chapter of sweet endings. Whether vanilla, chocolate, or strawberry is your flavor of choice (not to mention coconut, rocky road, or butter pecan), you'll find the perfect parfait, sundae, or sorbet to meet your expectations.

Once again, fruit is an integral part of fiber-rich desserts, and in these pages you'll see nothing less than a plethora of creative ways to include it in your repertoire. From caramel-drenched sautéed pears to the best strawberry sorbet ever, high-fiber desserts that cool and soothe will never be the same. A kicked-up banana split will satisfy even the most gigantic of appetites, while chocolate-hazelnut sorbet just might make you purr with pleasure.

Your Right to Partake

Frozen desserts such as sorbets are perfect venues for fruit as they incorporate much more fiber than you'd normally find in, say, a strawberry ice cream that's mostly dairy. They are also wonderfully refreshing and can be the perfect ending to a meal.

Creamy yet light, they provide the ideal finishing touch for a day in fiber land—and a well-deserved one at that!

Caramel, Pear, and Pine Nut Parfait

Sweet, buttery caramel enfolds succulent pears in this delicious dessert fit for special occasions but easy enough to prepare any day of the week.

4 medium ripe but firm *Bosc pears*, peeled and halved

¼ cup unsalted butter (½ stick)

¼ cup honey

2 TB. pine nuts

2 cups vanilla ice cream

Yield: 4 servings
Prep time: 10 minutes
Cook time: 14 minutes
Serving size: 1 pear
Each serving has:
2 g fiber
275 calories
15 g fat
32 g carbohydrate
3 g protein

1. Using a melon baller, remove core and trim bottom from each pear half, leaving stems intact.

2. In a large, nonstick skillet over medium heat, melt butter and whisk in honey. Add pears, cut side down, reduce heat to low, and cook, occasionally spooning sauce over pears, for about 12 minutes or until pears are fork-tender.

3. Meanwhile, toast pine nuts in a small, dry skillet over high heat, shaking the pan often. Set aside.

4. Using tongs, transfer pear halves to serving dishes, cut side up.

5. Increase heat to medium-high, and cook sauce for about 2 minutes or until sauce is bubbling and caramel-colored.

6. Scoop ½ cup ice cream on top of pears in each serving dish, and spoon sauce evenly over. Sprinkle pine nuts on top, and serve immediately.

 Fiber Optics

Bosc pears have long, tapered necks and russet-colored skin. They're denser and crisper than other varieties of pears, making them ideal for cooking.

Roasted Peach Parfait

Heightened sweetness and color are the result of roasting in this peachy delight of a dessert flavored with almonds and highlighted with tender, fresh raspberries.

4 ripe medium peaches	**⅔ cup fresh raspberries**
2 tsp. vegetable oil	**¼ cup sliced almonds**
2 cups vanilla ice cream	**Whipped cream (optional)**
¼ cup amaretto syrup	

Yield: 4 servings
Prep time: 10 minutes
Cook time: 45 minutes
Serving size: 1 peach
Each serving has:
3 g fiber
200 calories
8 g fat
30 g carbohydrate
3 g protein

1. Preheat the oven to 400°F.

2. Lightly coat whole peaches with vegetable oil, and place in a medium roasting pan. Roast for 45 minutes, occasionally shaking the pan to brown evenly. Allow peaches to cool until easily handled, and peel off skins. Pit and slice each peach into 6 wedges.

3. Scoop ½ cup ice cream into 4 parfait or wine glasses. Arrange peaches around the sides, and pour syrup over top. Top with raspberries, almonds, and a dollop of whipped cream (if using).

 Smooth Move _____

Look for amaretto and other nut-flavored syrups in the coffee aisle of your supermarket. Or use amaretto liqueur.

The Best Banana Split Sundae

An old-fashioned favorite gets a fiber makeover in this creamy, warm, and gooey sundae with caramelized bananas.

2 ripe medium bananas, peeled and halved lengthwise

4 tsp. dark brown sugar

1 cup butter pecan ice cream

1 cup vanilla ice cream

1 cup rocky road ice cream

¼ cup chocolate-covered peanuts

½ cup chocolate sauce, warmed

¼ cup whipped cream

¼ cup granola

Yield: 2 servings	
Prep time: 10 minutes	
Cook time: 2 minutes	
Serving size: 1 sundae	
Each serving has:	
7 g fiber	
750 calories	
25 g fat	
120 g carbohydrate	
10 g protein	

1. Preheat the oven broiler to high.

2. Place bananas, cut side up, on a baking sheet and sprinkle each half with 1 teaspoon brown sugar. Broil for about 2 minutes or until sugar melts and darkens. Transfer to 2 banana split dishes, caramelized side up.

3. Scoop ½ cup butter pecan ice cream, vanilla ice cream, and rocky road ice cream on top, and sprinkle with peanuts. Pour chocolate sauce over, top with whipped cream, and sprinkle with granola. Serve immediately.

Grist for the Mill

The banana split was invented by an apprentice at Tassel Pharmacy in Latrobe, Pennsylvania, in 1904. It cost 10 cents.

Hawaiian Pineapple Sundae

Fruit flavors of the tropics shine in this colorful and tangy sundae featuring sweet, fresh pineapple.

Yield: 4 servings
Prep time: 15 minutes
Cook time: 5 minutes
Serving size: 1 sundae
Each serving has:
4 g fiber
400 calories
12 g fat
44 g carbohydrate
3 g protein

2 cups fresh cubed pineapple

½ cup pineapple juice

1 TB. sugar

2 cups mango sorbet

2 cups vanilla ice cream

1 kiwi, peeled and diced

¼ cup dried banana chips

3 TB. shredded coconut, toasted

1. In a medium saucepan over medium-high heat, combine pineapple, pineapple juice, and sugar. Bring to a boil, cover, reduce heat to low, and cook, stirring often, for 5 minutes.

2. Transfer mixture to a food processor fitted with a steel blade, and pulse several times to chop—but not purée—mixture. Return mixture to the saucepan and keep warm.

3. Scoop ½ cup mango sorbet and vanilla ice cream into each of 4 sundae glasses. Spoon warm pineapple sauce over, and sprinkle with diced kiwi, banana chips, and coconut. Serve immediately.

 Smooth Move

To toast coconut, heat it in a dry skillet over medium-high heat, shaking the pan often, until lightly golden. For larger quantities, spread out on a rimmed baking sheet and cook in a preheated 350°F oven, stirring often, for 10 to 15 minutes.

Whole-Fruit Strawberry Sorbet

Smooth and creamy without a trace of fat, this easy-to-make sorbet with the intense flavor of strawberry is a heavenly end to any meal.

2 large egg whites

¼ tsp. cream of tartar

⅓ cup sugar

1 tsp. vanilla extract

½ cup light corn syrup

1 (16-oz.) bag frozen strawberries, thawed

1 cup diced fresh ripe strawberries

Yield: 6 servings
Prep time: 20 minutes
Serving size: about 1 cup
Each serving has:
3 g fiber
170 calories
0 g fat
40 g carbohydrate
2 g protein

1. In a large bowl, and using a mixer on high, beat egg whites and cream of tartar for 1 or 2 minutes or until soft peaks form. Gradually beat in sugar, and continue beating for about 2 minutes or until stiff peaks form. Beat in vanilla extract.

2. Slowly pour in corn syrup, beating on high speed, scraping the sides of the bowl often, for about 3 minutes or until very thick. Chill in the refrigerator for 15 minutes.

3. Purée thawed strawberries in a blender or food processor until smooth. Add to egg white mixture, and stir well to combine. Stir in fresh strawberries, and transfer to a clean bowl. Cover the surface with plastic wrap, and freeze for at least 3 hours before scooping and serving.

Smooth Move

If consuming raw egg whites is a problem (because of the risk of salmonella, this isn't recommended for pregnant women, babies, and the elderly), use the equivalent amount of meringue powder or pasteurized egg whites.

Coconut-Macadamia Sorbet

Fiberful coconut is featured in this creamy and delicious sorbet studded with toasted coconut and nuts.

Yield: 8 servings
Prep time: 10 minutes
Serving size: about ¹/₂ cup
Each serving has:
6 g fiber
350 calories
30 g fat
13 g carbohydrate
5 g protein

2 (15-oz.) cans *cream of coco-nut* such as Coco López

1½ cups ice-cold water

2 TB. fresh lime juice

⅔ cup shredded coconut, toasted and finely chopped

½ cup unsalted macadamia nuts, roughly chopped

1. In a large bowl, whisk together cream of coconut, ice water, and lime juice.

2. Pour into an ice-cream maker, and process, following the manufacturer's directions, until smooth and thick. Transfer to a bowl, and stir in toasted coconut and macadamia nuts. Cover the surface with plastic wrap, and freeze for at least 2 hours before serving.

Fiber Optics _____

Cream of coconut is an infusion of shredded coconut and water or milk. It's denser and sweeter than coconut milk.

Chocolate-Hazelnut Sorbet

Rich, intensely flavored, and undeniably decadent, this sorbet will satisfy any chocolate cravings.

2 cups water

1 cup sugar

¾ cup unsweetened cocoa powder

2 TB. hazelnut syrup

10 pieces (5 oz.) chocolate hazelnut candies, such as Perugina Baci, roughly chopped

Yield: 8 servings
Prep time: 15 minutes
Cook time: 2 minutes
Serving size: about ½ cup
Each serving has:
6 g fiber
350 calories
10 g fat
52 g carbohydrate
3 g protein

1. In a large saucepan over medium-high heat, whisk together water, sugar, and cocoa powder. Bring to a boil, and cook, whisking, for about 1 minute or until sugar is melted. Remove from heat and stir in hazelnut syrup. Transfer to a bowl, cover, and refrigerate until well chilled.

2. Pour into an ice-cream maker, and process, following the manufacturer's directions, until smooth and thick. Transfer to a clean bowl, stir in chopped candies, cover with plastic wrap, and freeze at least 2 hours before serving.

 Smooth Move

Always store leftover homemade ice creams and sorbets in airtight containers to prevent ice crystals from forming.

Glossary

al dente Italian for "against the teeth." Refers to pasta or rice that's neither soft nor hard, but just slightly firm against the teeth.

all-purpose flour Flour that contains only the inner part of the wheat grain.

almonds Mild, sweet, and crunchy nuts that combine nicely with creamy and sweet food items.

amaretto A popular almond liqueur.

anchovies (also **sardines**) Tiny, flavorful preserved fish that typically come in cans. Anchovies are a traditional garnish for Caesar salad, the dressing of which contains anchovy paste.

arborio rice A plump Italian rice used, among other purposes, for risotto.

artichoke hearts The center part of the artichoke flower, often found canned in grocery stores.

arugula A spicy-peppery garden plant with leaves that resemble a dandelion and have a distinct and very sharp flavor.

au gratin The quick broiling of a dish before serving, to brown the top ingredients. When used in a recipe name, the term often implies cheese and a creamy sauce.

baby corn This small version of corn on the cob, eaten whole, is a popular ingredient in Southeast Asian–style cooking.

bake To cook in a dry oven. Dry-heat cooking often results in a crisping of the exterior of the food being cooked. Moist-heat cooking, through methods such as steaming, poaching, etc., brings a much different, moist quality to the food.

balsamic vinegar Vinegar produced primarily in Italy from a specific type of grape, and aged in wood barrels. It's heavier, darker, and sweeter than most vinegars.

barbecue To quick-cook over high heat, or to cook something long and slow in a rich liquid (barbecue sauce).

basil A flavorful, almost sweet, resinous herb, delicious with tomatoes and used in all kinds of Italian or Mediterranean-style dishes.

baste To keep foods moist during cooking by spooning, brushing, or drizzling with a liquid.

beat To quickly mix substances.

black pepper A biting and pungent seasoning, freshly ground pepper is a must for many dishes, and adds an extra level of flavor and taste.

blanch To place a food in boiling water for about 1 minute (or less) to partially cook the exterior, and then submerge in or rinse with cool water to halt the cooking.

blend To completely mix something, usually with a blender or food processor, more slowly than beating.

blue cheese A blue-veined cheese that crumbles easily and has a somewhat soft texture, usually sold in a block. The color is from a flavorful, edible mold that's often added or injected into the cheese.

boil To heat a liquid to a point where water is forced to turn into steam, causing the liquid to bubble. To boil something is to insert it into boiling water. A rapid boil is when a lot of bubbles form on the surface of the liquid.

bok choy (also **Chinese cabbage**) A member of the cabbage family with thick stems, crisp texture, and fresh flavor. It's perfect for stir-frying.

braise To cook with the introduction of some liquid, usually over an extended period of time.

breadcrumbs Tiny pieces of crumbled dry bread, often used for topping or coating.

Brie A creamy cow's milk cheese from France with a soft, edible rind and a mild flavor.

brine A highly salted, often seasoned, liquid used to flavor and preserve foods. To brine a food is to soak or preserve it by submerging it in brine. The salt in the brine penetrates the fibers of the meat and makes it moist and tender.

broil To cook in a dry oven under the overhead high-heat element.

broth *See* stock.

brown rice Whole-grain rice including the germ with a characteristic pale brown or tan color. It's more nutritious and flavorful than white rice.

brown To cook in a skillet, turning, until the food's surface is seared and brown in color, to lock in the juices.

bruschetta (or **crostini**) Slices of toasted or grilled bread with garlic and olive oil, often with other toppings.

bulgur A wheat kernel that's been steamed, dried, and crushed and sold in fine and coarse textures.

Cajun cooking A style of cooking that combines French and Southern characteristics and includes many highly seasoned stews and meats.

cake flour A high-starch, soft, and fine flour used primarily for cakes.

canapés Bite-size hors d'oeuvres usually served on a small piece of bread or toast.

capers Flavorful buds of a Mediterranean plant, ranging in size from *nonpareil* (about the size of a small pea) to larger, grape-size caper berries produced in Spain.

caramelize To cook sugar over low heat until it develops a sweet caramel flavor. The term is also used to describe cooking vegetables (especially onions) or meat in butter or oil over low heat until they soften, sweeten, and develop a caramel color.

caraway A distinctive spicy seed used for bread, pork, cheese, and cabbage dishes. It's known to reduce stomach upset, which is why it's often paired with, for example, sauerkraut.

carbohydrate A nutritional component found in starches, sugars, fruits, and vegetables that causes a rise in blood-glucose levels. Carbohydrates supply energy and many important nutrients, including vitamins, minerals, and antioxidants.

cardamom   An intense, sweet-smelling spice, common to Indian cooking, used in baking and coffee.

cayenne   A fiery spice made from (hot) chile peppers, especially the cayenne chile, a slender, red, and very hot pepper.

cheddar   The ubiquitous hard cow's milk cheese with a rich, buttery flavor that ranges from mellow to sharp. Originally produced in England, cheddar is now produced worldwide.

chèvre   French for "goat milk cheese," chèvre is a typically creamy-salty soft cheese, delicious by itself or paired with fruits or chutney. Chèvres vary in style from mild and creamy to aged, firm, and flavorful.

chili powder   A seasoning blend that includes chile pepper, cumin, garlic, and oregano. Proportions vary among different versions, but they all offer a warm, rich flavor.

chilis (or **chiles**)   Any one of many different "hot" peppers, ranging in intensity from the relatively mild ancho pepper to the blisteringly hot habañero.

chives   A member of the onion family, chives grow in bunches of long leaves that resemble tall grass or the green tops of onions and offer a light onion flavor.

chop   To cut into pieces, usually qualified by an adverb such as "*coarsely* chopped," or by a size measurement such as "chopped into $1/2$-inch pieces." "Finely chopped" is much closer to mince.

chorizo   A spiced pork sausage.

chutney   A thick condiment often served with Indian curries, made with fruits and/or vegetables with vinegar, sugar, and spices.

cider vinegar   Vinegar produced from apple cider, popular in North America.

cilantro   A member of the parsley family and used in Mexican cooking (especially salsa) and some Asian dishes. Use in moderation, as the flavor can overwhelm. The seed of the cilantro is the spice coriander.

cinnamon   A sweet, rich, aromatic spice commonly used in baking or desserts. Cinnamon can also be used for delicious and interesting entrées.

clove   A sweet, strong, almost wintergreen-flavor spice used in baking and with meats such as ham.

coriander   A rich, warm, spicy seed used in all types of recipes, from African to South American, from entrées to desserts.

count In terms of seafood or other foods that come in small sizes, the number of that item that compose 1 pound. For example, 31 to 40 count shrimp are large appetizer shrimp often served with cocktail sauce; 51 to 60 are much smaller.

couscous Granular semolina (durum wheat) used in many Mediterranean and North African dishes.

crimini mushrooms A relative of the white button mushroom, but brown in color and with a richer flavor. The larger, fully grown version is the portobello. *See also* portobello mushrooms.

croutons Chunks of bread, usually between ¼ and ½ inch in size, sometimes seasoned and baked, broiled, or fried to a crisp texture and used in soups and salads.

crudités Fresh vegetables served as an appetizer, often all together on one tray.

cumin A fiery, smoky-tasting spice, popular in Middle Eastern and Indian dishes. Cumin is a seed; ground cumin seed is the most common form used in cooking.

curry Rich, spicy, Indian-style sauces and the dishes prepared with them. A curry uses curry powder as its base seasoning.

curry powder A ground blend of rich and flavorful spices used as a basis for curry and many other Indian-influenced dishes. Common ingredients include hot pepper, nutmeg, cumin, cinnamon, pepper, and turmeric. Some curry can also be found in paste form.

custard A cooked mixture of eggs and milk popular as base for desserts.

dash A few drops, usually of a liquid, released by a quick shake of, for example, a bottle of hot sauce.

deglaze To scrape up the bits of meat and seasoning left in a pan or skillet after cooking. Usually this is done by adding a liquid such as wine or broth and creating a flavorful stock that can be used to create sauces.

devein The removal of the dark vein from the back of a large shrimp with a sharp knife.

dice To cut into small cubes about ¼-inch square.

dill A herb perfect for eggs, salmon, cheese dishes, and, of course, vegetables (pickles!).

dollop A spoonful of something creamy and thick, like sour cream or whipped cream.

double boiler   A set of two pots designed to nest together, one inside the other, and provide consistent, moist heat for foods that need delicate treatment. The bottom pot holds water (not quite touching the bottom of the top pot); the top pot holds the ingredient you want to heat.

dredge   To cover a piece of food with a dry substance such as flour or cornmeal.

drizzle   To lightly sprinkle drops of a liquid over food, often as the finishing touch to a dish.

emulsion   A combination of liquid ingredients that do not normally mix well beaten together to create a thick liquid, such as a fat or oil with water. Creation of an emulsion must be done carefully and rapidly to ensure that particles of one ingredient are suspended in the other.

entrée   The main dish in a meal. In France, however, the entrée is considered the first course.

extra-virgin olive oil   *See* olive oil.

fennel   In seed form, a fragrant, licorice-tasting herb. The bulbs have a much milder flavor and a celerylike crunch, and are used as a vegetable in salads or cooked recipes.

feta   A white, crumbly, sharp, and salty cheese popular in Greek cooking and on salads. Traditional feta is usually made with sheep milk, but feta-style cheese can be made from sheep, cow, or goat milk.

fiber   The indigestible part of plant matter, either soluble or insoluble.

fillet   A piece of meat or seafood with the bones removed.

flake   To break into thin sections, as with fish.

flaxseeds   One of the few plant sources of omega-3 fatty acids. Used whole or ground.

floret   The flower or bud end of broccoli or cauliflower.

flour   Grains ground into a meal. Wheat is perhaps the most common flour. Flour is also made from oats, rye, buckwheat, soybeans, etc. *See also* all-purpose flour; cake flour; whole-wheat flour.

fold   To combine a dense and light mixture with a circular action from the middle of the bowl.

frittata   A skillet-cooked mixture of eggs and other ingredients that's not stirred but is cooked slowly and then either flipped or finished under the broiler.

fry *See* sauté.

garbanzo beans (or **chickpeas**)   A yellow-gold, roundish bean used as the base ingredient in hummus. These beans are high in fiber and low in fat.

garlic   A member of the onion family, a pungent and flavorful element in many savory dishes. A garlic bulb contains multiple cloves. Each clove, when chopped, provides about 1 teaspoon garlic. Most recipes call for cloves or chopped garlic by the teaspoon.

garnish   An embellishment not vital to the dish but added to enhance visual appeal.

ginger   Available in fresh root or dried, ground form, ginger adds a pungent, sweet, and spicy quality to a dish.

glucose   The simplest natural sugar.

Gorgonzola   A creamy and rich Italian blue cheese. "Dolce" is sweet, and that's the kind you want.

grate   To shave into tiny pieces using a sharp rasp or grater.

grind   To reduce a large, hard substance, often a seasoning such as peppercorns, to the consistency of sand.

grits   Coarsely ground grains, usually corn.

handful   An unscientific measurement; the amount of an ingredient you can hold in your hand.

hazelnuts (also **filberts**)   A sweet nut popular in desserts and, to a lesser degree, in savory dishes.

herbes de Provence   A seasoning mix including basil, fennel, marjoram, rosemary, sage, and thyme, common in the south of France.

hoisin sauce   A sweet Asian condiment similar to ketchup, made with soybeans, sesame, chile peppers, and sugar.

hors d'oeuvre   French for "outside of work" (the "work" being the main meal), an hors d'oeuvre can be any dish served as a starter before the meal.

horseradish   A sharp, spicy root that forms the flavor base in many condiments, from cocktail sauce to sharp mustards. Prepared horseradish contains vinegar and oil, among other ingredients. Use pure horseradish much more sparingly than the prepared version, or try cutting it with sour cream.

hummus A thick, Middle Eastern spread made of puréed garbanzo beans, lemon juice, olive oil, garlic, and tahini (sesame seed paste).

kalamata olives Traditionally from Greece, these long, medium-small black olives have a rich, smoky flavor.

knead To work dough to make it pliable so it holds gas bubbles as it bakes. Kneading is fundamental in the process of making yeast breads.

kosher salt A coarse-grained salt made without any additives or iodine.

lentils Tiny lens-shape pulses used in European, Middle Eastern, and Indian cuisines.

macerate To mix sugar or another sweetener with fruit. The fruit softens, and its juice is released to mix with the sweetener.

marinate To soak meat, seafood, or other food in a seasoned sauce, called a marinade, which is high in acid content. The acids break down the muscle of the meat, making it tender and adding flavor.

marjoram A sweet herb, a cousin of and similar to oregano, popular in Greek, Spanish, and Italian dishes.

medallion A small round cut, usually of meat or vegetables such as carrots or cucumbers.

mince To cut into very small pieces smaller than diced pieces, about $1/8$ inch or smaller.

nutmeg A sweet, fragrant, musky spice used primarily in baking.

olive oil A fragrant liquid produced by crushing or pressing olives. Extra-virgin olive oil—the most flavorful and highest quality—is produced from the first pressing of a batch of olives; oil is also produced from later pressings.

olives The fruit of the olive tree commonly grown on all sides of the Mediterranean. Black olives are also called ripe olives. Green olives are immature, although they're also widely eaten. *See also* kalmata olives.

oregano A fragrant, slightly astringent herb used in Greek, Spanish, and Italian dishes.

paella A Spanish dish of rice, shellfish, onion, meats, rich broth, and herbs.

paprika A rich, red, warm, earthy spice that lends a rich, red color to many dishes.

parboil   To partially cook in boiling water or broth, similar to blanching (although blanched foods are quickly cooled with cold water).

Parmesan   A hard, dry, flavorful cheese, primarily used grated or shredded as a seasoning for Italian-style dishes.

parsley   A fresh-tasting green leafy herb, often used as a garnish.

pecans   Rich, buttery nuts, native to North America, that have a high unsaturated fat content.

peppercorns   Large, round, dried berries ground to produce pepper.

pesto   A thick spread or sauce made with fresh basil leaves, garlic, olive oil, pine nuts, and Parmesan cheese. Some newer versions are made with other herbs.

phytochemicals   Specific nutrients in plants that have a protective effect on the body.

pickle   A food, usually a vegetable such as a cucumber, that's been pickled in brine.

pilaf   A rice dish in which the rice is browned in butter or oil, and then cooked in a flavorful liquid such as a broth, often with the addition of meats or vegetables. The rice absorbs the broth, resulting in a savory dish.

pinch   An unscientific measurement term, the amount of an ingredient—typically a dry, granular substance such as an herb or seasoning—you can hold between your finger and thumb.

pine nuts (also **pignoli** or **piñon**)   Nuts grown on pine trees, that are rich (read: high fat), flavorful, and a bit piney. Pine nuts are a traditional component of pesto, and add a wonderful hearty crunch to many other recipes.

pita bread   A flat, hollow wheat bread often used for sandwiches or sliced, pizza-style, into slices. Terrific soft with dips or baked or broiled as a vehicle for other ingredients.

poach   To cook a food in simmering liquid, such as water, wine, or broth.

portobello mushrooms   A mature and larger form of the smaller crimini mushroom, portobellos are brownish, chewy, and flavorful. Often served as whole caps, grilled, and as thin sautéed slices. *See also* crimini mushrooms.

preheat   To turn on an oven, broiler, or other cooking appliance in advance of cooking so the temperature will be at the desired level when the assembled dish is ready for cooking.

prosciutto A dry, salt-cured ham that originated in Italy.

purée To reduce a food to a thick, creamy texture, usually using a blender or food processor.

reduce To boil or simmer a broth or sauce to remove some of the water content, resulting in more concentrated flavor and color.

reserve To hold a specified ingredient for another use, later in the recipe.

rice vinegar Vinegar produced from fermented rice or rice wine, popular in Asian-style dishes. Different from rice wine vinegar.

ricotta A fresh Italian cheese, smoother than cottage cheese with a slightly sweet flavor.

risotto A popular Italian rice dish made by browning arborio rice in butter or oil and slowly adding liquid to cook the rice, resulting in a creamy texture.

roast To cook something uncovered in an oven, usually without additional liquid.

rosemary A pungent, sweet herb used with chicken, pork, fish, and especially lamb. A little of it goes a long way.

saffron A spice made from the stamens of crocus flowers, saffron lends a dramatic yellow color and distinctive flavor to a dish. Use only tiny amounts of this expensive herb.

sage An herb with a musty yet fruity, lemon-rind scent and "sunny" flavor.

salsa A style of mixing fresh vegetables and/or fresh fruit in a coarse chop. Salsa can be spicy or not, fruit-based or not, and served as a starter on its own (with chips, for example), or as a companion to a main course.

satay (also **sate**) A popular Southeast Asian dish of broiled skewers of fish or meat, often served with peanut sauce.

sauté To pan-cook over lower heat than used for frying.

sear To quickly brown the exterior of a food, especially meat, over high heat to preserve interior moisture.

sesame oil An oil, made from pressing sesame seeds, that's tasteless if clear, and aromatic and flavorful if brown.

shallot A member of the onion family that grows in a bulb somewhat like garlic and has a milder onion flavor. When a recipe calls for shallot, use the entire bulb.

shellfish A broad range of seafood, including clams, mussels, oysters, crabs, shrimp, and lobster. Some people are allergic to shellfish, so take care with its inclusion in recipes.

shiitake mushrooms Large, dark-brown mushrooms with a hearty, meaty flavor. Can be used either fresh or dried, grilled, or as a component in other recipes, and as a flavoring source for broth.

short-grain rice A starchy rice popular for Asian-style dishes because it readily clumps (perfect for eating with chopsticks).

shred To cut into many long, thin slices.

simmer To boil gently so the liquid barely bubbles.

skewers Thin wood, bamboo, or metal sticks, usually about 8 inches long, used for assembling kebabs, dipping food pieces into hot sauces, or serving single-bite food items with a bit of panache.

skillet (also **frying pan**) A generally heavy, flat-bottomed metal pan with a handle. It's designed to cook food over heat on a stovetop or campfire.

slice To cut into thin pieces.

steam To suspend a food over boiling water and allow the heat of the steam (water vapor) to cook the food. A quick-cooking method, steaming preserves the flavor and texture of a food.

steep To let sit in hot water, as in steeping tea in hot water for several minutes.

stew To slowly cook pieces of food submerged in a liquid. Also, a dish that has been prepared by this method.

stir-fry To cook small pieces of food in a wok or skillet over high heat, while moving and turning the food quickly to cook all sides.

stock A flavorful broth made by cooking meats and/or vegetables with seasonings until the liquid absorbs these flavors. This liquid is then strained and the solids discarded. Can be eaten alone or used as a base for soups, stews, etc.

succotash A cooked vegetable dish, usually made of corn and peppers.

tahini A paste made from sesame seeds, used to flavor many Middle Eastern recipes.

tarragon A sweet, rich-smelling herb perfect with seafood, vegetables (especially asparagus), chicken, and pork.

teriyaki   A Japanese-style sauce composed of soy sauce, rice wine, ginger, and sugar that works well with seafood as well as most meats.

thyme   A minty, zesty herb.

toast   To heat something, usually bread, so it's browned and crisp.

tofu   A cheeselike substance made from soybeans and soy milk.

turmeric   A spicy, pungent yellow root used in many dishes, especially Indian cuisine, for color and flavor. Turmeric is the source of the yellow color in many prepared mustards.

veal   Meat from a calf, generally characterized by mild flavor and tenderness.

vinegar   An acidic liquid widely used as dressing and seasoning, often made from fermented grapes, apples, or rice. *See also* balsamic vinegar; cider vinegar; rice vinegar; white vinegar; wine vinegar.

walnuts   A rich, slightly woody flavored nut.

wasabi   Japanese horseradish, a fiery, pungent condiment used with many Japanese-style dishes. Most often sold as a powder; add water to create a paste.

water chestnuts   A tuber, popular in many types of Asian-style cooking. The flesh is white, crunchy, and juicy, and the vegetable holds its texture whether cool or hot.

whisk   To rapidly mix, introducing air to the mixture.

white mushrooms   Button mushrooms. When fresh, they have an earthy smell and an appealing soft crunch.

whole-wheat flour   Wheat flour that contains the entire grain.

wild rice   Actually a grass with a rich, nutty flavor, popular as an unusual and nutritious side dish.

wine vinegar   Vinegar produced from red or white wine.

wok   A pan for quick-cooking.

Worcestershire sauce   Originally developed in India and containing tamarind, this spicy sauce is used as a seasoning for many meats and other dishes.

yeast   Tiny fungi that, when mixed with water, sugar, flour, and heat, release carbon dioxide bubbles, which, in turn, cause the bread to rise.

zest   Small slivers of peel, usually from a citrus fruit such as lemon, lime, or orange.

Resources

I hope I've helped satisfy your cravings for high-fiber foods, but if you want more information about ways to increase your fiber, or need to find retailers that sell fiber-boosting ingredients, you've come to the right place.

Fiberful Ingredients

The following retailers offer a great selection of ingredients to assist you in your high-fiber cooking. You can find everything from specialty flours to unusual dried beans and fruit.

Bob's Red Mill Natural Foods
1-800-349-2173
www.bobsredmill.com
Stone-ground flours and unusual grains are Bob's specialties. Find wheat berries, flaxseed meal, and a cornucopia of flours. Most health food stores and many supermarkets carry his products.

EthnicGrocer
1-866-438-4642
ethnicgrocer.com
Search by product or country at this online grocer. Find nuts, seeds, oils, and unusual spices and grains.

King Arthur Flour

1-800-827-6836

www.kingarthurflour.com

King Arthur makes white whole-wheat flour, as well as other grain flours and unusual ingredients. Look for them in your supermarket or order online from The Baker's Catalogue. Also have a look at their *Whole Grain Baking* book for advanced cooks.

Trader Joe's

1-800-SHOP TJS (1-800-746-7857)

www.traderjoes.com

This unique grocery store is cropping up all over the country with an evolving product list. Try its dried fruits, nuts, grains, and flours.

Informative Websites

Learn more about fiber and find tables listing fiber grams in common ingredients and food products at the following websites.

American Dietetic Association (ADA)

www.eatright.org or www.adajournal.org

The ADA provides important information on fiber as well as other nutrients and makes healthful recommendations on improving the diet of all Americans. Its journal regularly publishes ground-breaking articles on health.

The Mayo Clinic

www.mayoclinic.com/health/fiber

This famous clinic's website features a terrific discussion about fiber and its relationship to disease prevention.

National Fiber Council

www.nationalfibercouncil.org

All the latest news can be found here at this nonprofit organization's website devoted solely to dietary fiber.

USDA National Nutrient Database

www.nal.usda.gov/fnic/foodcomp/search

You can find out the amount of fiber in grams present in any ingredient you choose, as well as the content of specific vitamins and minerals.

Further Fiber Reading

Keep your mind on fiber with these titles.

Brumback, Mary, and Roger Brumback. *The Dietary Fiber Weight Control Handbook.* Charleston, SC: Booksurge Publishing, 2006.

Elkins, Rita. *Fiber Facts.* Utah: Woodland Publishing, 1999.

Grogan, Bryanna Clark. *Fiber for Life Cookbook.* Tennessee: Book Publishing Company, 2002.

Netzer, Corinne T. *Carbohydrate and Fiber Counter.* New York: Dell, 2006.

Sheasby, Anne. *High Fiber Cooking for Health.* London: Southwater, 2004.

Sperr, Shirley Lorenzani. *Dietary Fiber.* New York: McGraw-Hill, 1998.

Spiller, Gene A., and Monica Spiller. *What's With Fiber?* Laguna Beach, CA: Basic Health Publications, 2005.

Watson, Brenda. *The Fiber35 Diet.* New York: Free Press, 2007.

Index